BROWNS TOWN
1964

OTHER BOOKS BY TERRY PLUTO

ON SPORTS:
Glory Days in Tribe Town (with Tom Hamilton)
Joe Tait: It's Been a Real Ball (with Joe Tait)
LeBron James: The Making of an MVP (with Brian Windhorst)
The Franchise (with Brian Windhorst)
Dealing: The Cleveland Indians' New Ballgame
False Start: How the New Browns Were Set Up to Fail
The View from Pluto
Unguarded (with Lenny Wilkens)
Our Tribe
Browns Town 1964
Burying the Curse
The Curse of Rocky Colavito
Falling from Grace
Tall Tales
Loose Balls
Bull Session (with Johnny Kerr)
Tark (with Jerry Tarkanian)
Forty-Eight Minutes, a Night in the Life of the NBA (with Bob Ryan)
Sixty-One (with Tony Kubek)
You Could Argue But You'd Be Wrong (with Pete Franklin)
Weaver on Strategy (with Earl Weaver)
The Earl of Baltimore
Super Joe (with Joe Charboneau and Burt Graeff)
The Greatest Summer

ON FAITH AND OTHER TOPICS:
Faith and You
Faith and You Volume 2
Everyday Faith
Champions for Life: The Power of a Father's Blessing (with Bill Glass)
Crime: Our Second Vietnam (with Bill Glass)

BROWNS TOWN

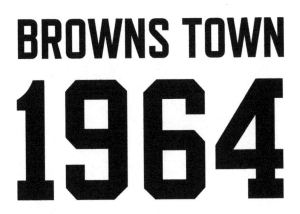

1964

THE CLEVELAND BROWNS
AND THE 1964 CHAMPIONSHIP

TERRY PLUTO

GRAY & COMPANY, PUBLISHERS
CLEVELAND

Gray & Company, Publishers
www.grayco.com

First paperback edition 2003.
First published in hardcover by Simon & Schuster under the title
When All the World Was Browns Town.

ISBN 978-1-886228-72-6

Printed in the United States of America
v2

To the memory of
Nev Chandler
*A true Browns fan
and a real friend*

CONTENTS

INTRODUCTION

They were Cleveland's last champions.

They were a team of men in the truest sense of the words, men who didn't expect to be coddled, men who didn't believe the world should genuflect at the mere mention of their names.

They had the greatest running back in the history of football, and a coach who wore a hearing aid. Their quarterback had a Ph.D. in math. They had a defensive end who was a preacher, and a halfback who became a millionaire.

These were the 1964 Cleveland Browns.

Just talking about this team brings tears to the eyes of Jim Brown. Picture Jim Brown: You can see him scowl. You can hear him growl. But can you imagine Jim Brown becoming sentimental?

That's what happens when he thinks of this team, when he embraces old friends such as John Wooten and Dick Schafrath, when he remembers how the aging coach, Blanton Collier, would quietly talk to him after practice—two men alone on the field as everyone else headed to the showers.

"We had the greatest, most overachieving team in the history of football," said Brown. "That was what football was like in Cleveland in 1964. It was a group of guys who never cheated the fans or each other. And the fans, they were there for us every week—all 80,000 of them. I'll never forget the cheering."

The 1964 Browns.

They were a team coming out of the shadow of Paul Brown. They were a team with much to prove, and so many guys willing to give.

The 1964 Browns were Frank Ryan, a quarterback who went to

school every off-season to earn his doctorate in math. During training camp, he carried around a huge textbook that included a single math problem covering 300 pages.

The 1964 Browns were Bill Glass, who wanted to become another Billy Graham, but found his real calling in preaching to prisoners.

The 1964 Browns were Galen Fiss, a linebacker who looked like everyone's grandfather and wore bedroom slippers in the locker room. They had another linebacker named Jim Houston, who, like Fiss, was an insurance man. "Jim wrote over $1 million in policies during the 1964 season," said Jim Brown in awe.

The 1964 Browns were men like Monte Clark, who took the money the team earned from beating the Baltimore Colts in the championship game and bought a Hammond organ.

"That check was for a little over $8,000," said Clark. "I made a photocopy of it before I cashed it. I figured I'd never see a check that big again. Then I used some of it on the organ. I had played the piano a little bit as a kid and I was in the band in high school. I always wanted an organ."

Monte Clark was an offensive tackle, a huge, physical man—but a man with music in his heart.

The 1964 Browns were Ernie Green, who spent his career taking care of others. First he blocked for Jim Brown. Then he blocked for Leroy Kelly. As a member of that championship team, Green said, "We were the best football team in the world. There were only forty men on that squad, and I was one of them. That was very hard for a humble man to accept."

Today, Ernie Green owns several companies and is a wealthy businessman, yet he approaches life like an unpretentious blocking back: He cuts no corners, asks for no favors, puts on no airs.

He is a true Cleveland Brown.

So is Paul Warfield, a rookie in 1964 who later became a member of the Hall of Fame.

"I grew up in Warren, Ohio, watching the Browns on TV," he said. "When I came to the team in 1964, I felt I had to prove I was worthy to wear their colors."

Remember that Paul Warfield was the team's No. 1 draft choice, a star at Ohio State. Today, most young players in that position wear their egos on their sleeves; Warfield checked his at the door. He lived in a small apartment on East 139th Street. He drove a small Corvair with a 4-speed on the floor. He knew he was the son of a steelworker with little time for fools.

"To me, football was not about appearing in Nike commercials or calling attention to yourself," Warfield said. "It was about winning, about fitting into the team. If I had been immature or not serious about my profession, they never would have accepted me. And more than anything, I wanted the acceptance and respect of those players."

The 1964 Browns were a defensive end named Paul Wiggin, a Phi Beta Kappa from Stanford, where he also earned his master's degree by going to school in the off-season. He then spent part of four years teaching education courses at San Mateo Junior College—all this while playing for the Browns.

The 1964 Browns were Gene Hickerson from Mississippi, who made more money wearing a suit and tie and serving as a manufacturer's representative than he did as a pulling guard in his Browns uniform. They were aging Lou Groza, his stomach hanging down over his football pants as he kicked one field goal after another, and they were Gary Collins, the man whose hands brought Cleveland its last NFL championship.

"Gary Collins ran that post pattern to perfection," said Jim Brown, "and he just may be the most underrated receiver ever to play this game."

Just ask the Baltimore Colts, who watched Collins catch three touchdown passes as the Browns pulled one of the biggest upsets in title game history, winning, 27–0.

The 1964 Browns were Blanton Collier coming home from the game to find that his wife, Forman, had a pot of chili on the stove and some ham and biscuits in the oven. Collier had a hearing problem that forced him to read lips. He could usually be found holed up in his study with a quart of ice cream, watching football films and plotting strategy.

"When we'd drive home from the games, Daddy always wanted to know if it had been interesting football," said Kay Collier-Slone, the coach's daughter. "He liked offense. He liked a team that was organized. He hated sloppy football. He'd die a million deaths watching today's game."

Most of the 1964 Browns had their college degrees. They had off-season jobs. Many of them even worked during the season. Few teams had players who sold more insurance or went to more business lunches than these Browns.

"They wanted to look the part of businessmen," recalled broadcaster Casey Coleman. "One day, Paul Warfield showed up on the road with a briefcase. All the players wore shirts, ties, and sport coats on the road, so the briefcase fit in. Some of the players asked Paul what he had in the case. It was his playbook. The next week, just about everybody had an attaché case. Some guys brought their business papers. Others just carried socks in there. The story was that Bob Gain carried his flask in there."

The 1964 Browns were a young owner named Art Modell, who had the guts to make some moves that led to this championship—and later had the audacity to steal the franchise away from the fans to whom it really belonged.

The 1964 Browns also were the fans and the old Stadium.

"My memory of the Stadium is that we're always playing in the snow or rain," said Paul Wiggin. "On one side of the field, there is a shovel just stuck in the ground. On the other side, there's a tractor with one of its wheels off. There's a couple of buckets overturned and some huge tarps rolled up. It was like going to work in a factory; Cleveland was that kind of town back then."

"When they'd introduce the players and you'd come out of the dugout, the fans would cheer so hard that the ground just shook," said John Wooten. "Just talking about it gives me goose pimples. I have spent my life in pro football, and there was nothing like the roar of those fans and that old Stadium rattling."

Browns fans should know this. You should know that when the players think of 1964, they think of you.

"I never played in another stadium where you could just walk out of the dressing room down that long tunnel to the field and just feel the drama," said Paul Warfield. "It was a long, dark, damp tunnel. At the end, you could see the light. You heard the fans, and they grew louder with every step. When you reached the light and ran onto the field, it wasn't just applause. It was thunder. It made your blood pump, your heart pound. You felt as if you had just gone to football heaven."

That was Browns football in 1964, when Cleveland was truly a Browns town.

ART'S
THUNDERBOLT

THE FOUNDER

They were men who could bend steel with their bare hands. They were men with scars and sandpaper hands. They were men from farms, mills, and mines—mean, tough men.

But with one look, Paul Brown could make these men shake in their spikes. He could make them cry. He could make them toss, turn, and churn in their beds.

He could do it without raising his voice.

He could do it without profanity, with few words at all.

He could do it because he was Paul Brown, and for nearly twenty years, Paul Brown *was* the Cleveland Browns.

"The worst thing anyone ever said to me came from Paul Brown," said former Browns defensive back Bernie Parrish. "It was during a film session, and I had messed up a coverage. He ran the film back and forth a couple of times and then said, 'Don't tell me that the great ones do it that way.' That was all he said, but I'm telling you, it nearly destroyed me."

Paul Brown always wore a hat. No one can remember the color of his eyes; some say blue, others say gray. But they all insist those eyes were fierce, those eyes could bore right through you, could crumble Mount Rushmore.

Paul Brown asked his players to call him "Paul" or call him "Coach," just never use his last name. And never smoke, swear, or drink around him. This was an era when most pro teams allowed their players to light up cigarettes in the dressing room at halftime. This was a group of men whose natural language was more than a little blue.

Not Paul Brown. Not with his Browns.

"When I joined the Browns [in 1957], we had a player named Junior

Wren," Paul Wiggin said. "Junior was just enraged at Paul. He told me, 'If Paul gets on me again like he did after last game, you know that hook where he hangs his hat?'

"I said I did.

"Junior said, 'I'm going to hang him right on that hook, I'm telling you. That last play, it wasn't my fault.'

"I just nodded and waited to see what happened.

"Paul came up to Junior and said, 'Junior Wren, I have seen better performances out of high school players.'

"Did Junior hang Paul on the hook? Of course not. All he said was, 'Yes, Paul.' That was it, 'Yes, Paul . . .'"

Wiggin laughed as he told the story. A veteran player, coach, and player personnel man, Wiggin has spent his life in the NFL.

"No one, I mean no one, has ever had total command and respect like Paul Brown," Wiggin said. "Not Lombardi, not Landry, none of them. I believe that Paul Brown could have been a general in the army . . . he could have taken over Ford Motor Company or IBM . . . you put Paul Brown in charge of anything and he would have been one of those special people who could organize and lead."

Wiggin said part of the reason was Brown's intelligence—and part was fear.

The play happened nearly forty years ago, but Wiggin will never forget it. He was on a punt coverage team. The Browns were ahead, 17–14. He rushed the punter, and knocked him down—drawing a roughing penalty, giving the other team the ball and a first down. The Browns went on to lose that game, 21–17.

The game was on a Sunday. Paul Brown did not believe in practices on Monday or Tuesday.

"For three nights, I didn't sleep," Wiggin recalled. "I was so terrified of what Paul would say about me when we had our film session on Wednesday. I was a young player, thinking about becoming a high school or college coach. My wife was telling me that if I was so upset about Paul and playing pro football that I couldn't even sleep, maybe I should just quit and go into coaching."

Wednesday's film session finally arrived. Paul Brown showed the play once, then stared hard at Wiggin and said, "Gentlemen, if we are not in the championship game on the twenty-seventh of December, we'll know who to thank."

No one said a word.

Wiggin was sure his heart stopped beating. He thought he was dead, but if he were dead, he knew he wouldn't feel so terrible. As the players filed out of the room, Brown stood in front of Wiggin and simply asked, "Why? Why would you do that?"

Wiggin said, "Paul, I just don't know."

Paul Brown stared for a few seconds, enough to turn Wiggin's knees to mush. Then the coach walked out. This twenty-three-year-old man who was 6′3″, 245 pounds was devastated, defeated, and convinced his career was over.

"I wasn't even a starter back then," Wiggin said. "A few days later, Paul came up to me and said I was starting at defensive end. I never would have believed it. I had three sacks in that game and was awarded the game ball. Afterward, I was talking to a few reporters, and I noticed Paul was waiting in the dressing room.

"The reporters left. Paul came up to me. I still hated him. At that moment, I didn't know if I hated anyone more in my life than I hated Paul Brown for what he had put me through that week. But Paul said, 'Hey, Wig, thanks.' That was it. He walked away, and I tell you, I never felt more appreciated by anyone in my life than I did at that moment, just because Paul Brown thanked me."

Paul Brown was pro football.

Over and over, you hear that from the players of the 1940s and 1950s.

He is the man who invented the face mask.

He invented the playbook.

He invented film sessions.

He invented the taxi squad, a place where five nonroster players could still practice with the team in case a regular player was hurt. Rather than being on the Browns' team payroll, they were on the payroll of team owner Mickey McBride, who also owned a cab company. They never drove cabs, they were just driven in practice by Paul Brown.

Paul Brown was also the first coach to have full-time assistants and the first coach to consistently call plays for the quarterback.

He also was the first to consistently use a number of black players.

"Paul was very pragmatic about it," recalled veteran Cleveland sportswriter Bob August. "There were good athletes out there of all

colors, and he wanted all of them he could get. He didn't make a big
deal about it. But I know that when we went out to Pasadena to play the
L.A. Rams, we stayed at a place called the Green Hotel. After a while,
it was pretty run-down, small rooms, no air-conditioning. But I found
out that Paul kept the team staying there because in the early days, the
Green Hotel was the one place that would accept the black players."

So who was Paul Brown?

"He was like Red Auerbach to the NBA, Branch Rickey to baseball,"
said former Browns coach Sam Rutigliano. "Paul Brown was a giant."

Paul Brown also won.

He made Massillon into what many considered the best high school
team in the country in the 1930s as he had an 81-7-2 record there.
Today, the Massillon Tigers play on a field called Paul Brown Stadium.

He won at Ohio State, taking the national title in 1942 in only his
second season of college coaching. He had an 18-8-1 record with the
Buckeyes.

He won at Great Lakes Naval Training Center during World War II,
upsetting powerhouse Notre Dame one year.

He won in the All-American Football Conference, which began in
1946. Brown was the first coach in the history of the Cleveland franchise later known as the Browns. He assembled a powerhouse team,
primarily composed of college players who were in the military for
World War II.

He signed Otto Graham while Graham was still in the military. Same
with Lou Groza. Same with many players. He'd send them a contract
and a bonus, telling them that a job in the new pro football league was
waiting once they were discharged.

Suddenly, the team from Cleveland in a league that no one ever
heard of had some of the best college talent in the country. That was as
much the genius of Paul Brown as anything—targeting the talent and
getting it first.

Paul Brown won four titles in four years in that All-American Conference; his record was 47-4-3. In 1950, the Cleveland franchise was
invited to join the established National Football League.

The Browns are named after their first coach. A "Name the Team"
contest was held in the local newspapers. Suggestions poured in.

"One of the names that received a number of votes was Browns," said
Mike Brown, the son of Paul Brown. "My father liked the name."

And that became the name of the team.

The legacy continued in the NFL. From 1950 to 1955, the Browns went to the championship game *every single season.* That's six years in a row, ten in a row if you go back to the AAFC. Otto Graham was the quarterback for all ten of those years. The Browns won seven championships with him calling the signals.

And every year, the legend of Paul Brown grew.

Otto Graham was the greatest quarterback in the history of the Browns, arguably one of the best ever in the NFL. Forty years after he threw his last pass for the Browns, Graham still wore a golf shirt that read "PAUL'S GUYS" over the pocket.

"When Paul Brown coached the Browns, he ruled with an iron hand," Graham said. "There were other men who owned the team, but the Browns were Paul's team. The men who played for him were Paul's guys. But you had better not cross Paul Brown.

"When Paul started in pro football, the image of the players was that of fat bellies, big cigars, foul mouths, and hard drinking. Paul would tell us that we were the New York Yankees of pro football. No drinking. No smoking. No swearing. No getting in trouble. Wear sport coats and ties in public. He really did trade players who were drunks and chased women. He'd tell us, 'One bad apple in a basket of apples will rot all the apples.' He really tried to run the team that way."

Graham's rookie year was 1946. The team captain was a center from Ohio State named Jim Daniell.

"Daniell and some other players went out on the town," Graham recalled. "He'd had a few drinks, then pulled up his car behind a police car. I don't know about you, but when I'm behind a police car, I don't honk the horn and tell the guy to get out of the way—but Jim did. The policeman got out of the car, talked to Jim, and there was a confrontation. The policeman took Jim to the station. Jim said he wasn't drunk and demanded a sobriety test. They gave him one, and he'd had enough alcohol to be considered legally drunk, and he was arrested."

The arrest of the team captain was in the morning paper.

"The next day, Paul called the team together after practice," Graham said. "He asked Jim, 'Is what I read in the paper true?'

"Jim said it was.

"Paul said, 'Fine, turn in your suit.'

"Jim said, 'Do you want to hear my side of the story?'

"Paul said, 'No, you're through.'

"Jim got up and left, and then it hit us: Paul Brown had just thrown off the captain of our team right before the championship game. We were a young team and he had us in the palm of his hand after that. We thought, if he could do that to Jim Daniell, he'd do it to anyone."

But Graham learned something else.

"Daniell's backup was a lineman who was just about as good as Jim," Graham said. "But I didn't realize that until later. What Paul did was get a message across to us, and not hurt the team, either. For years, veteran players told rookies about the day Paul Brown cut Jim Daniell, and that just made him even bigger and more powerful in the eyes of the young players."

Brown had theories about what made great players.

He thought the ideal pregame meal was as follows:

A steak, but no catsup.

A salad, no dressing.

A baked potato, no butter or sour cream.

"That stuff was so dry, it could choke you," Graham said.

Brown also did not want his players drinking water during practices or games; he thought it led to stomach cramps.

In training camp, you had better not wear a dirty T-shirt. At the evening meal, a dress shirt was required.

He wanted all of his players in bed by 10 p.m. the night before a game. He had assistants conduct bed-checks.

"Every year, Paul Brown gave the same speech about how he'd never fined a player in all his years as the Browns' coach," Wiggin recalled. "When I was a rookie, I asked Lou Groza how that could be true, if Paul was lenient. Lou said, 'No, no one ever breaks the rules.'"

Paul Brown did have one last rule: no marital relations from Tuesday night until after Sunday's game. But even Paul Brown knew better than to try and enforce what the players called "The Tuesday Rule."

Paul Brown's tentacles were everywhere.

Veteran Cleveland sportswriter Hal Lebovitz remembered a player named Horace Gillom, who felt Brown's wrath.

"Paul made every player keep a notebook," Lebovitz said. "He'd collect the notebooks and check to make sure that the players had written down the plays and notes neatly. He saw Gillom's was sloppy, and he told Horace, 'You are like an apple on a tree. When you get too ripe, you're going to fall off.' He could really scare the players."

Paul Wiggin will always remember those notebooks. "The same week that I was called for the roughing-the-kicker penalty that cost us the game, I had taken my notebook home with me," Wiggin said. "This was before the days of copying machines. I was copying all the plays out of it, because I wanted a copy of Paul Brown's plays in case he cut me and it was time for me to get on with my career as a high school coach. I was under so much stress that week, that when I went to practice on Wednesday, I left my notebook at home. In the classroom, every chair had a name on it. I was in the front row, so I knew that Paul would see that I didn't have my notebook.

"I went to Lou Groza and asked, 'What does the old man do if you forget your notebook?'

"Groza said, 'I don't know. I don't think anyone has ever forgotten his notebook before.'

"Lou's seat was way in the back. Paul never looked much at him. I asked Lou, 'Would you let me have your notebook while I'm sitting up front? I'm in so much trouble already, if I don't have my notebook, I don't want to think of what might happen.'

"Lou saw that I was a wreck, and he lent me his notebook. He probably saved my job by doing that."

Dick Modzelewski came to the Browns in 1964, two years after Paul Brown was fired.

"That was the first time I was handed a playbook," he said. "I had played in Washington, Pittsburgh, and with the New York Giants, and we never had one. Blanton Collier was using Paul Brown's system, and that book had every offensive and defensive formation in it. He wanted you to really understand the game."

Paul Brown also tested you.

In every training camp, Brown gave his players a football IQ test. The tests were infamous, a symbol of Brown's preparation and demands on the players.

"The thing was, everyone cheated like crazy on those tests," said Bernie Parrish. "They used crib sheets with all the answers. Hell, I remember seeing Chuck Noll do it, and Paul would brag about how smart Chuck Noll was."

In 1964, Jim Brown published a book in which he revealed the cheating on the tests. It was huge headlines in Cleveland, but no surprise to Paul Brown or anyone close to the team.

"I don't remember anyone caught cheating," Lou Groza said. "But I'm sure that guys did. I think Paul believed that by making up those crib sheets, the players learned the formations and the plays."

That was exactly it, according to Hal Lebovitz. "He had some real dumb guys, and Paul figured that by their copying down the plays a couple of times . . . hey, after a while, even the dumb guys start to remember it."

Defensive back Ross Fichtner recalled the tests vividly.

"Because I played quarterback in college, I was tested with the quarterbacks," he said. "There were sixty questions on the test and you had about twenty-five minutes to finish it. They'd start with basic stuff like a series of numbers: 1 . . . 2 . . . 3 . . . 5 . . . 6 . . . 8, and they'd ask you what two numbers were missing. That part was multiple choice. Then there were football-related questions. Usually, I got fifty to fifty-two questions completed. The only guy I know who was able to answer all the questions in the twenty-five minutes was Frank Ryan."

But Fichtner remembered a rookie quarterback who took the test along with him. When they finished, the rookie asked how many questions Fichtner had answered.

"About fifty," Fichtner said.

"I only got six," said the rookie.

"The next day," Fichtner said, "that rookie was gone. So Paul did take those tests seriously."

At least he did if the player was too stupid to even try and cheat.

———

It is obvious that even though Paul Brown wasn't the owner, he acted as if he were king. He hired the front office staff. He made the travel arrangements. He drafted and signed the players. He negotiated every contract.

Center John Morrow recalled talking contract with Paul Brown, and they agreed on a salary. "Then Paul said, 'Of course that includes the preseason.' I couldn't believe it. He had just talked me out of an extra $500 by refusing to pay for the preseason."

Ross Fichtner finally agreed to a $10,000 signing bonus/rookie salary when Brown told him, "You now realize that you are among the top 10 percent of income earners in this country, and you are just coming out of college."

Browns fullback Ed (brother of Dick) Modzelewski told Gene Hickerson that Paul Brown had a list of statistics that showed how different team members performed on special teams. Modzelewski was low on the list, and Brown showed it to him in order to justify the pay cut he offered.

"Ask Paul to show you the list," Modzelewski told Hickerson. "You're right at the top."

Hickerson asked. Brown refused.

"He looked at me with those eyes above his reading glasses and said, 'Well, you had a fair year on special teams,'" Hickerson recalled. "Old Paul Brown, he threw nickels around as if they were manhole covers. Art Modell was a real fish compared to Paul Brown."

"This was before agents," Lou Groza said. "We didn't know what anyone else made. Paul also made sure that the players' wives didn't sit together at games, so they wouldn't talk about salaries. But this also was a time when it wasn't considered good manners to talk about money like people do today."

Paul Brown also kept his players on edge, sometimes needlessly.

"During training camp, six rookies [and/or] free agents would be told to go to the office every Monday," Fichtner said. "These were guys on the verge of making the team. Each of the six players would be handed an envelope. In three of the envelopes, there were tickets home. The other three envelopes were empty, meaning you could keep practicing. Talk about going through agony. I mean, I went through three of those before I finally made the team for good. I never understood why Paul did that."

Those who disliked Paul Brown said those envelopes revealed the dark side of his personality. Why did Paul Brown have to worry these poor saps who were just trying to make the team?

Every player seems to remember something that Paul Brown said that hit them like a lightning bolt.

"He'd tell me, 'Galen, we can't do it for you,'" recalled defensive captain Galen Fiss.

The line that cut deep into Lou Groza was, "You're killing our football team."

Fichtner remembered a meeting of the quarterbacks that demonstrated how Paul Brown went right to the point.

"We were all sitting in a room, and Paul said, 'I'm going to explain the quarterback situation to you.'

"To Milt Plum, he said, 'You are the starter. It is your job to lose.'

"To Jim Ninowski, he said, 'We are going to make a deal for you.' And he did, trading Nino to Detroit.

"To Lenny Dawson, he said, 'You will be Milt's backup.'

"To another player, he said, 'You had better start looking for a different line of work, because you'll never make it in the NFL.'

"He said this matter-of-factly, and right in front of everyone."

Fichtner told another story. "We were running a play with the offense, and Paul Wiggin disrupted it by making a tackle in the backfield. Paul Brown really loved coaching the offense, and he was upset that Wiggin ruined the play.

"He told Wiggin, 'You aren't supposed to be in that spot.'

"Wiggin said, 'Paul, you don't know the defense.'

"Paul said, 'I know one thing, you're not going to be playing it come Sunday.' That man could really put you in your place."

Now you also know why longtime Cleveland radio talk show host Pete Franklin once said, "Paul Brown could be so cold that you'd get pneumonia just being in the same room with him."

Players loved Paul Brown's organization and his understanding of players' bodies.

"Paul would never let us kill each other in practice," Gene Hickerson recalled. "He said, 'We do the rough stuff on Sundays,' meaning in the games. A lot of our players lasted so long because he cut his practices short and didn't want us getting hurt. His favorite line in practice was 'Think, THINK, THINK!' He had practices timed to the minute, and there was this big old clock on the wall. He'd tell us at the start that we'd practice one hour, twelve minutes, and at one hour, twelve minutes, he'd stop practice even if we were in the middle of a play. Blanton Collier used the same system."

Paul Brown believed in drills; he always said, "Repetition is learning." But while Brown's practices were the height of rationality, he had his paranoid streak.

"One time, we were practicing at League Park and Paul saw a guy working on the roof of a nearby apartment building," John Morrow said. "Paul was convinced that the guy was from another team. He sent [trainer] Leo Murphy up there to check the guy out. It turned out the guy was a roofer."

Murphy said Brown once spotted someone sitting in a car near his practice.

"He had me go see who the guy was," Murphy said. "It was just some salesman, and the poor guy was asleep. He just wanted a nap, and I had to wake him up and tell him that Paul Brown didn't want him watching practice. The guy thought I was nuts."

———

Paul Brown is famous for being the first coach to call plays for a quarterback, but it wasn't always that way.

"In my first five years, I called all the plays," said Otto Graham.

For the record, the Browns also won five titles in those five years.

"Then one year [1951], Paul told me that he was going to call the plays," Graham said. "I didn't like it. We had some real battles."

Brown's point was that he and his coaches in the press box had a better view of the defense than the quarterback, who was bending down to take a snap from center.

"I couldn't disagree with that," Graham said. "But I also knew we had been successful with the quarterback calling the plays. I'd talk to the receivers and the other players, get input from them. I thought I had a pretty good feel for the game."

That's an understatement: Otto Graham was the Joe Montana of his era.

"Paul didn't want us changing a play at the line of scrimmage," he said. "Sometimes, I'd go to the line and see eight guys to the right—the exact direction we were supposed to run our play. It didn't make sense, but sometimes I'd change the play and pray that it worked, or I'd never hear the end of it."

Graham said when his changes went for big gains, Paul Brown never said a word to him. If he was wrong, Paul Brown would never let him forget it.

But after winning five titles, why would Brown change his play-calling system?

"Because he was Paul Brown," Graham said. "I love Paul, but one day Paul realized that he wasn't involved in the play-calling, and Paul wanted to be involved in everything. That was his personality."

So Paul Brown invented the messenger guard system. Players such as Chuck Noll and Gene Hickerson would alternate, Noll running off the field following a play and Hickerson running on to deliver the play call from Paul Brown to the quarterback.

"The quarterbacks didn't like it one bit," Hickerson said. "They thought it was degrading."

When Jim Ninowski was traded back to the Browns in 1962 and started that season—Paul Brown's last in Cleveland—Ninowski said he and Brown made a deal.

"I'd call some plays, and he'd call some," he said. "But a guard came in on every play, so everyone would think that Paul was calling all the plays. Paul said, 'It will protect you, and it will protect me.' But it was strange. A guard would come in and say, 'Call what you want.' By this point, the play-calling was a real source of controversy."

Paul Brown's final championship with the Browns was 1955, Graham's last season. He didn't coach the Browns into the championship game after 1957. Before the 1962 season, Milt Plum complained to reporters about Brown calling the plays—and was promptly traded to Detroit.

But that didn't stop the debate that Paul Brown was too much a dictator, that he took away the players' ability to simply play the game.

And around this time, a young guy from New York named Art Modell bought the team, and life would never be the same for Paul Brown.

ART MODELL

Paul Brown made a critical mistake when he met Art Modell: He underestimated this young man from New York.

Brown took one look at Modell and saw a thirty-five-year-old advertising and TV huckster who had never worn a pair of shoulder pads in his life. He heard the New York accent and assumed the fast-talking Modell was a nervous wreck.

Paul Brown thought Art Modell would be like all the other owners, that Modell would kiss his championship rings and never be seen except on Sunday afternoons.

He didn't know Modell. He probably didn't know many people like Modell, because few were as driven as this young owner of the Browns. Paul Brown didn't know that Art Modell had been rich and then poor. He didn't know that Modell became the man of his family at the age of sixteen. More than fifty years later, Modell was still haunted by his father's death in 1939.

"My father's name was George," Modell said. "I don't care what they say, I consider him a great man. In 1915, my father and his brother owned a radio store. He owned the first radio stores in America. By the 1920s, he was doing business with RCA, all the big electronic companies. He owned eleven stores and they sold those huge radios that you see in old movies, the ones where the family would gather around and listen to FDR give his fireside chats. Then came the crash. I mean, the Depression turned his business to tapioca."

Modell lived in a fine house with servants. His family was rich, and his father had made the money himself.

"Then it was gone," Modell said, snapping his fingers. "Just like that. The vacations to the shore, the Packard limousine, all of it. He was down to one store, and he gave that store to his brother, my uncle Henry. And my father went on the road to support us. I was five years old when it all changed, when our country had food lines and people selling apples on the corner. What you see in those old pictures of the Depression is true. That was my childhood."

George Modell became a traveling wine salesman in the 1930s. By then, the servants were gone. The car was old. He had enough money to support his family—but just barely, and certainly not in the style to which they had become accustomed.

"To go from having eleven stores to working for someone else and selling wine out of a suitcase," Modell said, pausing. "It was horrendous. The damage it did to his pride. He was such a good man, great sense of humor and he looked like Douglas Fairbanks. He was extraordinary. I was too young to realize what he was going through, how he cashed in all his insurance policies and worked so hard to keep the family going. I just knew I loved him. He was the original Willy Loman from *Death of a Salesman.*"

Then came 1939.

"My father and mother left New York together for an automobile trip to the South," Modell said. "It was going to be part business, part vacation. My mother got off in Shreveport, Louisiana, and she took the train home. He continued on to Austin, Texas, and that was where he died. I don't know what he died from, I just know that he died in Austin, Texas."

Modell paused.

"In the middle 1980s, the *Akron Beacon Journal* did a series of stories about me," he said. "The reporter went down to Austin and poked his nose into the records. He published the death certificate, which said my father died from acute alcoholism. It was the first time I had ever heard that. I read that story and cried, I just broke down in tears."

Modell worries about the man's reputation.

"No one in my family said he had a drinking problem. I don't remember him having a drinking problem. This was 1939, they put anything on death certificates back then. They found him in a hotel room. He had wine samples in his briefcase. They put that together and came up with alcoholism, and they did him and my family a terrible disservice. I wrote a scathing letter to the paper, and I said, 'You destroyed the myth that a young man had, the dream that I loved and how I loved my father. With no cause and no reason, you published it.' I'm telling you, that crushed me."

Modell's voice cracked as he talked about it.

"I carry such tremendous scars from those experiences that to this day, I refuse to go to Austin, Texas. I have no interest in going there. I don't care what is down there. I will never go there for any reason."

Modell made himself a promise.

"I was fourteen when my father died," he said. "I was determined to make it big, to do well and compensate for all those years."

Modell dropped out of high school and went to work in the shipyards to help support his family. He had two sisters. One taught piano upstairs, the other gave dance lessons in the basement. His mother found a job as a secretary.

"We had a mortgage at the Dime Savings Bank," he said. "We barely made the payments each month, but we made it. I earned fifty-eight cents an hour in the shipyards. I went to school at night. At seventeen, I joined the Air Force, and I had a job, too; from midnight until 8 a.m., I worked as an oiler on the Chicago/Rock Island Railroad. During the day, I did my Air Force duty. I nearly killed myself to send money home."

Modell had another way of picking up a few bucks: He was a very good pool player. Often, he could be found at Pacey's Pool Hall in Brooklyn, winning money from older men who were shocked at the kid's skill with a pool cue.

After leaving the Air Force, Modell returned to New York and used his GI Bill of Rights to attend college with a program specializing in a new medium known as television.

"This was 1946," Modell said. "Radio people said TV was a fad. Movie people said it would never replace motion pictures. I came in at the right time, the beginning. I wanted to be a producer. I wanted a field where I could make a name for myself, and something new like television seemed perfect. By 1947, I was producing twelve hours a week of programming for ABC. I went out, got the sponsors, and sold the commercial time myself. This was when there were only 5,000 TV sets in the greater New York area. People would stand in front of department stores and watch TV through the windows, those old black and white sets."

Modell was successful in TV, but more intrigued by advertising. In

1954, that became his main interest, and he was a vice president by 1960 when he received a phone call that changed his life—and Paul Brown's.

If you want to blame someone for Art Modell's becoming owner of the Browns, start with a guy named Fred "Curly" Morrison.

He was a former Browns fullback who had connections with the Browns' owners in the early 1960s. They told Morrison they wanted to sell, and asked Morrison if he knew anyone who was looking to get into the football business.

Curly Morrison had never heard of Art Modell and had no idea that Modell would become the man who'd fire Paul Brown, own the Cleveland Browns for thirty-five years, and then move them to Baltimore.

But Curly Morrison knew Vinnie Andrews, who was a New York theatrical agent. Morrison was aware that Andrews moved in the circles where men had big money, men who liked action and were willing to take a gamble. Compared to investing in a Broadway show, buying into the NFL was safer than loading your bank account with U.S. Savings Bonds.

"I have a client in the television business," Andrews told Morrison. "He's a real football nut."

So if you are going to blame Morrison, you must blame Andrews as well. The man Andrews knew was Arthur B. Modell of Brooklyn, New York.

According to Modell, Andrews called him one day and the conversation went like this:

"Art, how would you like to buy a football team?" Andrews said.

"I have no interest in the New York Titans," said Modell, who had heard that the AFL team was for sale.

"I don't know if it's the Titans," Andrews said.

"Is it the Giants?" asked Modell.

"I don't know," Andrews said.

"Well, what league is it in?" asked Modell.

"I don't know," said Andrews.

"Come on, how am I supposed to know if I want to buy it, when you can't tell me what team—or even what league it is?" Modell said, growing agitated.

Modell asked for a meeting with someone who had the answers. Andrews agreed, and Modell found himself talking to Curly Morrison and Andrews. Modell already thought this was great, because he knew that Morrison had been a star at Ohio State and later played for the Browns. The only people Modell enjoyed having around more than show business types were athletes, so he was trying not to be starstruck when meeting with Morrison.

"It's the NFL," Andrews said. "But I can't tell you the name of the team until you express a real interest. I don't want you blabbing about this all over town."

"How am I supposed to make a judgment about this when I don't know what the hell it is?" Modell asked. "You have my promise. I will keep this in the strictest confidence. If I don't want the team, you'll never hear about it from me again."

"Art," Andrews said, pausing. "It is the Cleveland Browns."

Modell sat there, dumbfounded. For one of the few times in his life, he had nothing to say.

The Cleveland Browns? Paul Brown's team?

"This was 1960," Modell later recalled. "This was like having a chance to buy the New York Yankees dynasty. At that point, I didn't know what the team would cost. I didn't know where I'd find the money. I just knew that these guys were offering me a chance to buy the Cleveland Browns, and I was going to get it done—no matter what."

There was another character in this story, a stockbroker named Roger Struck who had an interest in the team. He arranged for Modell to attend a Browns–Chicago Bears game on December 11, 1960. Struck was there to put the finishing touches on the sales job to Modell, but he could have saved his breath; from the moment Modell heard about the Browns being for sale, he was obsessed with buying them.

"I wasn't thinking clearly," Modell said. "It was December and I went to that football game in nothing more than a raincoat. I was sitting at the north end of the Stadium. The wind was whipping off Lake Erie and around the scoreboard. I froze my ass off."

But his fire for the team burned hotter. The Browns hammered the Bears, 42–0, that day. Modell saw Paul Brown stand stoically on the sidelines, arms folded, watching his team perform with precision. Modell sat there with 38,155 fans and thought, "This could be mine." He thought how Paul Brown could be *his* coach, Jim Brown *his* running back. He looked at over 40,000 empty seats for this great team, and *he*, Art Modell, was sure that *he* was the guy who could bring some New York sizzle to this town and sell out this huge stadium.

The snow was falling. The skies were gray. The wind was cutting him in half. He was smoking cigarette after cigarette, throwing down one cup of coffee after another. None of it helped. It was freezing, but he was smiling. The Cleveland Browns. His Cleveland Browns. Arthur B. Modell, who never even finished high school, the same Arthur B. Modell could own all this. Owner of the Cleveland Browns. He ran that phrase through his head, over and over.

Later, Modell asked his contacts, "How much do you want for the team?"

"Four million," they said.

It was an outrageous price. It was worse than robbery. Few teams were worth even $1 million in 1960. While the Browns were on their way to an 8-3-1 record and a second-place finish, attendance was down to 57,000 per game; two years before, the team averaged 63,000.

"Four million," repeated Modell. "You've got a deal."

Modell kept thinking about being owner of the Cleveland Browns.

"I never had been to Cleveland in my life until I came out on that snowy Sunday to see the Browns play the Bears," he said. "I was a New York guy, never wanted to live anywhere else. You know what they used to say, 'Anything outside of New York was Bridgeport.' That was my attitude until I had a chance to buy the Browns."

And a chance to prove to his dead father that he had really become somebody.

Now that Modell had a crack at the Browns, all he needed was the money—and the time to raise it.

"I didn't have a nickel," Modell recalled. "I did well in television. If I liquidated everything, I could come up with about $250,000. I had a partner, but he defaulted. The $4 million was a record price for an NFL franchise, and now that I realized how high that price was, I wasn't sure where I'd find the money. But damn it, I was determined to get it."

Modell went from bank to bank. He found new partners. Deals were made, then fell through.

"I found a banker named George Herzog," he said. "He knew me from New York. He was the kind of guy who bet on people, not balance sheets. At this point, I still needed $2.8 million. There was no way my signature could support that kind of loan. But George was with the old Union Commerce Bank in Cleveland and he gave me the $2.8 million, basically against the value of the franchise."

Modell later learned that the only other offer for the team was from a Cleveland group.

"They were willing to pay $2.8 million," he said. "So I probably over-paid by $1.2 million. But I was convinced I could make money on the Browns. I knew that football and television would be a great marriage. Football is made for TV. The rectangular field is perfect. Baseball is terrible on TV because of the shape of the diamond."

Modell was right about the future of football and television, and he later became the point man when the NFL negotiated contracts with various television networks.

On January 25, 1961, Modell closed the $4 million deal to buy con-trolling interest in the Browns. One owner who kept his share in the team was Robert Gries, who had been one of the franchise's original stockholders. He kept his 20 percent interest.

"Paul Brown was a key asset," Modell said. "When I bought the Browns, I thought Paul would remain the coach forever."

Brown had about 15 percent ownership in the club at the time of the deal.

"You can take this how you want," Modell said, "but when I gave Paul his $500,000 check for his share of the team in the boardroom at the Union Commerce Bank, well, that was the last time he ever said hello to me."

Brown also had an eight-year contract with the team worth about $50,000 annually—and that deal was part of the sale agreement between Modell and the old owners.

At the time of the sale, Brown told the *New York Times:* "I retain control over those things I consider essential to the operation of the team."

Modell agreed that Brown would "have a free hand" in running the team, but he also said, "I've loved football since I was seven years old, and I pledge to devote 99 percent of my effort to producing a winning team in Cleveland."

"Most people didn't know Modell when he bought the Browns," said Hal Lebovitz. "Some didn't trust him because he was from New York. Others, because he was Jewish. Every time I wrote a nice story about him, I got a couple of 'Dirty Jew' letters. That was always there for Modell."

Modell knew what many fans were thinking: "They believed I was just coming to town to milk the team for a few years, then sell out for a higher price," he said. "They never understood why a New York advertising man would want to come to Cleveland."

Paul Brown didn't care that Modell was from New York, or that he was Jewish, or that he was in advertising. But the part about Modell moving to Cleveland so he could immerse himself in the football business—well, that made Brown nervous.

"Not long after Art bought the team, I went in to see Paul Brown about my contract," Bernie Parrish recalled. "Paul had already been moved out of his big office—Art had taken it over. Paul was in a smaller office, and he told me, 'This guy paid way too much money for the team, he'll never get it back. And Bernie, you don't want to know where he got his money.'"

As for first impressions of Modell, the *Plain Dealer* called him "An intense man who can rarely be found at ease. He is static tension, three packs of half-smoked cigarettes and a peripatetic schedule."

Not long after buying the team, Modell took Lou Groza to dinner. Groza had been one of his favorite players.

"I surprised Lou by naming eight members of the 1946 team that was in the old All-American Conference," Modell told the *Plain Dealer* in 1961. The newspaper also reported, "There was a touch of the autograph seeker or the hero worshipper when [Modell] talked about that dinner with Lou Groza."

Reading those things was alarming to Paul Brown, who read every word about his team in the Cleveland papers. He knew that Modell was only thirty-five, and that he had become very full of himself after buying the team and seeing his picture and name regularly in the newspapers.

Modell was on a cloud. He was a self-made man, a man who came from nothing to buy the Cleveland Browns. When the purchase was announced, there was Modell's name in headlines on the front of the New York Times sports page. His friends looked at him differently, asked his opinion on football, and wanted to know, "What is Paul Brown really like?"

Art Modell was about to find out.

THE LAST DAYS OF PAUL BROWN

Even before Art Modell bought the Browns, there were whispers about Paul Brown. Not long after he bought the team, Modell heard the whispers; he realized that there was a ghost in the dressing room, the ghost of 1958, the ghost of the fake field goal.

After a while, that ghost took the shape of a question mark, and the questions were about Paul Brown. Those questions were first whispered among the players. As far as the fans knew, Paul Brown was still Paul Brown. But something had happened at the end of the 1958 season, something the players from that team still talk about.

"That damn fake field goal," said Gene Hickerson. "I hate to say it, but Paul Brown cost us that game."

It cost the team a trip to the 1958 championship game. But even worse, it made some of Brown's players begin to wonder if the old man was losing it.

It was the final game of the 1958 regular season. The Browns had a one-game lead over the New York Giants. All they had to do was win or tie in New York to play Baltimore for the NFL title. The Browns believed they had earned that title shot. They were better than the Giants. They had opened the season with four consecutive victories and had been in first place virtually all year.

Yes, it was the Giants, and yes, New York had beaten the Browns, 21–17, earlier in the season at Cleveland Stadium. But they were still the Browns, and Paul Brown's Cleveland Browns just didn't lose this kind of pressure game.

It was a cold, snowy, bone-rattling day in New York. It was not a day to get tricky. It was a day to hand the ball to Jim Brown and block your man into the Harlem River. It was a day to play the game by the book.

At halftime, the Browns had a 10–3 lead. Jim Brown had run 65 yards for a touchdown, and Lou Groza had kicked a 33-yard field goal.

The Giants tied the game at 10–10 early in the fourth quarter.

"We still were in good shape," recalled linebacker Galen Fiss. "We had a better record than New York, so even if the game ended in a tie, we were fine. I wasn't worried."

New York had a chance to take the lead, but Pat Summerall missed a 36-yard field goal and missed it badly. "Flubbed it to the left," he recalled. "There were five minutes left, and I was convinced I had blown the game."

The score was still 10–10. All the Browns had to do was chew up the clock, but the offense coughed up the ball. Snow had turned the field white and slippery. The skies were death gray. New York had the ball.

"In that last drive, there was a play where Frank Gifford caught a short pass in the backfield," Fiss said. "I hit Gifford and knocked the ball loose. Our defensive back, Walt Michaels, picked up the fumble and ran it all the way for a touchdown. That should have been the game."

Nearly forty years later, Fiss found himself so upset about the play that he could barely finish the story.

"The official's name was Charley Berry, I'll never forget that," he said. "He ruled it an incomplete pass. Gifford had caught the ball and taken two steps when I hit him. It was a fumble."

But it wasn't ruled a fumble, or a Browns touchdown, which would have given them a 17–10 lead.

The Giants kept the ball, and Pat Summerall was presented another chance at a field goal.

"And the man kicked a 49-yard field goal right through a driving snowstorm," Fiss said. "I couldn't believe it."

Despite Summerall's outrageous field goal, many Browns players believed they still should have won the game. They point to a decision by Paul Brown late in the third quarter.

The Browns had the ball on New York's 16-yard line. They had a 10–3 lead. It was fourth down and four yards to go. In the players' mind, it was easy: You send Lou Groza out there and you kick the field goal. That would have made the score 13–3. Yes, Groza had missed two field goals earlier in the game. One was from 37 yards, another from 38 yards. Yes, it was snowing and the footing was treacherous. Yes, it wasn't simple to kick on a slippery turf. But the Browns had Lou Groza. If Paul Brown invented pro football, then Lou Groza was the father of placekicking. Others had kicked before Groza, but none as well—at least not in the minds of the Cleveland players.

And didn't Paul Brown so love Groza that this cold, unfeeling coach often called him "My Louie"?

Groza had made a field goal from 33 yards earlier in the game—the same distance this third-quarter kick would have been. The players just knew that Groza would not miss again.

"Originally, Paul was going to have Groza kick the field goal," said backup quarterback Jim Ninowski, who was standing next to Paul Brown when the decision was made. "But then he called timeout. Bobby Freeman was Lou's holder. When Bobby came to the sidelines, Paul changed his mind. There were several of us around Paul. I couldn't believe it. Even though I was just a rookie, I said, 'Paul, let's kick. All we need is a tie.'

"But Paul said, 'No, we're going to fake it.'

"Think about this for a moment. You are on the defensive team. You see the other team getting ready to kick a field goal, then they call timeout and there is a debate on the sidelines. What are you thinking? Don't you think they might be faking it, or why else would they call a timeout?" Ninowski's instincts were correct.

"We went out there, and all of the Giants on defense were yelling, 'Watch the fake . . . watch the fake,'" recalled guard Gene Hickerson. "They were ready for us."

"Bobby Freeman took the snap, started to run, and the defense swarmed him," Ninowski said. "The play had no chance. But when Bobby came off the field, Paul glared at him and said, 'You've lost some of your agility.' Paul didn't want to take the blame for that play."

Later, Brown tried to explain his decision by saying his team had a 10–3 lead; a field goal only would have made it 13–3 . . . a touchdown, and the Browns would have been ahead, 17–3. Since the Giants couldn't afford to tie—they had to win—they would have needed three scores to pull out the game.

"A touchdown there would have put New York in a real hole," Brown explained.

Fans were so baffled by Brown's decision that veteran Cleveland *Plain Dealer* sports editor Gordon Cobbledick wrote, "[There are] the people (and don't think there aren't plenty of them) who are saying the Browns threw the game to New York so they could get another gate and another payday [from a playoff game]."

Cobbledick went on to dismiss the rumors, but it is remarkable that a respected sportswriter such as Cobbledick believed that such rumors had to be addressed in print, so you know they were rampant.

Losing 13–10 to the Giants was not the end of the season. All it did was force a playoff game to determine the conference winner.

"But we had nothing left," Fiss said. "We thought about Summerall's field goal in the snowstorm, the fumble that wasn't called, the fake field goal that didn't work . . . it was like we weren't supposed to win. We took the field that day with a lot of baggage."

And the Browns were beaten, 10–0.

"From that point on, Paul never had quite the same respect from the players," recalled Bob August, who covered that game for the old *Cleveland Press*. "The Giants suddenly became a big issue."

New York beat the Browns three times in 1958. Tom Landry was the Giants' defensive coordinator. According to author Jack Clary in his book *Pro Football's Great Moments*, "Landry predicted that if the Giants smothered Cleveland's running attack, Coach Brown could be depended upon to call a prearranged sequence of pass plays."

In other words, the Giants had a pretty good idea what was coming from the Browns' offense—and they stuffed it. Remember, Paul Brown was calling the plays for quarterback Milt Plum, and he didn't give Plum much freedom to change those plays at the line of scrimmage. Time after time, Browns players lined up and realized they were running a play right into the teeth of the New York defense—and they couldn't change it.

In 1958, the Browns scored only three touchdowns in three games against New York. That season swung the power in the NFL East from Cleveland to New York. In 1959, the disheartened Browns stumbled to a 7-5 record. In 1960, they won their last three games to finish at 8-3-1, but were out of the conference race with two weeks to go.

Then Modell came on the scene.

When Modell took over the Browns, he said all the right things.

"The depth of Paul Brown's genius is incredible," he told reporters. "My job is to supplement the team effort with a zealous promotional program and make it a financial success while Paul Brown continues to produce winning, colorful teams on the field."

What about Brown calling the plays and the messenger guard system?

"As far as I'm concerned, Paul Brown can send the plays in by carrier pigeon," he said. "In my opinion, he has no peer as a football coach. His record speaks for itself. I view our relationship as a working partnership."

And Modell added, "I am assuming responsibility for finances, promotions, that type of thing. We will be consulting frequently. I don't like to outline any delineation of power. We'll be partners in the Browns operation."

Paul Brown read that in his morning newspaper and knew his world was about to change. Since when did he have to consult with anyone? Who was this Modell to expect Paul Brown to confide in him, to ask advice of some kid advertising man from New York?

Paul Brown read that and seethed.

"I meant no harm," Modell later insisted. "I worshiped Paul Brown. I idolized the man. The first time I met him was in the lobby of the Grand Concourse Hotel in the Bronx, right by Yankee Stadium. It was December 17, 1960. I told him, 'I've watched your career and you're a living legend. I love pro football and I want to buy the Browns. . . .' It was a great meeting. He was very warm and wished me well."

Paul Brown had a different memory. In his book, *The Paul Brown Story*, he wrote, "Phil Harber, a member of the team's law firm, brought him [Modell] to our hotel. I had no idea then who he was or that he was involved in the team's sale. I was led to believe that he was a football buff and we had a very pleasant chat. Later, he would tell me, 'I'm buying the team because of you. . . .'"

Not long after closing the sale, Modell began to meet some of the players. They said little about their coach. That bothered Modell. Why didn't these guys like Paul Brown? Didn't they know he was the best coach in the NFL? But as he talked to more players, he began to hear that the players had another opinion. They told him about losing to the Giants in the 1958 game, the fake field goal. They told him that he took their freedom away by calling all the plays.

"It didn't take long for me to discover the truth about the Browns," Modell said. "The team was on the decline. I also had a lot of people telling me that the game was starting to pass Paul Brown by a little bit."

When he bought the team, Modell's favorite Browns player was Lou Groza, who had retired before the 1960 season.

"I had been an offensive tackle and a kicker," Groza said. "I hurt my back and couldn't play tackle anymore. Heck, I could barely walk, so I took 1960 off and did some scouting and worked in my insurance business. I was thirty-six and I thought I had retired."

One day, Modell called Groza, just to introduce himself as the new owner of the Browns. That was one of the wonderful perks of the job. Modell could just call anyone associated with the NFL, and they'd talk to him! Just like that!

"Lou, do you still work out?" asked Modell.

Groza said he was retired.

"But do you think you can still kick?" asked Modell. "I bet you'll be able to kick straight from your grave."

Groza began to feel his heart beat a little faster. Was Modell saying what he thought? Did the Browns want him to come back and kick? Lord, he missed the Browns. He missed kicking. He missed the players. He missed smoking a big cigar with friends after practice.

"I have an idea," Modell said. "Why don't you meet me at that high school field near your house? We'll throw a football around."

Modell spotted Groza at the high school. He threw him a pass, and Groza caught it. The two men, both in their middle thirties, laughed like a couple of kids.

"Hey, Lou," Modell said. "I'll hold and you kick some."

He set up at the 20-yard line. Groza's boot split the uprights.

They moved back to the 25 . . . the 30 . . . the 35 . . . the 40 . . . the 45 . . . it was boom, Boom, BOOM! The big man was kicking like he always kicked, like no man in the NFL had ever kicked before.

According to Modell, the next day he approached Paul Brown and said, "I saw Lou Groza kicking the other day. I don't want to interfere. It's your show. But if you bring Groza back, just let him kick."

And according to Modell, Brown replied, "That's impossible. He's washed up. He's over the hill."

Modell said the next night, he was home and turned on the television news, "And there was Paul Brown announcing that he had brought Groza back to kick. I thought, 'Boy, are we in for a great relationship.' That was just the start of a lot of things that disturbed me."

Paul Brown wanted to keep everything the same.

He would make assistant coach Howard Brinker walk with him every Sunday when the Browns were at home, walk that long mile down East Ninth Street from the team hotel to the Stadium. Rain or snow, they walked. On some of those fall Sunday mornings, the frigid gusts felt like a hacksaw. Brinker had to wish that they took a cab or a team bus instead of walking. Often, Brown said nothing, but it was understood: Come seventy degrees or a blizzard, they walked to the Stadium.

Then there was the team's training camp in Hiram, where Brown's players ran the 40-yard dash on the first day of camp. Today, a player's time in the 40-yard dash is a universally accepted measure of a football player's speed. But it was Paul Brown who used it first, believing that the average punt went 40 yards and he wanted to see how fast his defensive players could go that distance to cover the punt.

And Paul Brown continued to come up with new gimmicks. A couple of his blockers complained that defensive linemen were grabbing them by their face masks (face masks were another Paul Brown invention to protect Otto Graham's broken nose). But now, opponents were grabbing some of the Browns players by the mask and throwing them to the turf. Paul Brown had the face masks taped, and on the inside he attached tacks, pointing out. When the defender put his hands around the mask, his fingers were cut to shreds by the tacks. That was one way to stop the illegal play of face-masking linemen.

And Paul Brown still kept a box of chocolates on top of his desk in his Hiram College dorm room. When kids visited camp, sons and daughters of players, coaches or friends, Paul would excuse himself, go to his room, and return with the chocolates. One big family was what they were, with Paul Brown in charge. That was how he wanted it to remain.

But now there was Modell . . .

There was Modell riding around town in that maroon and black Cadillac as if he were Mr. Cleveland.

There was Modell in the office at seven every morning, taking over the big office and sticking Brown in the smaller one down the hall.

There was Modell hanging out at the Theatrical Grill, a Cleveland nightclub, acting like he was the reincarnation of old Indians owner Bill Veeck, telling jokes, taking players to dinner, buying them drinks. Didn't he know that Paul Brown had rules against drinking? Didn't he care about the image of his team? Didn't he realize how it looked to have the owner of the team out sharing cocktails with his players?

There was Modell living in his swanky bachelor pad on the West Side, right on Lake Erie. He had big stereo speakers, and he told anyone who could hear him, "I love my music, and I play it *loud.*" He nearly destroyed your eardrums with those Broadway show tunes. And women—Art Modell was seen with more women than some of his players. How was Paul Brown supposed to tell his guys to stay out of bars and stay away from the women when the owner was out on the town every night? So what if Modell was single? He should be an owner first, a bachelor second.

There was Modell at practice, almost every day. Didn't Modell realize that practice was a sacred time between the coach and the players? Didn't Modell know that he hated the idea that any stranger might even just walk by and take a peek? Didn't he know that the owner had no place in practice?

And then there was Modell in the dressing room before a game . . .

"It was during my first year as owner," Modell said. "I stopped in the locker room to see the players. Paul called the team together for his pregame talk. I sat on a duffel bag in the back of the room as he told the players, 'Play hard . . . no mistakes . . . Okay, let's go.' The players filed out and then Paul called me over and said, 'I'd appreciate it if you never came in here again. This is private, between myself and the players. You don't belong here and don't come back.' That hurt me. I didn't think it was necessary for him to talk to me that way."

Modell paused as he told the story.

"Paul didn't understand," he said. "I wanted to be his friend. But he viewed me with suspicion. He wasn't used to having an owner who wanted to talk to people in the front office, an owner who wanted to hire people for some of those front office jobs. He was used to owners who showed up on Sundays with a drink in their hands and a tag that said 'Owner' on their chests. But those guys had other businesses. The Browns were almost like a hobby to them. To me, the Browns were my life. I had leveraged myself over my eyeballs. I quit my job in New York.

The Browns were my only business and I was going to keep my hands on it."

Modell did approve a ten-year contract extension for Brown, beginning in 1961. Brown would be paid $82,500 annually with a chance to buy stock in the team each year. He also had bought out Brown's old shares in the team for $500,000.

"It didn't take us long to realize that Art was closer in age and interest to the players than he was to the coaches," said Galen Fiss. "Art was single, and the guys—especially the single players—would see him at places around town. Art was having a tough time. He wanted more authority with the team, and thought he deserved it because he was the owner. He was a young man with a tremendous amount of confidence, and Paul Brown wasn't giving Art the respect Art felt he deserved."

Which made Modell someone for players to go to complain about Paul Brown. They knew Modell was having trouble with the coach, so he'd be sympathetic—and he was.

In his book, Paul Brown wrote that he was becoming disturbed about Modell's press releases, "which continually referred to us having the best at this position or that position until any reasonable person could only assume we were promising a championship."

Paul Brown told Modell this. Modell said he knew about publicity and advertising; that was where he made his money in New York. What was wrong with hyping the team a little bit, creating conversation? We're a business, right? We have to sell tickets, right?

But Paul Brown worried that he was being put in the position where he had to win a championship or else. Then he heard that Modell would watch games in the press box, second-guessing and complaining about the players and coaches right out loud.

"That doesn't mean anything," Modell said. "I'm just a fan."

"No," Paul Brown sternly informed him. "You are the owner and the position requires that you conduct yourself a bit differently in public, particularly when sitting among the press."

Modell did tone down his press box act, but he continued to pepper Brown with questions: Why run inside so much? Why wasn't the pass rush better? Why this? Why that? Why not make a trade?

Brown was disturbed when Modell told fans and writers, "No matter how much money it takes, I'm prepared to guarantee that we will win an NFL title."

Then there was Jim Brown.

At his first press conference, Art Modell referred to the star running back as "my senior partner."

If Jim Brown was the owner's senior partner, then where was Paul Brown in all this? Besides, until Art Modell showed up, the players believed there was no owner—at least none that counted—except Paul Brown. And as sure as Paul Brown could cut their heads off with one razor-slash line during practice, they knew that Paul Brown had no partners. God doesn't have a partner, does He?

Paul Brown viewed football as a sacred calling. To Modell, it was show business and Jim Brown was his star. If you don't have a star, you create one. If you're lucky enough to have the greatest player in the game, you promote him. You get him in the newspapers, on radio and television. You use him to sell tickets.

That was how Modell was raised.

It turned Paul Brown's stomach. No one player was greater than the team or the coach. No player was allowed to have his own radio show or newspaper column. Rules were rules, and what was best for one player was best for every player. Modell changed that. Modell made exceptions. Modell put Jim Brown together with Cleveland sportswriter Hal Lebovitz, and the two combined for a radio show and a newspaper column. Modell thought it was good publicity for the team. It meant a few extra bucks for Jim Brown and Lebovitz, so they were happy. Besides, who got hurt?

Paul Brown believed that players with their own shows were pushed to say controversial things—and eventually they would. Paul Brown would rather eat a bucket of rusty nails than have any controversy on his team. But he couldn't overrule Modell on this. The owner *just went out and did it,* and he didn't even ask Paul Brown. So by the time the coach found out about it, he would have had to take the show (and the money from it) away from his running back and Lebovitz. That would have made three important people angry—Modell, Jim Brown, and Lebovitz. So Paul Brown let it go and waited for the storm.

"When Milt Plum spoke out against Paul calling all the plays, Jim Brown backed him on his radio show," Lebovitz recalled. "There also was a controversy among the fans about who should be the starting

quarterback, Milt Plum or Jim Ninowski. Jim backed Plum. No sooner
was the show over than I got a call from Paul Brown. He was very upset
about what Jim had said. He was starting to yell at me. I stopped him
and said, 'Paul, I just wrote what Jim told me he wanted to say. Here is
Jim's number, you call him and talk about it.' Then I called Jim and told
him to expect a call from the coach. But Paul never called."

Why not?

"The truth was that Paul was scared of Jim Brown," Lebovitz said.
"He'd tell any other player, 'You are like an apple on a tree—one day
you'll get too ripe and just fall off.' But he'd never say anything like that
to Jim Brown. In fact, when I told Jim that Paul would call, Jim said,
'No, he won't.' Jim Brown had the same kind of chip on his shoulder as
Paul Brown."

"It's true," said Ninowski. "Paul would never criticize Jimmy. I don't
know if it was because Jimmy was such a great talent or what. I can
recall a play where Paul crawled all over me for a mistake that Jimmy
made. I knew it was Jimmy's fault—so did Paul, and so did Jimmy. After
the meeting, Jimmy came up and apologized to me for getting me in
trouble. I said, 'Jimmy, he wants to stick the needle in you to play better,
but he doesn't have the guts to do it to your face. That was just his way
of giving you the message.' Maybe because he worked Jimmy so hard,
running him thirty, even thirty-five times a game, he just wouldn't confront him."

The closest Paul Brown would come to zapping his running back
would be at a banquet, where he introduced Jim Brown, "Jimmy is the
greatest runner in the game—and I pay him that way." Or he'd say, "The
only thing fat about Jim Brown is his wallet."

"I never had any real problems with Paul Brown," said Jim Brown.
"When I came to the Browns, I loved the idea that he was strict. I loved
his organization and administrative skills. I appreciated it when he'd
call the team together and say, 'We are the Yankees of pro football.'
Then he'd tell us how he expected us to speak, act, and dress to a certain
standard. The one strange thing he'd say was, 'I don't want any butch-
ers on this team.' I was never quite sure what that meant, and I was not
about to ask."

There was another reason Jim Brown respected his coach.

"Paul Brown integrated pro football without uttering a single word
about integration," he said. "He just went out, signed a bunch of great

black athletes, and started kicking butt. That's how you do it. You don't talk about it. Paul never said one word about race. But this was a time in sports when you'd play in some cities and the white players could stay at the nice hotel, but the blacks had to stay in the homes of some black families in town. But not with Paul. We always stayed in hotels that took the entire team. Again, he never said a word. But in his own way, the man integrated football the right way—and no one was going to stop him."

Some suggested the problems between Paul Brown and Jim Brown were racial, that the older white coach was just not ready to deal with an emerging young black superstar. But race wasn't the issue. Jim Brown believed that after accomplishing so much on the football field, he had the right to supply some input into the offense. That is why he supported Milt Plum. He thought players had the right to make suggestions about the game plan.

"The only trouble I ever had with Paul Brown was that he became too conservative with his play-calling," Jim Brown said. "It wasn't just me, but a number of players felt that. Players on defense, too. I felt that I was sort of boxed in, running from tackle to tackle. That was tough, inside running. That was fine, but I also wanted a chance to run outside on sweeps, but that wasn't in Paul's offense."

Jim Brown thought it should be, and let others know.

"Art Modell sensed the dissatisfaction with Paul," Jim Brown said. "He picked up on that."

In the end, it came down to Modell and Paul Brown.

In his first season as owner, the Browns had an 8-5-1 record, but won only one of their last four games. After that 1961 season, Paul Brown was determined to trade for another running back to play next to and block for Jim Brown. Bobby Mitchell had been the halfback, but Brown thought the slight and swift Mitchell was better suited for wide receiver. He certainly didn't picture Mitchell as a rugged blocker for Jim Brown.

Paul Brown was in love with a runner named Ernie Davis, who had just broken all of Jim Brown's rushing records at Syracuse. Paul Brown liked Mitchell, but Mitchell weighed only 188 pounds and did not have the kind of frame that would easily add bulk. Mitchell also was serving military duty and would be available only on weekends in 1962, meaning he'd miss practice. The Washington Redskins were looking for a player to break their color line (yes, Washington had no black players until 1962), and the Redskins knew that Mitchell was classy and bright, the perfect guy to do it. So the Browns traded Mitchell and a No. 1 pick to Washington for the draft rights to Syracuse star Ernie Davis.

"One day, I got a call from [Redskins owner] George Marshall," Modell said. "He asked me, 'What do you think of our trade?'

"I said, 'George, what trade?'

"He said, 'Mitchell and your No. 1 pick for our No. 1 pick.'

"I was embarrassed into silence.

"Then George said, 'Aren't you running that franchise?'

"I stammered, 'George . . . well . . . I don't know . . .'

"He said, 'Don't ever let that happen again. You are the owner. You own the franchise. It's *yours.*'"

Modell went to see Paul Brown.

He told the coach he was embarrassed by the conversation, asking Paul Brown how he could make a trade of that magnitude and not tell the owner.

"I mean, you could have asked or consulted or at least given me a warning," Modell said.

Paul Brown just looked at Modell as if he were a petulant child. What was this young man from New York thinking? Didn't he know that Paul Brown didn't consult with an owner? He was the coach. He had always made all the football decisions and always would.

"Paul had no idea where I was coming from on this and he didn't care," Modell said. "He was used to owners like Mickey McBride, who just paid the bills and wouldn't even know who Bobby Mitchell was, or if they should trade him for Ernie Davis."

Modell sensed that most fans liked the trade. Davis was a great college player. So he took over the contract negotiations—something Paul Brown had always handled. He signed Ernie Davis to an $80,000 deal—$30,000 more than Jim Brown made in 1961.

Paul Brown knew that was trouble.

Then Modell said that the addition of Davis virtually "guaranteed" a championship. At a Sigma Delta Chi journalism fraternity dinner, Modell told the audience, "The Browns will win their first championship since 1955 and the team will be the finest in years. Spectators will feast on a brand of professional skills unmatched since the Golden Days of ten years ago . . . if we don't win, we'll have a rough time finding excuses."

Paul Brown bristled. Modell had set him up to fail. Only one team wins a championship. But to Modell, this was just creating interest in the team; he was still an advertising man, believing that no one would remember what he said yesterday. Hey, every year some product is "New and Improved," right? Why not a "new and improved" Browns?

Paul Brown wasn't buying.

Modell also told reporters, "Paul has my unqualified support. I'm a Paul Brown man. I believe in him. He's one of the greatest coaches of all time. I'm sure if there are any adjustments to make, he'll make it."

Paul Brown wasn't buying that, either.

Then Ernie Davis was diagnosed with leukemia just as training camp opened.

Things became very ugly, full of charges and countercharges between Modell and Paul Brown. A few weeks into the season, Davis went into remission. He was convinced that he was getting better, that he'd beat the disease. He was working out with the team—not in contact drills, but in the conditioning drills and even sitting in on team meetings.

Modell believed that Davis deserved a chance to play in a game, almost as a dying wish. Davis also had been cleared by one doctor to play.

Paul Brown loved Ernie Davis, because he not only was a great talent but a superb human being. It tore up the veteran coach to see this young man at practice, this young man who was dying. In his book, Paul Brown wrote, "Modell told me, 'Put him in a game, let him play. We have a big investment in him, and I'd like to get some of that back. It doesn't matter how long he plays, just let him run back a kick, let him do anything so we can get a story in the paper saying he's going to play and the fans will come to see him. If he has to go, why not let him have a little fun?'"

Modell heatedly disputes that he wanted to bleed some dollars out of Ernie Davis, insisting he wanted Davis to play because it was what Davis wanted.

"Ernie really did want to play," recalled Hal Lebovitz. "His doctor was a childhood friend of mine, and he gave Ernie permission to play. But Paul refused to do it. I can't say that I blame Paul. If I were a coach and had a player with leukemia, I don't think I'd play him and take that responsibility. Later, Paul would claim that Ernie did not have a doctor's permission, but I know for a fact that he did. They finally compromised by putting the poor kid in a uniform, introducing him before a game and having him run across the field in a spotlight."

Davis received a standing ovation. It probably was the best course of action, but so much bad blood had been spilled between Modell and Paul Brown over the incident that it became yet another wedge between them.

A sign that all the pressure from Modell was wearing on Paul Brown could be seen in his relationship with Blanton Collier.

If ever two men were destined to be best of friends, it was Paul Brown and Collier.

They met during World War II, when Paul Brown was coaching at Great Lakes Naval Training Station. That was in 1943. Brown noticed a sailor in glasses always hanging around his practices. Turned out the man was Blanton Collier, who had been a high school football coach. He had heard of the famed Paul Brown, and when he discovered that Paul Brown was coaching right near his naval station, Collier was a regular at practice, taking notes and hoping to learn something he could take back to his high school in Kentucky after the war. Brown began talking to Collier, and soon Collier was helping Brown as a volunteer assistant coach. When Paul Brown moved to Cleveland and pro football in 1946, Collier went with him.

"My father did more than coach under Paul Brown," said Kay Collier-Slone, Blanton's daughter. "The two families became extremely close. Paul Brown came to our family weddings. To me, he was like an uncle, and I knew that he was my father's best friend. I found out that he had put himself through college playing dance band piano. I was a young musician, and Paul Brown would sit with me at the piano, and we'd play duets. I remember him trying to play my French horn."

In 1954, Collier left the Browns to become head coach at the University of Kentucky.

"They still talked often," Collier-Slone recalled. "We went up to Ohio during the summers so Daddy could go to training camp with Paul. The families got together at Turkeyfoot Lake. When Daddy was having trouble at Kentucky, my mother called Paul—not for football advice, but to invite Paul and his wife down to just be there for Blanton. Paul Brown came down and offered support for my family, all the way to Lexington, Kentucky.

"That is the kind of friends the Browns and Colliers were."

Collier was fired at Kentucky after the 1961 season. He had a respectable 41-36-3 record, but was only 5-5 in his final season.

"Daddy had replaced Bear Bryant at Kentucky," Collier-Slone said. "He made it very clear that the alumni were not going to buy his house for him. He was not going to be beholden to anyone, and his players were going to attend class and graduate. The faculty had a lot of respect for him. He was the Southeastern Conference Coach of the Year in his first season."

But Collier never won as big as the alumni thought he should. In his high school, his nickname was "Brainy." At Kentucky, he wore horn-rimmed glasses and talked like a math professor. The alumni just didn't think he had enough blood-and-guts football in him to lead Kentucky to an SEC title.

"Toward the end, the fans hung Daddy in effigy on the courthouse lawn," Collier-Slone said. "My mother was a very social being, very gregarious. But she stopped going downtown to shop. She loved to entertain, but she stopped that, too. It just became uncomfortable to see people, even some of our friends. There were threatening telephone calls in the middle of the night. My mother took it harder than Daddy."

It was almost a relief to the Collier family when the school bought out Blanton's contract, which had three years left and was worth a total of $50,000. (Yes, a Division I football coach made under $20,000 a year back in the early 1960s.)

The Collier family was overjoyed when Paul Brown called and hired Blanton as the Browns' offensive backfield coach for 1962.

"My happiest days were coaching the Browns," Collier told the *Plain Dealer* when he was hired in 1962. "I'm pleased and grateful that Paul wanted me back. We'll be in Cleveland lock, stock and barrel as soon as we can sell our home and clean up some odds and ends. This is like returning home."

Paul Brown told reporters, "Blanton is a scientific football man, a very unusual one. He has ideas and is an outstanding teacher. He rates with the best in the scientific aspects of the game, but he also is a wonderful gentleman and one of my closest friends."

During the 1962 exhibition season, Paul Brown made some changes in the messenger guard system. He also allowed Collier to use a "checkoff system," which gave the quarterback freedom to switch from the play called by the coaches to one of several other options.

"The checkoff system became a point of contention between Blanton and Paul," Lebovitz recalled. "Frank Gibbons wrote a flattering piece about Blanton (in the *Cleveland Press*) and gave credit to Blanton for the Browns being undefeated in the exhibition season. Paul read that and put Blanton in the corner. The checkoff system was over, and that was the beginning of a split between those two good friends."

"That's true," said Bernie Parrish. "Blanton was as loyal to Paul as anyone could be. But when the newspapers gave him a little credit for the offense, Paul took away Blanton's authority. It got to be petty."

"The players believed that Paul was upset when Blanton received some good press," Jim Ninowski recalled. "Paul just junked Blanton's system, as if to say, 'Hey, I'm running the show now.' I know this happened."

As the 1962 season progressed, Paul Brown relied less and less on his old friend. He withdrew into his coaching foxhole, feeling pressure from all sides—from Modell, from some of the players, from Davis's illness, and from the press, who seemed too anxious to embrace Collier as if they had forgotten all the good things Paul Brown had done for Cleveland.

"Daddy was a self-taught psychologist," said Collier-Slone. "He knew that Paul was under strain and feeling paranoid. He simply was not the same Paul that he had been in the past. Daddy never talked about how Paul changed the offense, but we know it was true. We also know that he never assigned Daddy a desk or an office. It was a difficult situation, because Paul wanted Daddy there, but became upset when Daddy got a little bit of credit."

Collier loved to break down game films. He spent hours charting plays and tendencies. He could tell you the favorite moves of every player in the league. Certain runners loved to fake with their left shoulders, others with their right hips. Collier reveled in this minutiae.

Art Modell spotted this quiet man in the corner of the office, watching films by the hour and taking notes. Since Modell wanted to spend time with anyone who'd talk football and was closed out by Paul Brown, he gravitated to Collier, who he sensed had also been left out in the cold by the coach. By nature, Collier was a friendly man and loved to talk football. Modell had found a teacher.

Collier was just happy to have a little company. He found himself in a tough spot: Modell was the owner, his boss—but so was Paul Brown, and he knew that Brown didn't want his coaches talking to Modell. But what was he supposed to do, tell Modell to take a hike? He had just been hired as an assistant. He didn't even have a desk. So he was patient with Modell, continued to work hard for Paul Brown—and prayed that somehow this mess would work out.

Meanwhile, Modell was spending more and more time with the players. He was the Man About Town, the team's bachelor owner who drove fast, smoked three packs of Marlboros a day, and had special tables at Cleveland's premier nightclubs.

Paul Brown wrote that when his team beat the New York Giants, 17-7, to open the 1962 season, Modell rushed into the dressing room and "threw his arms around me and kissed me. I couldn't stand to be around him, especially since I knew that while he was displaying all this affection, he was also working against me among the players. No wonder he told people that I was cold and unemotional toward him."

When the Browns opened the 1962 season with a 2-3 record, there were no more hugs from Modell. Instead, he would buy the players drinks after games—even though he knew that Brown objected to drinking on the team. The coach believed Modell was undermining the discipline on his team—and he was right.

"We had a game in New York where we ran into the old actor George Raft in a hotel lobby," Gene Hickerson recalled. "Paul Brown said it was time for the team to leave for the airport, but Art held up the bus for thirty minutes so he and some of the players could talk to George Raft. That obviously didn't sit well with Paul Brown."

There was a time when the Browns were fogged in at the Sacramento airport, and Modell bought the players drinks in the airport bar. This was the day before the team would play the San Francisco 49ers. It was the final sign that the coach had lost control of the team.

Linebacker Jim Houston and defensive back Ross Fichtner both tell this story about a practice before that same game in San Francisco—the last game of the 1962 season:

Cleveland had been blanketed by a blizzard. Paul Brown always kept his practices short, and he didn't see any reason to put his players through long drills in the middle of a snowstorm. "But that day, he had us on the practice field at League Park," Fichtner recalled. "Instead of being on the field with us, Paul sat in his car, about twenty yards behind the offense. The quarterback would go to Paul's car after every play, and Paul would roll down the window and give him the play. The players were all freezing, and Paul was in his warm car."

"The snow was over your knees," Houston said. "Paul had the players out there. It made no sense, because afterward we had to catch a train to New York—the weather had closed the Cleveland airport—and then we were flying from New York to San Francisco for the game. It was so out of character for him that, to this day, I don't understand it."

Modell heard about this, and really began to believe the players were right in everything they said about Paul Brown. Of course, the team was finishing up a 7-6-1 season, so he was also looking for reasons to make a coaching change.

"I think that the guys felt that Paul Brown wanted a winning season rather than a championship," said Fichtner.

Why?

"Because it was the best deal for the team financially," he said. "These were the days of one-year contracts. By finishing second, you still drew good crowds because you almost won. But you also could tell your players at contract time that they didn't win a title, so they weren't entitled to much of a raise. You saved money on salaries, and you didn't have to buy championship rings, either."

Can this be true?

"That's what the players talked about," Fichtner insisted.

While it's hard to believe that Paul Brown set out to finish second, the fact that some players began to suspect as much demonstrated that there were more problems on the team than the relationship between the coach and the owner.

"In my first two years, I was a Paul Brown man," said Bernie Parrish. "But I had a lot of veterans telling me, 'Wait until you get to know him.' They hated his guts, but I thought Paul was doing a great job. It turned out that they were right. Paul didn't adjust to the changes in the game. By 1962, he was more worried about protecting his reputation as the Greatest Coach Who Ever Lived than he was about winning a title. But he had not been to a title game since 1957, and many of us on the 1962 team were not around back in 1957. We felt his strategy held us back, and the guys on defense believed Paul was more interested in the offense. By the end of the 1962 season, a lot of us wanted to be traded because we were convinced that we'd never win a title with Paul Brown—and we never believed Paul Brown was going anywhere."

Bill Glass said that on that final train trip to New York and then on the flight to San Francisco, Modell was talking to different players about Paul Brown's future.

"At Art's request, he wanted to know what I thought of Paul Brown," Glass said. "I had just been with the team for a year. I got along fine with Paul. But I also was very aware that a lot of the key players didn't like him. It was kind of weird, Modell asking the players about the coach on that final trip. He also was asking us about Blanton Collier. It wasn't even if we thought Blanton would make a good head coach. It was almost as if the situation had been decided, and Art wanted to check our feelings about Blanton. I thought Blanton was a genius when it came to football, and I said so. I don't think Art Modell wanted to fire Paul Brown because he was sensitive to public opinion, but the more he heard from the players, he knew he had to fire Paul Brown."

The players told Modell of a game where Ray Renfro dropped a pass, and when he came to the bench, Brown told his aging receiver, "Well, you just can't make the big catch anymore." Several players insisted that Renfro broke down and cried, right there in the middle of the game.

"I remember that San Francisco trip," Parrish said. "I was telling [broadcaster] Ken Coleman how so many guys just couldn't bear the thought of playing for Paul for another year. Ken told me to take it easy, everything was going to work out. It was later that I realized Paul Brown was fired on that trip to San Francisco, only no one told him."

Paul Brown never saw it coming.

He just never thought anyone would dare fire Paul Brown. The Browns were his team. He created them. And some kid huckster from New York was going to take them away?

The day before he was fired, Paul Brown called groundskeeper Harold Bossard. The coach was unhappy with the playing surface at League Park, where the team practiced. He wondered if Bossard had any ideas about how to improve it.

Meanwhile, Modell had just returned from the NFL meetings, where he cornered Pete Rozelle. A close friend and the NFL commissioner, Rozelle was surprised when Modell said they needed to talk in private, and talk *now*. They went to Rozelle's hotel suite. There were two double beds in the room. Modell sat on one, Rozelle on the other.

"Pete," Modell said, "I've got to do something that I know you're not going to like, and the other owners aren't going to like it, either."

Rozelle sensed what was coming, but still didn't believe it. No one in the NFL could imagine Art Modell firing Paul Brown.

"I've got to make a coaching change," Modell said.

Rozelle just stared at him for a moment.

For one of the few times in his life, Modell also was silent.

"Gee," Rozelle said. "I mean, Art, you've only been in this business for two years. Are you sure you want to do this?"

"It's either him or me," Modell said. "He is determined to drive me out."

According to Modell, Rozelle then said, "Well, Art, I respect you for being a man of your own convictions." Rozelle also said he wouldn't want to be in Modell's shoes when that bombshell dropped.

Sometimes Art Modell says that he had no other choice—he had to fire Paul Brown. Other times, he'll tell you, "If I had to do it over again, I would not do what I did to Paul on January 9, 1963. I was more brazen. I had more courage or more stupidity back then. Now, I'd try to work it out with the man who was a giant among coaches."

What Modell did on January 9, 1963, was to ask Paul Brown to see him at the Browns' offices. Since it was three weeks after the Browns' final game of the 1962 season, Paul Brown perhaps thought he was safe for another year. If Modell were going to fire him, he would have done it right after that final game in San Francisco, when Paul Brown was aware that the owner was talking to the players, asking them about the coach.

"I've made a decision," Modell told Brown. "You have to step down as coach and general manager."

Brown was thunderstruck. He just stood and stared at Modell. Brown thought, "He really did it . . . he fired me."

Finally, Paul Brown said, "I really don't know what to say. I have a contract for six more years."

Then, according to Paul Brown, Modell told him, "This team can never fully be mine as long as you are here because whenever anyone thinks of the Browns, they think of you. Every time I come to the Stadium, I feel that I am invading your domain, and from now on, there can be only one dominant image."

Modell disputes this. He claims that he said Paul Brown would be paid for the remainder of his contract (all six years), and that there was no discussion about whose team the Browns were—because Modell owned them.

"I can still see that meeting like yesterday," Modell said. "Paul Brown was the same Paul Brown, the same bald-headed, thin man you see in pictures. I told him, 'I've made a decision, Paul, and I hope you understand. I think we have to part company. I'm going to ask you to step down as coach and general manager, and you are to be reassigned.' He was horrified. He stormed out of the office before I could say much else."

Other than the fact that Paul Brown was fired, everything is disputed between the two men. Modell owed Brown $82,500 annually for six years, having extended Brown's contract in 1961. Modell's and Brown's lawyers were soon sparring over the clauses of Brown's contract.

"My father thought he controlled his own destiny," said Mike Brown, Paul's son. "He was shocked that he could have a contract and not be allowed to fulfill it. It broke his heart when he was fired. There has always been a lot of talk and rationalizations [about the firing], but it came down to the fact that Art wanted to run the Browns and couldn't as long as my father was there."

There is even controversy over what happened the day following the firing.

"The next morning, I found the contents of my desk, the pictures of my family, all of it in a cardboard box," Brown wrote in his book. "It was left on the front porch. The message was clear. Don't ever come back to the office."

"I wasn't in the office when this happened," Modell said. "But the day after I fired him, Paul came in to the office to clean out his desk.

He saw that his six assistant coaches were still there, still at work. He had hoped to find the office empty, that they would walk out in protest. Instead, they were looking at films. That just killed him. He died. He was so unforgiving and angry at the coaches for not showing their respect and walking out. But I had called in the coaches and said, 'Look, I had to do this. I'm asking you to stay. You're a great bunch of coaches. You're good people. Please stay on board and give me a chance to make a decision about hiring a new head coach.' And they did. Paul Brown didn't cotton to that. He thought the whole world would stop [after he was fired]."

Trying to get to the bottom of this is impossible. Paul Brown is deceased. Modell has his version. Others claim to know the truth, but they weren't there for every incident.

So Modell either gave Paul Brown the "It's You or Me" speech . . . or he didn't.

Either Modell had Brown's belongings sent to his house and dumped on the front porch . . . or Brown came to the office to clean out his desk and saw the assistant coaches . . . or maybe he went to his office, saw his coaches were still there, went home without cleaning out his desk—and then Modell sent the stuff unceremoniously to his house.

Either the players forced Modell's hand in the firing . . . or Modell used the players as an excuse to make the move he wanted.

It is known that Modell issued this statement: "Paul E. Brown, head coach and general manager of the Cleveland Browns, will no longer serve the team in those capacities. Brown will remain as a vice president and be assigned other duties. He will finish out the balance of his six-year contract at the same compensation and will continue as a stockholder."

Paul Brown's final record with Cleveland was 164-53-8 with seven conference championships. In his two years with Modell, he was 15-11-2.

After the firing, Paul Brown told reporters, "Mr. Modell is young and aggressive. Often he has said he wants to be a 'playing owner,' which means he wanted to take over some of the duties which were mine under the contract. Well, he has put me on the shelf and now he is in complete charge . . . I am a Vice President in Charge of I Don't Know What."

Modell's reply?

"If Paul would only let me, I could make him an idol of America," he said, only a few days after he fired Paul Brown.

———————————

One of the many theories about the firing is that Modell waited until three weeks after the season to fire his coach because Cleveland was in the middle of a newspaper strike.

"It was during the forty-fifth day of the strike," Modell said. "People acted like I waited until day one of the strike, when it was forty-five days old. Frankly, I couldn't wait for the papers to end their strike just so I could fire Paul on their timetable."

"Did Art do it intentionally during the strike?" asked Hal Lebovitz. "I wouldn't be surprised if he did. But I don't know."

But Lebovitz knew that people wanted to read about the firing. He put together a twenty-four page pamphlet titled *The Play Paul Brown Didn't Call*. It featured stories by sportswriters from both striking Cleveland newspapers, covering virtually every angle of the firing.

"I sold over 50,000 of them at 50 cents each," Lebovitz said. "Today, it's a collector's item. The original sells for $250. I paid all the writers $75 each. At the time of the strike back in 1963, $75 was a lot of money. It was so even-handed that both Modell and Paul Brown were angry about it. In my opinion, Modell did the right thing when he fired Paul Brown. The players weren't in a mutiny, but it was pretty obvious a change had to be made."

In Cleveland, a chain of weeklies called the Sun Newspapers ran a poll that found fans to be split on the firing—perhaps a few more favoring Modell.

"Even though Paul Brown was respected, he hadn't won lately," recalled veteran *Cleveland Press* writer Bob August. "Fans were more stunned than upset. No one thought he'd be fired. But after it happened, people were very divided."

The newspaper stories and the memories of those who were there sharply conflict with the revisionist history of today in Cleveland, which insists that Modell caused a huge outcry and had few supporters when he fired Paul Brown—much as he did when he cut Bernie Kosar in 1993. But that simply wasn't the case.

Nonetheless, it does tell you something about Art Modell.

"Paul Brown used to tell us that no one would ever buy the team and replace him," said Jim Brown. "But here comes a thirty-five-year-old Art Modell. He scrapes together the money. He takes away Paul Brown's big office and puts him in the back. Then he fired Paul Brown, this brash young man from New York firing this legend in Ohio. That showed you he wasn't afraid to make any move he believed was in his own best interests."

With Paul Brown gone, Modell was free to speak his mind. He said that Jim Ninowski would be the quarterback, "and he'll run the show. He'll occasionally receive advice from the bench, but the days of messenger guards are gone. Sideline play-calling is no longer the accepted practice."

And Modell said, "Jimmy Brown, my senior partner, will have his greatest season."

And Modell said, "I consider myself a student of football, but not an overly qualified one. Even if I could coach, I don't want to coach."

The amazing thing was that Modell was saying all these things before he even had a new coach.

"The dismissal of Paul Brown is a move that defies comprehension," wrote Arthur Daley in the *New York Times*. "The moody genius from the lakefront had achieved an eminence in his profession that lifted him far above the pack, virtually exalting him to a class by himself. If he was unloved, he was admired and respected by all. He was a man who built a better mousetrap. . . . What nudged Modell into dismissing him was a personality conflict."

That was tougher on Modell than anything written in Cleveland after the firing. The reaction at home was best summed up by former *Cleveland Press* columnist Frank Gibbons, who wrote: "It was like the Terminal Tower toppling," the Terminal Tower being the tallest building and the most famous Cleveland landmark in the early 1960s.

"After Paul was fired, he talked to Herb Eisele, the football coach at John Carroll University and a dear friend of mine," Lebovitz recalled. "He told Herb, 'If I ever get back into coaching, I'll never let a team get away from me again.' Paul realized what had happened with the Browns, and when he did come back and coach in Cincinnati [where he was also the principal owner], he never again lost control of his team."

BLANTON COLLIER
TAKES OVER

Even before he fired Paul Brown, Art Modell knew whom he'd hire as the next Browns coach.

But he couldn't just do it. He wanted a few days of publicity. Let the newspapers speculate; Modell was quick to help them by floating a few names.

"Yes," he'd say. "Blanton Collier is a candidate, but not the only candidate."

Who else?

"I can't say," Modell would explain.

Only Modell would stay on the line. And then the reporter would ask for more names. The reporter might mention a name of his own.

Otto Graham?

"That's a good name," Modell would say.

But Modell had long since made up his mind. Blanton Collier, who had followed Bear Bryant at Kentucky, would have to follow Paul Brown in Cleveland.

Art Modell loved Blanton Collier because Collier was a gentleman. "He taught me more football than anyone I've ever met," Modell said. "I used to watch films with him. I'd ask him a question, and he'd explain things." It is hard to know if Modell would have made this same move later in his career. At the time he was hired, Collier was fifty-six years old. He had a hearing problem. He did not have a flashy personality that would project well on TV or sell tickets. He had never been a head coach in the NFL. He had been fired at Kentucky. But Modell had been in the NFL for only two years when he fired Paul Brown; he had few contacts, and he really didn't know where to look for a coach if he had to find one outside the Browns organization. In the 1970s, 1980s, or 1990s, Modell would have had one of his "nationwide searches," the kind of hunting expedition that led him to Bill Belichick.

Back in 1963, he almost had to hire Blanton Collier. He really didn't know anyone else. Besides, the same players who said they didn't want to play for Paul Brown told Modell that Collier was the right choice for the job.

Modell also knew Collier would talk to him. He knew that Collier would treat him like an owner, an equal, not an interloper. Modell's business manager and confidant with the Browns was Harold Sauerbrei, who lived next door to Collier—and he was a Blanton booster.

"I asked Harold to bring Blanton to my apartment on the Gold Coast [in Lakewood]," Modell said. "I told Blanton that I wanted him to be the next coach of the Browns. I expected him to accept it on the spot. But he told me, 'I'm flattered. I'm overwhelmed. But first I have to get a blessing from Forman [Collier's wife] and from Paul Brown.' I was surprised to hear him say that about Paul, but now that I think about it, I would not have expected Blanton to do anything else."

"After the 1962 season, Daddy was approached by Green Bay and Baltimore. Both wanted to hire him as an assistant," Kay Collier-Slone said. "But he always said that the only places he ever wanted to coach were Paris High, Kentucky, and Cleveland—the three places he had already coached. I'll never forget the day Paul Brown was fired. Daddy was in agony. When Art offered him the job, it should have been the happiest day of his life, but Daddy was still torn because of the grief he felt over what had happened to Paul."

Collier called Paul Brown and told him about Modell's offer.

"You have to take it," Brown said. "You have to think of your family."

Still Collier wrestled with the decision. Finally, he called his family together.

"I can picture Daddy standing in front of us, saying, 'I owe this to you. Your mother has been through all these terrible things at Kentucky.' Daddy knew he had to take the job," said Kay Collier-Slone.

A week after Paul Brown was fired, Blanton Collier was hired as only the second coach in the seventeen-year history of the Cleveland Browns. He signed a three-year contract worth $35,000 annually—

less than half the $82,500 Paul Brown was being paid *not* to coach the Browns. The morning Collier was hired, he looked out the window at the thermometer at his home in Aurora. It was 0 degrees. He wasn't sure if that was a good omen or not, but he knew he'd never forget the temperature on the day he became the head coach of the Browns.

"When Blanton was hired, I thought it was a bad choice," recalled Bob August. "He was a very nice man, a scholarly man and a true gentleman. But how many gentlemen win football games? I knew he was a brilliant assistant, but, again, how many nice guys win games? I also knew that he'd been fired at Kentucky, and that was a concern."

Modell knew that, too.

"Kentucky was a basketball school and Adolph Rupp ran roughshod over Blanton," the owner said. "Also, Blanton just didn't have the stomach for recruiting. Woody Hayes would come into a player's home, romance the family, and get the uncle a job—he did what he had to in order to get the kid to Ohio State. But that just wasn't Blanton Collier."

Browns linebacker Jim Houston confirmed this.

"I had been recruited by Kentucky when Blanton was the coach," he said. "I made a weekend visit, and maybe talked to Blanton for five minutes. I just thought the head coach would spend more time with a recruit, but Blanton didn't seem very comfortable. He said hello to me, shook my hand, and that was it."

Houston played for Woody Hayes at Ohio State.

Ohio State had better talent, but no head coach had a stronger staff than the one assembled by Collier at Kentucky: Don Shula, Chuck Knox, Bill Arnsparger, Howard Schnellenberger, Ed Rutledge, and Ermal Allen. "Blanton was a soft-spoken man who looked professorial with his glasses on," Modell said. "He was the kind of coach that other coaches loved. If you were around him, you learned something about football each day. And Blanton, he also dressed well. He wore a fedora. I have known a lot of good people in my life, but none better than him."

That is the refrain you hear over and over about Collier: He was a good man. He had no vices, unless you have a problem with a man who eats a quart of ice cream while watching football films.

"What I didn't realize is that by being so different from Paul Brown, Blanton was the perfect choice to replace him," said Bob August. "He had the players in his corner, especially Jim Brown, and Jim was a very powerful figure on the team. I really believe that part of the reason the players performed so well for Blanton is that they wanted to justify Paul's firing."

Despite August's reservations—which likely were shared by other Cleveland writers—Collier's hiring was greeted enthusiastically in the press. They all knew and liked Collier. While some writers were in Modell's corner and others didn't trust the owner, to a man they all wanted Collier to do well and were willing to give him the benefit of the doubt. That was yet another reason why choosing Collier was the best football decision Art Modell ever made.

———————

But many fans wondered, "Who is this guy?"

They knew he had been on Paul Brown's staff for years, but he was not an assistant who was in the public eye. Of course, when you worked for Paul Brown, you knew that it was best to keep your name out of the newspapers.

On the day of his hiring, Collier paid tribute to Brown. He said all the assistant coaches would stay. He added, "We don't know much else but the Paul Brown system. All of us have been associated with Paul for years and we believe in his system."

Collier did say that he planned to let the quarterback call most of the plays and seek more input from the players. But Hal Lebovitz realized that fans wanted to know more than about Collier the coach. He wrote a wonderful column, revealing this about Collier:

- He shook hands with his left hand, "because the left hand is the closest to my heart."
- He refused to return to the Browns as an assistant in 1962 until he was sure that no other coach would lose his job to make room for him.
- His nickname was George, because when he taught high school, he called most boys "George" and most girls "Martha," after George and Martha Washington. Soon, the kids called him "George," and that nickname followed him to the pros. He also used "George" and "Martha" as a way to entice people to own up to their mistakes. When something went wrong and no one knew why, Collier would say, "I guess George and Martha did it when no one was looking."

- His favorite breakfast was sausage and eggs.
- Before dinner, he liked a good shot of Kentucky bourbon and water.
- As a teenager, he picked tobacco in the dusty Kentucky fields. He joined the Navy when he was thirty-seven because he felt it was his duty during World War II, even though he probably could have avoided serving because he was nearly forty, married with a family, and was a teacher.
- When Paul Brown made up his first rooming list, he picked Collier as his own roommate.

Certainly, none of his coaching peers had the same hearing problems as Collier.

"As far as I know, Daddy had no problems hearing until he went into the Navy," said Kay Collier-Slone. "The first time it became an issue was when his name was called several times over the loudspeaker to report to his ship. He never heard it. Then they checked him and realized there was a problem. He had been teaching survival swimming, and the doctors suggested that maybe he damaged his hearing when he was working in the tidal pool—all the reverberations from the waves. Another theory was that the damage was done on the marksmanship range. Daddy did say that there were a few times when he was younger that he'd been in a crowd of people who were having casual conversations, and he couldn't hear that well—there was too much noise interference. But it never became an issue until the Navy, when they figured he had less than 40 percent of a normal person's hearing."

Collier became a shrewd lip-reader.

Some people would shout at him, because they were aware of his hearing problems. But volume wasn't the issue. If more than one person spoke, it didn't matter how loud they yelled, he couldn't hear them. He was best in one-on-one situations, where he could see the person's lips.

"We [the players] knew that Blanton couldn't hear very well," recalled defensive end Bill Glass. "It was strange, because sometimes he could hear, and sometimes he couldn't. Some guys accused him of having a convenient loss of hearing, as if he heard only what he wanted to hear. I didn't believe that. But I do know that he'd be in front of the team, and he couldn't hear what was being said in the back of the room. Some of those guys would make fun of him, because sometimes a player would ask Blanton one question, and he'd completely misunderstand and answer a totally different question. It also made Blanton a bit paranoid, because he'd imagine people were saying things about him—and they weren't talking about him at all."

"Frank Ryan told me that he sometimes believed Daddy would act like he didn't hear as a teaching tool," Kay Collier-Slone said. "He'd ask Frank a question. Frank would answer. Then he'd ask the same question, saying he didn't hear the answer. Then Frank would have to rephrase his answer, and sometimes Frank said he learned more by answering it a second time."

Back then, few players wore beards or mustaches. "But Daddy couldn't have anyone he dealt with having a lot of facial hair," Kay Collier-Slone said. "He couldn't read their lips. After he retired, there was a priest at the Episcopal church that Daddy attended, and the man had a beard and mustache. That frustrated Daddy because he couldn't read the man's lips."

Modell was concerned about Collier's hearing, but he also was aware that the players knew the coach well and were used to communicating with him.

"But you couldn't talk to him on the phone," Modell said. "So when I called Blanton, I'd talk to his wife, Forman. Then she would relay the message to Blanton, and he'd tell her what to say to me. Or else I'd send Harold Sauerbrei to Blanton's house, because they were next-door neighbors, and Harold would talk to him in person. If you talked to Blanton square in the face, everything was fine."

When a friend called and Collier wished he could be on the extension to at least overhear the conversation, his wife worked out a system. Blanton would sit next to Forman. She held the phone in one hand, and wrote out short notes about the conversation with her other hand. They became so good at this that often only a few words were needed to convey a long message. Then Blanton would tell her what he wanted to say, and she'd relay the message to the person on the line.

Was it ideal? No. Was it time-consuming? Of course. But did it work? Most of the time.

As Kay Collier-Slone said, "Daddy liked to hear what was being said, so we created ways to get it across to him."

Meanwhile, Modell was continually digging up new doctors to examine Collier.

"He even tried acupuncture," Kay Collier-Slone said. "He tried so many different hearing aids. Nothing much helped, because his problem was not volume—it was discriminating between sounds. I have a low voice and move my lips when I talk, so Daddy never had problems hearing me. Art was so worried, there were times when he found a new doctor and he'd drive Daddy to see him. Daddy's hearing did get a little worse every year, but he just worked around it."

"Blanton often told people, 'Don't yell at me, I just got this new hearing aid,'" recalled Dick Modzelewski. "In one game, I got into an argument with him on the sidelines, and then I stormed off. I thought I had my back to him, and I called him a name. Next thing I know, Blanton grabbed me by the shoulder and said, 'Don't you ever call me that again.' I still don't know how he heard me."

"Press conferences could be difficult for Blanton," recalled Akron sportswriter Tom Melody. "Sometimes, we'd ask him one question, and he'd guess wrong and answer another one. We liked Blanton so much that no one would say, 'Hey, I didn't ask you that.' Rather, another reporter would ask that same question a few minutes later. We sort of took care of each other and Blanton that way."

It would seem that a football game would be the worst place for a person with Collier's handicap.

"I just know that Daddy blocked out the stadium noises," said Kay Collier-Slone. "He had tremendous concentration. Bill Glass told me that Daddy was able to compensate for his hearing loss with his other senses. Even though he wore glasses, he had excellent eyesight. He could just feel the game. He caught all the details."

Part of the reason Collier trusted his players is that he had no choice. He couldn't be on the headset with the coaches upstairs. He couldn't have three people yelling at once. He had to keep the lines of communication simple, just one-on-one. And with this group of players who felt squashed by Paul Brown's heavy hand, that was the perfect approach.

Offensive lineman Monte Clark made an excellent point when he said, "A less intelligent group of players may have made fun of him. But we had so much respect for Blanton that we worked with him. Besides, we were a very mature group, and we knew better than to ridicule someone such as Blanton."

But the players did have some jokes about Collier's hearing, jokes that even Collier enjoyed.

One of them was when the Browns were in a playoff game. It was a hot day, and Paul Wiggin wondered if the players had to wear their coats and ties to the game.

"No ties," Collier said. "It's a playoff, sudden death."

All he heard was the word "ties," and he was thinking about the game. "I often kidded Blanton about the ties and sudden death," said Modell. "That was another reason we loved the man—he took things so well."

In the summer of 1963, the Browns reported to Hiram College, a small, sleepy campus about forty miles from Cleveland, for their first training camp ever with someone other than Paul Brown in charge. It was Brown, of course, who had picked Hiram as the team's training site back in 1946. This was one more part of the Paul Brown system that Blanton Collier felt comfortable leaving in place.

Collier had his sixty players (thirty-seven veterans and twenty-three rookies) gather around him. They saw an elderly man peering at them through horn-rimmed glasses. Many of the players suddenly realized that Collier was older than Paul Brown. And yes, the team was in his hands—but it also was in theirs. Most fans believed that the players had as much to do with the firing of Paul Brown as Art Modell.

Collier stood in front of them, a little self-conscious. It was finally hitting him, here at Hiram with 120 eyes staring at him, that he was standing where Paul Brown had once stood, telling the players many of the same things Paul Brown once told them. But first, he had to say something about what had happened to Paul and what it meant to the team.

According to newspaper reports, Collier told the players, "We're going to be watched by the entire football world in the coming season, and we'll be judged by one standard—did we win or lose? It's the law of the range. I've learned it the hard way. The world doesn't want the nice guys. The world wants the winner to be a nice guy, but first he has to be a winner. Each of you has to produce or get out. That's not Collier's law or Modell's law, it's the law of professional sports . . . I'm not a tough person, and I don't try to be. But I do get fired up about things, especially a lack of effort and a lack of attention to detail. What you do and how well you do it will show me how dedicated you are. My coaches have worked harder for the last six months than any coaches

I've known. They gave up much of their vacations to prepare for this camp. Now it is time for everyone to get down to business."

It wasn't a Speech for the Ages, but it was sincere.

The "Produce or Get Out" theme was at the center of Paul Brown's coaching style, and Collier was not about to change that.

"When Blanton took over, it was like someone had their hand up the back of his jacket and was moving his mouth," Ross Fichtner recalled. "It was like Blanton's mouth was moving, but Paul Brown was talking. You would not have known the difference, except for Blanton's voice. It was as if Paul had written his script. We cut out the IQ tests. Blanton also got rid of that thing where the players [who were on the edge of being cut] had to go down to the office to get the envelopes. But nothing else changed. He ran training camp and practices much like Paul Brown did. Why would it be different? Blanton had learned his football from Paul Brown."

Bernie Parrish agreed.

"The difference was that we were just so damn happy that Paul was gone," he said. "We never believed it would happen. But suddenly, the players realized that the burden was on us. We had to go out and prove we were right about Paul, that we'd be a better team without him. We also were convinced that Blanton believed in us. Since we already knew Blanton, we didn't think there would be a big adjustment."

Collier inherited a team that was 7-6-1 in 1962, and it hadn't helped itself in the draft. The only notable player selected was Jim Kanicki, a second-rounder who became a starting defensive tackle in 1964. But the first-round pick was Tom Hutchinson, a wide receiver from Kentucky (where he had played for Collier) who never met Collier's expectations in Cleveland. The Browns were picked no higher than third in the seven-team Eastern Conference, and most writers predicted they would be lucky to finish at .500 and in the middle of the pack. Even those who respected Collier and believed the change of coaches was a good idea still thought the Browns would struggle because of their questionable talent. If the best Paul Brown could do was 7-6-1, why expect any better from someone else?

The Browns went to training camp in 1963 not knowing if Jim Ninowski or Frank Ryan would be the starting quarterback, and neither made anyone believe that the Browns had the second coming of Otto Graham.

Collier hoped Ernie Green could be the other running back next to Jim Brown, but he wasn't sure because Green's experience was limited. He also had to replace two starters on the offensive line and find a couple of starting defensive backs.

Meanwhile, Collier was in the middle of stories such as this one in the *Saturday Evening Post:* "A Team on Trial: The Browns Fight to Prove They Can Win Without the Man Who Invented Them."

Over and over, Collier found himself telling out-of-town reporters, "I'm not Paul Brown. I don't want to be Paul Brown. I just want to be Blanton Collier."

The remarkable thing is that Collier seemed so tranquil. He was just Blanton, the same Southern gentleman the Browns players knew so well. Yes, he made it clear that all decisions came from him, but he wasn't a bully about it. He didn't set out to prove he was in charge, he just treated it as a given—and so did the players.

Meanwhile, Modell was a wreck. He was puffing away on his three packs of cigarettes a day. He was getting to the office even earlier, staying later—although he really had no more to do than before. He just felt he should be there. He should be working even harder. Hey, he fired Paul Brown. His butt was on the line. He couldn't blame Paul if this season went up in flames. Collier sensed this. He was patient with his young owner, showing Modell films, explaining things. Just being able to communicate with his coach calmed Modell, at least for a few hours. "Daddy never talked about the pressure of replacing Paul Brown," recalled Kay Collier-Slone. "He had been there before, when he coached after Bear Bryant at Kentucky. Daddy just immersed himself in the work and preparation, but he was very serene and confident."

If you want to know why the Browns became champions in 1964, you just had to see Blanton Collier with the players in 1963. You had to watch him after practice for a half hour, talking with Jim Brown. The fullback would be sweating, holding his helmet under his right arm. Sometimes they walked around the field; other times, they just stood there, talking, for a half hour.

Collier asked Brown what plays worked, what didn't. How was the blocking? How could they make him a better player, a better runner?

Brown loved it. While he respected Paul Brown, he also knew that Paul Brown didn't care what he thought—or what anyone thought. Paul Brown told you what to do, and you did it. He had heard that Paul

Brown once told his assistants, "We're going to let the animal loose." The coach meant they were going to have Jim Brown run the ball even more often. Jim Brown didn't consider Paul Brown to be a racist; he knew that as much as anyone, Paul Brown integrated football. But he also came to see that Paul Brown just didn't know much about people. To him, all of the players were sort of like animals—and he was the lion tamer, trying to entice them to perform tricks.

Collier was different. Collier listened. Collier asked questions.

And most of all, Blanton Collier knew his stuff, knew it cold. He talked about football differently from any man who had ever discussed the sport with Jim Brown before. Sometimes, Jim Brown knew that Collier went into one of their after-practice talks with an idea for him, and that Collier had a way of taking his idea and making it seem like it was yours all along.

"I loved talking to that man," Brown said years later. "He had a way of making you feel important. He allowed you to breathe, to grow. Paul Brown scared you to death. You dropped a pass and you looked over your shoulder. What was Paul thinking? With Blanton, we just played the game."

"The relationship between Blanton Collier and Jim Brown was almost father and son," said John Wooten, Brown's best friend. "You just don't see a relationship like that between a superstar and a coach. They'd walk away from those meetings after practice, arms around each other."

"Most people would talk about how Jim Brown never missed a game," said Kay Collier-Slone. "Daddy would say, 'Jim never even missed a practice.' He found Jim to be one of the most astute players on the team." Brown exploded under Collier. He gained 996 yards in Paul Brown's last year—and 1,863 in 1963 under Collier.

"Vince Lombardi has always received the credit for 'Running to Daylight,' where the back just ran to the hole, regardless of where it was," Wooten said. "But Blanton was doing it first with us. It began with Blanton's blocking schemes. He believed in something called 'option blocking,' where you didn't just have to block a man in one direction. If it was easier to move him left, then block him to the left. It gave the offensive linemen more options in blocking. Then you take a back like Jim Brown and you tell him just to run wherever he sees a hole, and look out. Jim would start left, then cut back to the right when he saw how the blocking was developing."

The players talked about the freedom: The freedom to block. The freedom to run. The freedom to change plays at the line of scrimmage. That was Collier's message for Frank Ryan: Just play. Trust yourself. Trust your talent. It doesn't matter how many degrees you have in mathematics, go with your gut. You are a football player first.

Paul Brown did not want plays changed at all. Collier allowed the quarterback to make adjustments, but not just call anything. If the bench sent in a play (and Collier did that less than half the time) and the quarterback saw that play would not work, he already had an option of maybe six other plays from which to pick.

"I relied a lot on the input from the players," Ryan said. "Gary Collins would tell me that he could beat his man in a certain direction, and I'd keep that in mind. If Jim Brown believed that our strength was running the ball, and he wanted the ball, believe me, I heard him. The key was that the players were telling me things they thought would work—not just because they wanted the ball."

There was a point during the season when Collier called quite a few plays. He thought Ryan had become too conservative, and he wanted his quarterback to open up the attack—to rely on his own ability and that of his teammates to make big plays. When Ryan began to be more daring with his play-calling, Collier gave him more freedom.

The Browns jumped off to a 6-0 start, and in five of those games, they scored at least 35 points.

All of this made Art Modell very happy.

It no doubt ate away at Paul Brown.

As for Collier, there was a feeling of contentment. He had many theories about football, especially on offense. His running to daylight, option blocking, and other schemes had created a scoring machine.

"Blanton believed that the offense began with blocking, and blocking started in the mind," said Monte Clark. "To me, football was contact. In my first pro game, I went back to pass-block. The veteran rushing against me grabbed my helmet and pulled it right down over my eyes. I couldn't see. He did it again on the next play. He noticed my helmet was a little big, and he kept grabbing my face mask and pulling it down over my eyes. I came to the sidelines, asked a teammate what I should do about it. He said, 'Don't let the guy do it.' That was it. Don't let him grab the face mask."

Collier would tell a player how to prevent that: where to stand, where to put your hands, what foot to move first, and how far you should step.

"One day at practice, I was really busting my ass—and getting my ass kicked," Clark recalled. "Blanton yelled, 'Monte, you need movement.'

"I said, 'I have movement.'

"Blanton said, 'Ah, you're just a con artist. I can't even talk to you.'

"That bothered me because it was so out of character for Blanton. So we talked about it, and he opened my eyes. He started telling me about his concept of detail, how every little thing was so important. He believed in psychocybernetics, which is a form of visualization. Physically, you can only block so many times in practice. But you can picture yourself blocking hundreds of times, and if you create the proper mental picture with all the right details, you are more likely to physically execute it. At first, I thought it was nonsense. I didn't want to read the book [*Psycho-Cybernetics*, by Maxwell Maltz], but Blanton kept talking to me about different chapters in it. I had to read it just to keep up with him, and it worked. I ended up priding myself on details."

Or as Clark's good friend Paul Wiggin said, "When I came to the Browns, I thought football was blood and guts. But these guys were a bunch of scientists. The first thing I did was take an IQ test for Paul Brown. Blanton had his psychocybernetics. But all this made me a better player."

Under Collier, the Browns were a football classroom, and the coach expected the players to do some of the teaching themselves. The night before games, Frank Ryan would meet with the offensive linemen to discuss blocking schemes and just make the linemen feel as if they were more than guys paid to sacrifice their bodies. Then guard John Wooten and tackle Dick Schafrath would meet in Jim Brown's room.

"The three of us would talk over the plays, maybe pick six of them that we were sure would work well for the running game that week," Schafrath said. "Then I'd take those plays to Frank Ryan."

It can be dangerous, allowing so many players to get together without coaches. But while Collier believed in sketching the outline of a game plan, he wanted the players to supply some of the colors.

"Blanton's willingness to accept advice helped me swallow not being the starting quarterback," said Jim Ninowski. "The first game we played was against the Redskins, and a couple of the plays I suggested went for touchdowns. In our team meeting the following week, Blanton said, 'We can win if we have the attitude of pulling together. For example, even though Nino didn't play, two of his suggestions went for touchdowns.' Just by saying that, he brought me over to his side—even though I was very upset about not playing and thought I should have been the starter that year. He also hired Dub Jones as offensive coordinator, and you could sit down with both of them and talk football. I used to kid Blanton, saying, 'You're a great teacher. But when the game starts, just stand there and we'll take care of the rest.' Blanton took that the right way. You'd never dare say anything like that to Paul Brown."

But the players did learn there were limits to their suggestions.

When Frank Ryan was in a slump during the second half of the season, Dick Schafrath went to Collier to say that a number of the players thought Ninowski deserved a chance to start.

Schafrath was the team captain, and it was true that some of the players were concerned about Ryan. Collier didn't say a word when Schafrath mentioned changing quarterbacks. Then Collier gave him The Stare. Schafrath could have sworn Paul Brown had just shown up. It was a look that said, "And who are you to dare tell me what I should do with my quarterbacks?" Schafrath slinked back to his room, end of discussion. Collier made it very clear that some decisions would always be his.

After that 6-0 start, the Browns were spanked 33–6 by New York. They ended up a strong 10-4-0, but were only 4-3 in the second half.

"We should have won a title in 1963," said John Wooten. "But dissension hit our club, racial dissension."

This is something few players wanted to discuss. Others said they didn't recall it happening. But, clearly, something was wrong.

"The Browns always took such pride in how racial issues were handled," said Wooten. "We were so far ahead of the rest of the league. When we played in Dallas, we stayed at a Ramada Inn near the airport because that hotel would take all of our players. A lot of other teams stayed in a nice hotel downtown, but their black players had to stay in the homes of black families. On airplanes, the players who weighed over 260 pounds sat in first class—it had nothing to do with color, just size. We had three buses. One for the coaches and writers, one for the rookies, and one for the veterans—again, it wasn't by race."

So what happened?

"We were 6-0, and suddenly everyone wanted to play all of the time,"

Wooten said. "And when one guy was playing over another, it took on racial connotations. If anything blew us apart that season, it was these racial problems. I know that some players couldn't believe that 'some black guy' was playing in front of them, even if it was obvious to almost everyone that the black player was better."

Bernie Parrish agreed.

"Wooten was right," he said. "Some of the white players believed that Ernie Green was not the answer at halfback, that we needed to get a big, white blocking back to play next to Jim Brown, sort of a John David Crow type. I know some of the black players picked up on that, and it really bothered them. I can't remember all the names, but I know that some black players thought they should have had more time—that they weren't playing as much because they were black. There was a lot of whispering going on."

Some black players thought Walter Beach should have played in the defensive secondary for more than three games; in 1964, Beach became a starter.

"It seemed like the black players were gravitating to one bus, the whites to another," Schafrath said. "No one said it had to be that way, but it was happening."

Schafrath ended up an unwilling symbol of the racial divide, which pains him to this day. He always was close friends with Wooten and Jim Brown. They invited Schafrath to their room for informal pregame meetings.

"But think about this," Wooten said. "Jim Brown set an NFL record for yards rushing in a season. He was the league's MVP in 1963. But who was voted the MVP on the Browns?"

Schafrath?

"Right," Wooten said. "And he was voted by the players. Jim would never admit that he was hurt by that, but he was very aware of it. We talked about it. Jim was in a sensitive position. Many blamed him for getting Paul Brown fired, which just wasn't true. He was very frustrated about how things were under Paul, but so were a lot of other players— they just weren't as outspoken as Jim. Then he had a career year, and he wasn't even MVP of his own team?"

The Cleveland media sensed something was wrong. While they sidestepped the racial issue, they kept asking how Schafrath could be the MVP over Jim Brown.

"I'll tell you, the writers tore the team apart for not voting for Jim," Schafrath said. "They kept asking me about it. They wanted to know how this tackle could get more votes than Jim Brown when Jim broke all these records. I voted for Jim. I told them, 'I didn't vote for myself, so I know that Jim got some votes.' But it was a sticky situation. It never became a problem between Jim and me; we were friends before and even better friends after. We didn't have to discuss it. He knew that I considered him our MVP."

Quietly, Blanton Collier called together the team leaders, men such as Wooten, Brown, Schafrath, Ryan, Parrish, and Galen Fiss. He told them that he would not have any more of this racism on his team. It was not how he did business. It was not how the Cleveland Browns did business. He asked the players what was going on. He listened.

"After 1963, Blanton cut the problem right out," Wooten said. "He made some trades. He got people to talk to each other more. He did it in his own, subtle way—but he did it. And by 1964, we had no racial problems. None. We were a team again."

Collier also was shrewd enough to keep the media on his side.

"On the Monday after games, Blanton would take out a 16-millimeter projector and set up the game films to be shown against his office wall," Modell recalled. "Then he'd invite all of the beat writers and columnists in, and he'd dissect the game. I loved to sit in on those sessions. He taught everyone there how to watch a football game, and he'd show us who made mistakes and who did things right. It was all off the record, just background for the writers."

"Blanton would not allow us to use any individual criticism of players," recalled Hal Lebovitz. "But we learned so much, things we could use later, questions to ask. Do you know that Paul Brown never had a postgame press conference in Cleveland? When the game was over, we just went into the dressing room, talked to the players, and wrote what we saw. Sometimes you could find Paul in the corner of the dressing room and ask him something, but it was nothing formal."

Collier relished talking football with everyone, and he couldn't help but teach the game to anyone who seemed the least bit interested. But his film sessions also encouraged the writers to see the game through his eyes. He was teaching them to react as he would react, and that helped the press understand why Collier made certain moves without even asking him. But this was also when no more than five writers went on the road, and when there was no such thing as talk radio. TV was in its infancy. Writers weren't looking to make their reputations by taking on coaches.

"Blanton would sit in front of the media and just talk to us," said Pete Franklin, who pioneered sports talk radio in Cleveland. "He'd give us inside stuff, and to my knowledge no one ever violated it. Then he'd do one-on-one interview sessions so you'd have something to take back to the office. We'd have lunch. Blanton probably had his one drink a week—a Kentucky bourbon—and we'd talk football. After you were finished, he'd say, 'Sure y'all got enough?' And if not, he'd talk to you some more. The man was magnificent. He didn't just like reporters, he liked everyone. I can't imagine a coach today handling the press like he did, telling them really what was going on with the team and expecting them to keep it as background. But that was Blanton's style, and it was why we all appreciated him."

Akron sportswriter Tom Melody recalled that Collier did have a way of getting his message across if he was unhappy with something you wrote.

"One day, Bill Scholl [of the *Cleveland Press*] and I were at practice," he said. "The Browns were trying out a kicker, and there weren't many people around. Blanton asked us to stand in the end zone and catch this guy's kicks. We did, and it seemed like the balls were dropping from the heavens. We dropped some, and nearly got hit in the head with others. As we walked off the field, Blanton put his arm around me and said, 'The next time you criticize someone for dropping a punt or a kick, I want you to remember this day.' And it worked, because I always thought about that whenever I saw a guy mess up a kick."

———

The 1963 season saved Art Modell's football career. He was vindicated in the firing of Paul Brown. *Sports Illustrated* wrote, "There can be no doubt about it, the major factor in the improvement of Jimmy Brown and his teammates is the absence of Paul Brown."

Ten games were the most the Browns had won since 1953. That 6-0 start combined with Collier's wide-open offense had fans packing the Stadium. Fans loved watching Jim Brown break all of his own NFL rushing records. They were pleased when Gary Collins set a team record with 13 touchdown catches, and Frank Ryan tied Otto Graham's team record with 25 TD passes—although Ryan had fourteen games to do it, while the Browns only played a twelve-game schedule during Graham's era (1946–55).

In 1962, the Browns drew 422,043 for their seven home games. In 1963, the attendance was 487,430, so Art Modell also was making more money.

The Browns ended the 1963 season by playing in the now-defunct Playoff Bowl that matched the second-place teams from each conference in a completely meaningless game. They were crushed, 40–23, by Green Bay.

There was nothing but praise for Collier, who obviously deserved it, in the season-end wrap-ups. Not one prominent writer in Cleveland or nationally suggested that the team had made a mistake by firing Paul Brown.

1964

HIRAM

When Paul Brown went shopping for a training site, he thought of one thing: isolation.

He thought of trees.

He thought of a small college in a town that wasn't even a dot on the map.

He thought the only light at night should come from the moon.

When Paul Brown heard about Hiram College, he heard about huge oaks, rolling hills, a campus with only one outdoor phone booth that was forty rural miles from Cleveland.

Then someone told Brown, "The town is dry."

No bars. Heck, no restaurants—just one store with a small snack bar. The closest place to buy a beer was ten miles away in a small town called Garrettsville.

So it was to Hiram that Paul Brown took the Browns every summer, and it was in Hiram that they assembled under Blanton Collier to start the 1964 season.

Like his mentor, Collier loved Hiram. He relished its serenity. He knew this was a place where players would be forced to pay attention to football; they had just each other and their thoughts. Long before "getting away from it all" and "learning about yourself" reduced this experience to meaningless psychobabble, the Browns were almost using Hiram as a retreat.

"In Hiram, there was one gas station," Jim Brown said. "We slept in these little beds in tiny rooms that were the girls' dorms. There was this big hill down from the dorms to the practice field. I remember trudging up that hill after practice. You'd go through two workouts a day, then walk up that hill—it felt like Mount Everest."

Jim Brown saw tremendous signs of unity in that 1964 training camp.

He watched Bernie Parrish holding special film sessions for defensive backs. He saw John Wooten and Dick Schafrath leading the offensive linemen on long runs and short sprints, watching those elephants nearly drown in their own sweat. He knew that it would pay off; he knew that if he broke through the line of scrimmage, as he headed downfield Gene Hickerson or Wooten would be out there in front, knocking some defensive back into oblivion.

"That's what made our line so great," Brown recalled. "These guys would throw a block at the line of scrimmage, then they'd get up, run 10 or 20 yards down the field, and nail someone else. It was common for Hickerson and Schafrath to throw three blocks on one play."

Schafrath came up with an idea called "the healing towel." It was a towel he brought into the huddle, a towel soaked in ice water.

"As the game went on, it got pretty grungy," he said. "We'd suck on it to get the water. We'd use it to wipe off the sweat. We'd use it to stop bleeding, to get mud out of our eyes. That was why it was the healing towel; we could use it for almost anything."

The Browns' offensive line seemed never to rest under that unrelenting July sun in Hiram. Assistant coach Fritz Heisler would scream, "Don't stop. Don't look back. You'll turn into a pillar of salt."

They invented a play called "Mash to It."

"It meant we'd give the ball to Jim," Schafrath said. "Then we'd just mash the guy right in front of us. No strategy. Just block the hell out of the closest guy and let Jimmy run the ball. The defense really couldn't prepare for it, because it was so simple it confused them."

When the Browns were only a few yards from the end zone, this became one of their favorite plays.

Quarterback Frank Ryan would sometimes ask key players for input in the huddle. The receivers favored a pass play. The backs wanted to run. Then Schafrath or Wooten or Jim Brown would scream, "The hell with it, just Mash to It."

And they did.

This was exactly the spirit that Collier wanted. He'd give the players the structure, he'd work on their individual skills, he'd get them in shape, he'd prepare them for the plays the opposition would employ. But in the end, it came down to the players. They had to make key decisions. They had to knock the other guys on their butts. They had to believe in the system and themselves.

The best way to do that was to let the players feel they were creating that system, that their voices were heard.

In 1963, Collier saw some of that happen—but some players acted as if they had been released from prison. While some were still convinced they were weighed down by the strategic ball-and-chain that was Paul Brown's philosophy, others took advantage of Collier's light hand, pushing freedom a bit too far.

By 1964, they were learning what it took to be champions, and to play for Blanton Collier. And the groundwork for this championship season was being laid down at Hiram.

———

Collier made a couple of shrewd moves to bolster his roster.

When it came time to make their top pick in 1964, everyone wanted Paul Warfield. Interestingly, Paul Brown was the first to suggest that the Browns keep an eye on the running back from Ohio State.

For his $82,500 each year, Paul Brown was still listed as vice president, but all he did was turn in a few scouting reports. Having coached at Ohio State, he still had tremendous connections in Columbus. He knew that Warfield was not only an amazing athlete, but also a disciplined person, a Paul Brown kind of player. Brown filed this report right before he sold his home in the Cleveland suburb of Shaker Heights and moved to La Jolla, California, outside of San Diego. The move was understandable; it had to be gut-wrenching for Paul Brown to be in Cleveland and no longer coaching the Browns, especially when the Browns were the talk of the town.

After Warfield, the other significant draft pick in 1964 was Leroy Kelly, who was picked in the eighth round from Morgan State.

"I had never been to Cleveland before," Kelly said. "Playing at a small school like Morgan State, you don't even know if the NFL notices you. I didn't even know if I'd play pro football."

Kelly flew from Baltimore to Cleveland. This was before rookies were wined, dined, and led by the nose to their destinations by NFL teams. In the 1960s, the assumption was that these were college men, and college men should be able to travel from Point A to Point B by themselves.

Kelly did just fine going from Baltimore to Cleveland. But then he had to catch a bus in Cleveland to Hiram.

That was trouble.

Kelly watched the steel mills and stores out the window turn into chickens and cows. The gray skies of the inner city were now country blue. He was going to Hiram, wherever Hiram was—and few people on the bus were sure. No one else was headed there. Even the driver wasn't sure where Kelly should get off. So the driver and Kelly guessed—and guessed wrong.

They overshot Hiram by a couple of stops. Kelly had to sit in a gas station in the middle of nowhere for three hours waiting for the bus coming in the opposite direction.

This time, he walked off the bus at the one gas station in Hiram. He grabbed his bags and walked down that huge hill to the football field and the gym. There he saw Blanton Collier.

"Well, Leroy, it's almost five o'clock," said Collier, looking at his watch. "If nothing else, you made it in time for supper."

Welcome to the Browns for this scared young man who later would replace Jim Brown and find his way to Canton and the Football Hall of Fame.

Collier also signed a free agent from San Jose State named Walter Roberts. He was called "The Flea." He was listed at 5′10″ and 170 pounds.

No one believed it.

The Flea earned his nickname because he was small and fast, especially on kickoff and punt returns. He was spotted by a Browns scout named Sarge McKenzie, an old Army buddy of Paul Brown's who lived on the West Coast. Sarge didn't think Roberts was an inch over 5′7″ or heavier than 150, but he clocked the kid at 9.6 in the 100-yard dash. He saw him play nearly every down at San Jose State—flanker on offense, safety on defense, and deep man on the return teams. He was a Flea all right, but with the toughness of a roach.

Collier said fine, "We'll take a look at him."

No one even drafted Roberts. He didn't rate a plane ticket to Cleveland, just bus fare. The Flea spent three full days and nights on a bus from San Jose to Hiram. He said he ate nothing but hamburgers for three straight days, those little White Castle burgers that cost a dollar for a dozen.

After a few practices, Collier was very glad he had taken Sarge McKenzie's word. "That Roberts is like a fox terrier running around the legs of an elephant," he said after watching the rookie return a few punts for long yardage, leaving bigger men facedown in the dirt as they literally fell for his fakes.

A few days later, Collier was calling Roberts "a rabbit in a wheat field."

Collier's other key addition was Dick Modzelewski, a veteran defensive tackle acquired from the New York Giants. Modzelewski had been in the middle of the Giants' defense that had been stuffing the Browns for years. His brother, Ed, was a running back with the Browns in the 1950s. When Dick came to the Browns, he was thirty-three—too old, according to the Giants.

Collier thought Modzelewski was exactly what the Browns needed. Old or not, he had played in 138 consecutive games, the longest streak in the NFL. He was 6-foot, 250 pounds, a square of flesh on two legs.

The Browns' other defensive tackle was Jim Kanicki, the second-year man from Michigan State. He had two nicknames. In public, he was called "Smokey the Bear," because he was a bearlike 6´4˝ and 275 pounds. But some of his teammates called him "Baby Huey." He was more fat than muscle, more jolly than mean. Collier not only believed that Modzelewski would help on the line, but he knew that the veteran would teach Kanicki. That was Modzelewski's nature, and Collier believed that one day the tackle would make a fine coach. This was a chance for him to coach and still play. Just as Bernie Parrish would tutor inexperienced defensive backs such as Larry Benz and Walter Beach, Modzelewski would work with Kanicki. Former Browns receiver Ray Renfro was also brought to training camp, to tutor Paul Warfield.

Modzelewski said Collier would stop by his dorm room after practice; the two men would discuss line play, and suddenly Collier would have several chairs lined up, displaying different defensive formations. It reached the point that when Modzelewski saw Collier coming, he went down the hall, found extra chairs and took them into his room so the coach would have plenty of props for that day's lesson.

Collier also was smart enough to know that there were only so many hours he could keep players on the field, and that there wasn't enough time for him to work with everyone. So he put the tutoring system into place, his veterans helping the assistant coaches school the rookies.

This gave players more individual attention, and it made the veterans feel they had even a bigger stake in the game.

For example, Modzelewski noticed that receiver Gary Collins could be a little tense. Modzelewski had experimented with yoga and meditation and discovered it relaxed him and enhanced his concentration. He took Collins aside for a few lessons, and had the receiver take nine short, quick breaths, then exhale deeply. Collins was not especially comfortable with it, but the fact that Modzelewski was willing to spend that time with Collins pleased the coaches. To them, that was leadership.

There was something else unusual about the Browns' training camp during the 1960s: the media was welcome to watch every practice from the sidelines, not far from the coaches. And writers stayed in the same dorms as the players.

"Paul Brown felt in real competition for the sports fans with the Indians," recalled former Cleveland sportswriter Bob August. "He thought his teams were better than the Indians—and they were, although the Indians were terrific for most of the 1950s, too. Anyway, Paul wanted the attention and he was glad to have the local writers around."

Collier took the same approach, welcoming writers and fans to his practices at Hiram. Nothing on the field was closed to the public. Players were encouraged to sign autographs.

Yes, there were football cards back then. The Topps Company came to Hiram every summer to take photos for their cards. Each player received $5 as a signing bonus with the company, and $125 for each year that his picture was used. Topps was the only football card company, and it was a take-it-or-leave-it deal—and the players were glad to take it. Back in the 1960s the Browns were a popular team not just because they won, but also because they truly appreciated the fans' support.

But Paul Brown's training camp did have its quirks.

"Paul did not believe in cohabitation during training camp, not even for his married players," recalled Akron sportswriter Tom Melody. "There was a family day when they had a cookout for the players and their families. If Paul noticed that a certain player and his wife had been gone for a while, he sent Blanton to track the guy down, to knock on all the dorm rooms until he found the blissful couple. Blanton made a lot of noise and let them know he was on the way, and they soon rejoined the group. Paul's idea of family day was everyone sitting under the trees, eating hot dogs, hamburgers, and drinking lemonade—then the wives were to go home."

As head coach, Collier wasn't quite so strict.

That 1964 training camp was a time like no other for the Browns.

It was Frank Ryan trying to roll down a hill on a skateboard.

It was Jim Brown dancing to Motown tunes blaring from Hiram's one jukebox.

It was players sneaking off ten miles to Garrettsville, then slipping back to Hiram with six-packs of beer.

It was Wiffle ball games, throwing Frisbees, and family picnics.

"It was a summer I'll never forget," said Casey Coleman.

In 1964, Coleman was thirteen years old. He is the son of Ken Coleman, who was the Browns' TV voice. Casey spent that summer in Hiram as an assistant to equipment manager Morrie Kono. Now a veteran TV sportscaster in Cleveland and the last Browns radio play-by-play man, Coleman sounds like an excited thirteen-year-old when he talks about that summer.

"I brought my skateboard with me," he said. "There was that steep hill that went from the dorms to the field house. I'd go flying down that hill. I could have fallen and broken my neck, but when you're thirteen, who thinks about that? Anyway, Frank Ryan saw me on my skateboard. He wanted to try it. There went Frank down the hill."

But here was the team's starting quarterback, perhaps the smartest man in the NFL, rolling down the hill on a skateboard as if he were thirteen.

"The next day, Blanton Collier came up to me," Coleman said. "Usually Blanton was really nice to me, but he had this stern look on his face. Somehow he had heard about Frank on that skateboard, and he told me that the skateboard was to disappear, or I would face dire consequences. I never rode it at Hiram again."

Center John Morrow recalled the bar in Garrettsville.

"There was nothing special about the place, except they kept Rolling Rock beer just above freezing," he said. "After those two-a-day practices, we'd go down the road, throw down a few of those Rolling Rocks—

nothing tasted better. Then we'd go back to camp in time for supper and eat like a horse."

Some of the players brought beer back with them and hid it from the coaches. The problem was that the rooms were so small, and there were no refrigerators, so the players had to drink the beer that night or it really wasn't much good.

"The food at Hiram was the best, especially after Modell bought the team," said Gene Hickerson. "He'd get these huge tenderloins, top-grade steaks. You'd smell fifty steaks outside on the grill, the smoke dancing up to the sky, your mouth was watering. That was the best smell in the world after those long practices."

A cold Rolling Rock. A good steak.

That is what these men remember about Hiram.

When he was bored, Jim Brown wandered into the small snack bar, the only business establishment in Hiram. He took a handful of quarters, poured them into the jukebox and danced to the early Motown stars. There was Jim Brown, a 230-pound fullback, the greatest runner of his era, dancing by himself in a small snack bar in Hiram.

"One time, I put my quarter in," Casey Coleman said. "I loved the Beach Boys and punched up one of their tunes."

Jim Brown was waiting for the next song, when he heard these wailing white boys.

"Man, what is that?" he asked Coleman.

"It's the Beach Boys," Coleman said, feeling as if he should crawl under the chair.

"What is wrong with you?" he asked. "Don't you know that no one can dance to the Beach Boys?"

Brown sat down next to Coleman, and they both waited in silence for the song to end. Then came more Motown (Brown loved the Four Tops), and Brown was back dancing again.

There were only two TVs at Hiram. Gene Hickerson had one in his room, a portable he brought from home. The other was in the lounge area of the dorms.

"Whoever got there first could turn the TV to what he wanted to watch," Coleman recalled. "But this was when you had those old rabbit-ear antennas, and you had only three stations from Cleveland. The reception was pretty fuzzy and the TV was a black and white. Some nights, no one watched it at all. More often, some of the guys would sit down there while [offensive tackle] John Brown brought out his guitar, and strum and sing."

If you are starting to see Hiram as a summer camp, you are getting the idea.

"One day, [defensive back] Ross Fichtner showed up with this big box," said Tom Melody.

The players asked, "What's in the box?"

Fichtner said, "It's a mongoose."

Then Fichtner told the players how the mongoose was the cleverest, most dangerous animal in the wild. It could kill you on sight. More and more of the players gathered around, listening to Fichtner's account of men dying from just looking at a mongoose.

"Finally, he had about half the team around him," recalled Melody. "Then Ross said he'd open it just a crack, so the guys could take a peek. You had all these huge men, leaning over, trying to see what was in the box. Ross slightly lifted the lid and a tail jumped out."

Players scattered as if they were convinced they were to be the next victim of the mongoose.

"I remember seeing big Jim Kanicki knocking over chairs to get out of the way of what was just one of those toy tails that would spring out of a box," said Melody.

This also was the era of crew cuts.

"All the guys had really short hair," said Coleman. "There was no place to get your hair cut in Hiram, so I decided to go to Garrettsville for a haircut. It was ten miles away, and I needed a ride. I walked down to the parking lot, and I saw that [defensive back] Bobby Franklin had just come back from somewhere. He had this big Pontiac with Mississippi plates."

Coleman was only thirteen, and didn't have a driver's license.

"'Hey, Waxy,' I said. They called Franklin 'Waxy,' because he used so much wax in his hair. Anyway, I asked Waxy if I could borrow his car to get a haircut."

"Do you know how to drive?" asked Franklin.

"That was a great question for me," Coleman said. "He didn't ask if I were old enough or if I had a license. He just wanted to know if I could drive. Well, I had driven my dad's car up and down the driveway a few times, so I figured I could do it."

Coleman said, "Sure I can."

Franklin threw Coleman the keys. The kid drove down that two-lane blacktop to Garrettsville.

"I'll never forget that feeling, driving Franklin's Pontiac," he said. "But I paid the price for the haircut. I got it cut really short. It was lunchtime, and when I returned, I was on the field for most of the afternoon, helping at practice. About two in the morning, I woke up. It felt like the top of my head was on fire. I had this awful sunburn."

Sometimes, Coleman and the rookies would meet on the lawn in front of the dorm after supper, and they'd throw a Frisbee around.

Usually, it was Leroy Kelly, Paul Warfield, Clifton McNeil, and the thirteen-year-old clubhouse kid.

"Then we started playing Wiffle ball games," Coleman said. "You had to call your field—are you going to hit the ball to left or right field? If you hit it to the wrong field, you were out. One day, Warfield hit a two-run shot that landed on the roof at Centennial Hall."

All the players stood, staring at the roof, waiting for the ball to come down.

Warfield was circling the bases, figuring he had a home run. But the ball never did return to the ground.

"It got stuck in the gutter on the roof," Coleman said. "That was the end of our Wiffle ball games, because all we had was only one ball."

And no one was about to risk climbing on the roof to get it down—not because they might fall, but because they knew the coaches wouldn't like it if they saw Warfield or Kelly risking a fall just to get on the roof for a Wiffle ball.

"I spent a lot of time with the rookies such as Kelly and Warfield," Coleman said. "They didn't have cars or money to leave campus and go to Garrettsville at night."

Yes, Kelly and Warfield were two future Hall of Famers with no cars, no cash.

———————

The Browns had a preseason game in Detroit, a night game.

"We were taking a bus back from the Cleveland airport," Coleman said. "I don't know why, but there were only about six guys on that bus. It was about three in the morning, and [defensive lineman] Frank Parker got all over the bus driver about going too slow.

"This went on for a while, and finally the bus driver got mad, pulled over and told Parker to drive. I mean, we must have been airborne going over those hills and country roads to Hiram."

When the players got off the bus, they were hungry. But the kitchen was closed.

"Parker broke into the kitchen," Coleman said. "He led us to the icebox, where they had this huge vat of chocolate ice cream. A couple of guys had ladles and were just scooping out gobs of that ice cream. Other guys were frying up bacon and eggs. They made dozens and dozens of eggs."

The Browns had only one trainer in camp, Leo Murphy, and Murphy couldn't tape everyone's ankles and ice everyone's bruises.

"One of my jobs was to rub Paul Wiggin's back," said Casey Coleman. "He had a bad back, and needed it loosened up. I remember him yelling at me, 'Lean on it. *Lean on it!*' I was only thirteen, and I couldn't push on him hard enough."

But apparently, Wiggin was a happy customer.

"Then Gene Hickerson wanted me to rub his back," Coleman said. "So every day, I did Wiggin first, and then Hickerson."

Can you imagine an NFL team today letting a ballboy anywhere near a player's back?

Collier also had a special assignment for young Casey Coleman.

"I'd bring the towels to the field for the morning practice," Coleman said. "Then my job was to catch the kicks from Dick Van Raaphorst, a rookie placekicker from Ohio State who was trying out for the team. It was just Dick and me. Blanton had me keeping a chart.

"After I caught the ball, I threw it back and recorded how far he'd kicked it. I'd write, 'He kicked 30 times, 15 went into the end zone, 10 landed inside the 10-yard-line and 5 went out-of-bounds.' I thought this was an awesome responsibility, like the future of the free world depended upon me keeping track of those kicks just right."

Art Modell had his own dorm room at Hiram and was a constant presence at practice.

"Art paid me $25 for working two months at training camp," Coleman said. "I still have the receipt from that check, because it was my first paycheck. But Art would throw all his change into the top drawer of the bureau in his dorm room, and every few weeks, he'd let the two of us [ballboys] come in and divide up that change. It usually was at least a couple of bucks, which was great because a dollar could buy a lot back then."

Modell liked to tell Buddy Hackett stories. He was friends with the comedian, and Hackett was hot back in 1964. Modell also was dating Suzanne Pleshette, the actress.

"She was one of the most beautiful women in the world in 1964," said Coleman. "Art liked to drop the names of show business people."

One day, Coleman ran an errand for Modell. When he was finished, he noticed that Modell had boxes and boxes of football cards in the corner of the room.

Model said, "Casey, help yourself."

Coleman carried away all he could, stacks and stacks of cards.

"I got home, opened them up, and realized that all the cards were the same," he said. "I had about 300 Maurice Bassett cards, box after box of Maurice Bassett. At first, I wasn't even sure who he was."

Bassett was a backup running back with the Browns from 1954 to 1956.

Now, it's hard to imagine star players being on the special teams, but that was common in 1964. Leroy Kelly blocked a punt that year. Gene Hickerson led the team in tackles on special teams, and Jim Houston was right behind.

Walter Roberts and Kelly returned kicks and punts.

"Back then, no one thought they were too good to be on special teams," said Houston. "You just wanted to play as much as you could."

That was because little distinction was made between the players. Yes, Jim Brown was the franchise. And yes, you didn't have your quarterbacks making tackles on the punt teams. But everyone else helped out.

Asked what he did in his off-season, Frank Ryan talked about how he and his wife, Joan, remodeled and painted several rooms in their house. "We decided to save the money and do it ourselves," he said. "We painted until we were blue in the face."

Here is another story that says so much about 1964.

"Every morning, we'd put together a bundle—each player received a pair of socks, some shorts, a jock strap, and a T-shirt. We'd tie them together in a towel and give them to each player," said Coleman. "There were no sizes. Everyone got the same size shirt, jock, and shorts—no distinctions were made and no one whined that this stuff wasn't their size. Back then, they were just happy to have someone wash their clothes every night."

That was life at Hiram, a simple place where football players came together to become a football team.

THE BROWNS
BREAK CAMP

Trade Jim Brown?

That was what the Browns should do—or at least, that is what former Browns quarterback Otto Graham suggested the team do unless Jim Brown shaped up.

Graham stunned his former team when he appeared at a luncheon in Canton, Ohio, and told 150 fans, "If I were the Browns' coach, I would tell the fullback that I would trade him if he didn't block and fake. The Browns will not win anything as long as Jim Brown is there. Chew on that for a while."

There was more.

"There is no comparison between Jim Brown and [former Browns running back] Marion Motley," Graham said. "Motley was the greatest all-around fullback."

And more.

"As each year goes by, I gain more respect for Paul Brown," Graham said. "The world could use more Paul Browns."

And even more.

"His teammates have told me that he doesn't block or fake," Graham added.

Graham remains the greatest quarterback in Browns history. While he battled with Paul Brown over play selection, the two men were very close. Graham also was aware that many people believed Jim Brown led the "player rebellion" that led to Paul Brown being fired.

When he made those remarks, Graham was the coach of the Coast

Guard Academy in New London, Connecticut. He spoke out two weeks before the regular NFL season was to open. Jim Brown dismissed the comments by saying, "Every fan has a right to his opinion." But the rest of the team circled the wagons around the fullback.

"What Graham doesn't realize is that the pro football parade has passed him by," Frank Ryan told Cleveland writers. "There have been many changes since he played. It wasn't Jim Brown's fault that we lost out on the title last year, it was mine. If Otto Graham has any advice, he should direct it at me."

Cleveland sportswriters examined Graham's charges. It was true that Jim Brown was not a good blocker. Sometimes, he didn't block at all. But he carried the ball on 74 percent of the running plays in 1963. As Bill Scholl wrote in the *Cleveland Press,* that meant there were only seven running plays a game where Jim Brown had the opportunity to block for someone else.

On pass plays, Brown was usually sent out as a receiver, an option for a short pass if the quarterback could not find anyone open downfield.

"Don't blame him until we ask him to do that consistently," Blanton Collier said. "Blame me, not Jim. He has done everything I asked."

Art Modell jumped mouth-first into the fray, insisting, "It's tragic that a man who has taken so much out of pro football and played so brilliantly himself sees fit to demean one of the greatest players of all time, especially at the outset of a new season. It's obvious that Otto Graham is not the coach of the Browns."

Virtually every Cleveland writer came to Jim Brown's defense, the summation best expressed by *Plain Dealer* sports editor Gordon Cobbledick, who wrote, "In the judgment of his coach, Blanton Collier, he performs a more useful function in other areas, as a decoy rather than a blocker. This is an opinion that also was shared by Paul Brown."

Modell then gave Jim Brown a contract for $50,000—which was a $10,000 raise from 1963, and made him the highest paid player in the NFL.

While Collier and Modell were surprised and upset by Graham's last blast, it served to unify the team behind Jim Brown. It also told Brown how much he was appreciated by his coaches and teammates.

And it did something else.

If you tell a proud, stubborn man such as Jim Brown that he can't do something, he'll do it just to make his critics gag on their words. During the 1964 season, Jim Brown blocked better and harder than he ever had in his life. Nothing Collier or anyone could have said would have so inspired Brown as Graham's attack.

Graham was stung by the backlash from the Cleveland media, who always had praised this wonderful quarterback. Furthermore, Graham also is a true gentleman, which is why his charges about Jim Brown made such huge headlines. Graham probably thought he was supporting Paul Brown, but no one read it that way.

Later, he said, "I hope what I said about Brown makes Jimmy so mad that he becomes a better player. He could be the greatest football player of all time."

Well, in 1964, there was none better.

What made Collier happiest in training camp was Paul Warfield, whom veteran *Plain Dealer* football writer Chuck Heaton characterized as being "perhaps the best player to crash the Cleveland football scene since Jim Brown in 1957."

He wrote this in July, before Warfield even played his first exhibition game.

A month later, Heaton wrote, "We predict that the Warfield–Gary Collins combination will make the fans, even the old-timers, forget all about Mac Speedie and Dante Lavelli. Warfield has more speed than either of them. Collins is bigger and catches the football just as well."

Speedie (who had a great last name for a split end) and Lavelli were considered the greatest receivers in Browns history, the favorite targets of Otto Graham. Even Graham liked Warfield: "He should be an outstanding pro. He's very quick and has terrific moves."

Warfield was indeed exactly as advertised, not just as an athlete, but as a gentleman. This was one smart, hardworking guy.

The Browns had been drafting receivers in the first round for several years: Rich Kreitling (1959), Bob Crespino (1961), Gary Collins (1962), Tom Hutchinson (1963), and Warfield (1964). Only Collins was worthy of being a first pick, at least until the arrival of Warfield from Ohio State.

Warfield credited Collier.

"He talked about football, man versus man," Warfield said. "By that,

I mean that Blanton talked about you and the man who was covering you. He'd show you that player's tendencies, and then show you how to beat him. No detail was too small. His thinking was that if you used the proper technique and your man beat you, he could live with that."

Warfield said that Collier did insist that "football is a tough game," but also said it was much more than blood, mud, and guts.

"Blanton would tell us to have some fun, to enjoy what we were doing," Warfield said. "He said there was no way to play this game like a powder puff, but his approach was analytical. At that time, the belief was that you just beat the stuffing out of the other team. We weren't viewed as a very physical team, but we won because we had skilled players. Blanton didn't think football had to be a heavyweight fight where the only way to win was to pound the other guy into submission. He was convinced that games were won by the team that made the fewest mistakes and executed best."

Collier would tell players that execution was harder than it seemed. It could be raining. You could slip. It could be 90 degrees, when the heat robs you of your concentration. Or it could be snowing and you couldn't even feel your fingers.

"No matter what the weather, what the crowd was like, or where the game was played, nothing was to interfere with your concentration," Warfield said.

What if it did?

"We'd have film sessions," Warfield said. "He'd stop the film and say, 'We have a good play drawn up here. The guards, the tackles, the center—they all executed their blocks. The backs ran their patterns. The quarterback threw a perfect pass—but I guess that we can't depend upon Paul Warfield to run the correct pattern and make the catch.' And it was right there on film, so you couldn't argue with him."

Collier liked how his team was coming together.

Dick Modzelewski and Jim Kanicki solidified the defensive line. Warfield and Collins gave the Browns the best receivers in the league. Jim Brown by himself composed the best backfield, and Ernie Green wasn't just another back, as he showed when he was named to the Pro Bowl the year after Brown retired.

Quarterback was still an issue: Jim Ninowski or Frank Ryan?

As training camp opened, Bob August wrote in the *Cleveland Press:* "The tag on Frank Ryan was 'not good enough.' . . . Ryan was to be a fill-in for Ninowski, marked for emergency use only. He never would have been here if Len Dawson, the No. 2 quarterback, hadn't balked at the bargaining table. The emergency developed when Ninowski was injured [in the middle of the 1962 season], and Ryan has been a regular ever since. . . . Before the Pro Bowl Game in January, Ryan commented that he could be another Y.A. Tittle. 'Too bad about Ryan,' said an office cynic. 'He must mean that he's losing his hair [like Tittle].' . . . Ryan is starting his sixth season as a pro, but only his second as a regular, and the quarterback is the most important man in the team's immediate future. . . . Ryan has made himself a success only by stubborn insistence on his ability, even when it was widely doubted."

There still were doubts at the start of 1964, even though the Browns were 10-4 with Ryan the previous year. Part of it was that Ryan didn't throw like a quarterback. His passes were soft, often high lobs.

"And when Frank was off, he was way off," said Casey Coleman. "He'd overthrow a wide open receiver by 15 yards, the kind of pass even a high school kid wouldn't make."

By contrast, Ninowski had a powerful arm. If anything, his critics insisted that Nino threw too hard.

"As a ballboy, I would warm up both quarterbacks during training camp," Coleman said. "Marty Murphy [son of trainer Leo Murphy] was the other ballboy. We'd take turns, and neither one of us wanted to warm up Nino. We loved Nino as a person, but he'd throw the ball 90 miles per hour. You'd end up with bruises on your arms and chest from Nino's passes. Frank was just the opposite, so soft. But Nino was a more accurate passer, and as is the case with most talented backup quarterbacks, on certain Sundays Jim Ninowski was the most popular man in town, even though he never got into the game. The fans would chant his name."

Paul Brown had obtained Frank Ryan from the L.A. Rams at the start of the 1962 season to back up Ninowski. But once Ninowski separated his shoulder, Ryan played, and Paul Brown changed his mind— he liked Ryan better.

So did Collier, when he took over in 1963.

But the doubts lingered during camp in 1964. Maybe Ryan wasn't quite good enough. Maybe this man with the Ph.D. in math was too smart, too intellectual, to lead a football team. Ninowski had gotten a raw deal: He lost his job to an injury, and never was given a real chance to regain it.

Then the Browns opened the preseason with a 26-7 loss at San Francisco. Ryan had one of those games where you wondered if he knew what color jersey his team was wearing. The ball went everywhere, except to his receivers. Art Modell paced and muttered to himself in the press box, his main theme being, "Thank God this game isn't on TV back in Cleveland."

The only time the Browns did move the ball was when Ninowski played in the second half, and that brought back cries for Ninowski to start (at least from the fans) when the team returned to Hiram.

"It was a poor performance by Frank," Collier said. "But when a pitcher gets knocked out of the box, that doesn't mean he won't be back out there in four days. That is how I feel about Frank."

Collier wanted the world to know that Ryan was his quarterback. Over and over, he professed his faith in the math professor from Rice University.

In the next three exhibition games, the Browns won by scores of 56-31, 42-7, and 35-14—and that ended the rumblings about Ryan.

They finished the preseason with a 20-17 victory over Green Bay, and their record was 4-1. Ticket sales were booming. The Browns were ready to open the season, and they would win a title if . . .

If Collier could put together a decent secondary.

He was confident in cornerback Bernie Parrish. He had faith in safety Ross Fichtner.

That still meant he needed another safety and cornerback.

Collier resisted the temptation to use Paul Warfield on defense, which was Paul Brown's idea. It had merit; Warfield was such a gifted athlete and such an intelligent guy that he probably could have become an All-Pro safety.

But Collier was a coach who loved offense, and he was not about to change his vision of Gary Collins at one end of the offensive line, Warfield at the other—and the two flashing down the field, either sprinting under Frank Ryan's passes or simply stretching the defense, allowing Jim Brown more room to run.

Leroy Kelly played some defensive back at Morgan State, but Collier saw that this rookie was awed by the NFL. In training camp, Jim Brown told Collier that he only would play two or three more years, and Collier saw Kelly as Brown's replacement. So he decided not to try and turn Kelly into a defensive back.

Collier and Bernie Parrish lived in the same Aurora housing development. While Parrish didn't have the official title of assistant coach in the team's media guide or program, he was treated as such by Collier. A year after the death of close friend Don Fleming, the Browns' starting safety who was killed in a construction accident before the 1963 season, Parrish still seemed stunned. It wasn't easy for him to discuss who ought to play in Fleming's spot. Collier was intrigued with rookie Lowell Caylor, primarily because he was 6′3″ and 205 pounds. Most defensive backs were under 6 feet and weighed about 185. But Collier saw receivers becoming bigger every year, and if he could find someone with size, Collier wanted to try it.

But Parrish thought Caylor didn't have the experience the team needed. While Larry Benz was small (5′11″, 185 pounds), Parrish thought Benz was a good football player, period. Benz had been a quarterback and defensive back at Northwestern. He even threw two touchdown passes when Northwestern upset Notre Dame, 14–6, in his junior season, but he was not a pro-caliber quarterback. Nor was he seemingly talented enough to play in the defensive secondary, so he was completely passed over in the NFL draft. Former Browns player Ara Parseghian called both Paul Brown and Collier, pushing the team to invite Benz for a tryout; he did and won the starting safety job in 1963, replacing Fleming. It was hard for Parrish to accept anyone replacing Fleming. Parrish was harsh with Benz; he picked, sometimes even nit-picked. There were days when Benz had to wonder if anything he did was right. But Benz started every game and intercepted seven passes as a rookie in 1963.

Parrish believed there was no reason to change for 1964.

"If nothing else, I didn't want to train another new guy," he said. "Besides, Benz was a tough little guy. When he tackled you, you knew it."

The Browns would have a new right cornerback, as Jim Shofner retired after starting at that position for the previous six years. The new man was Walter Beach, who was signed a free agent in 1963, but played in only three games.

Who was Walter Beach?

The 1964 Browns media guide stated mysteriously: "reported to the Browns camp in 1963 for one final attempt to make good in professional football after a curious succession of efforts with other clubs."

The media guide really didn't explain, other than to say that Beach had been originally picked by the New York Giants in 1960, but was cut. He also played for Hamilton in the Canadian Football League and the Boston Patriots of the American Football League. He had attended Central Michigan University, where he was a track star who ran a 9.6 in the 100-yard dash.

He also had spent four years in the military after high school. When he was cut by the Patriots, he taught fourth grade for a year in his hometown of Pontiac, Michigan. He received an invitation to try out with the Browns in 1963, and made the taxi squad. He dressed for only the final three games of the season.

Now, in 1964, be the events "curious" or not, Beach was the starting right cornerback—the league's oldest first-year starter at the age of twenty-nine.

"I liked Walter," said Bernie Parrish. "This was when the black consciousness movement was beginning. Walter was reading the Koran and things like that. He was a smart, smart guy. But he never tried to rub your nose in his politics. Some of the other teams he was with maybe were uncomfortable with him because of his interest in black politics, but he was great with us."

As a player?

"After myself, he was our best cover man," Parrish said. "He was not a good tackler, but he could cover anybody."

Jim Kanicki knew Beach because they both attended the same high school, although not at the same time. "Our family and Walter's family knew each other," he said. "He could be outspoken about civil rights, and maybe that was why sometimes we heard he was a rebel who created problems with black players when he was with other teams. That just wasn't the case. Walter was a good man, a heady individual who thought about things. We had a lot of black leaders on our team, such as Jim Brown and John Wooten. The Browns were always ahead of most teams when it came to race relations, so Walter probably felt comfortable with us."

Or as Bill Glass said, "Walter came to us with a bad reputation, but I respected him. He was a nice guy, and frankly, there were a number of players on our team who were more radical than Walter Beach. I always thought Walter was like the entire defensive backfield that year—they were better than anyone thought they'd be."

So what was the Browns' secondary?

There was Parrish. At twenty-eight, he was the only established star, having been to two Pro Bowls.

There was Fichtner, who had been a quarterback at Purdue and was nearly cut in his first training camp back in 1960.

There was Benz, who wasn't even drafted in 1963.

There was Beach, who certainly didn't have the usual NFL pedigree.

And to think that defensive backfield would help shut down the Baltimore Colts in the 1964 championship game.

Most national publications were not impressed with the Browns as the 1964 season opened. They didn't believe that the team could repeat its 10-4 season. No one thought they'd win the title—no one but Chuck Heaton of the *Plain Dealer.*

The veteran Browns writer simply thought the team had greatness about it, and he was in love with Paul Warfield. He considered Collier a coaching genius and thought this would be the season that "everything comes together."

The respected preseason guide *Street and Smith's Magazine* picked the Browns to finish in second place, behind the Pittsburgh Steelers in the East. They thought the offensive line "isn't the best, and isn't the worst." They thought the pass rush was weak and worried about the defensive secondary. Even the great offense could not overcome those problems.

But this turned out not to be one of *Street and Smith's* better years, as the magazine picked the Baltimore Colts to finish in fourth place in the West. "Few teams will stop the Colts from scoring, but the Colts will stop few teams themselves." Defense was supposed to be the Colts' trouble.

The Scripps Howard newspaper chain polled its seventeen NFL writers, and the Browns were picked to finish third in the East, behind the New York Giants and St. Louis Cardinals.

They also picked the Colts to finish fourth in the West.

Sports Illustrated had the Browns finishing second, with Green Bay and St. Louis meeting in the title game. Then there was that great prognosticator, Ted Stepien. This man would purchase the Cleveland Cavaliers in 1980, and within three years the team would be near financial ruin and become one of the laughing-stocks of the NBA. But back in 1964, Stepien was just another sports fan.

He wrote this letter, which appeared in the *Plain Dealer:* "In the past several years, you writers have set up Jim Brown like a great idol. I read his article in *Look Magazine*—this was enough for me. I have no regard for someone who takes this kind of position. His personal attitude about the races—and his lack of blocking ability won't produce a winner here."

THE SEASON

Art Modell did Blanton Collier a favor: He didn't predict a champi-onship for the Browns. He didn't tell reporters that his team had the most talent in the NFL. He didn't tell some rotary club the Browns just might be the best team in NFL history.

He thought those things, but somehow he controlled himself. He didn't just blurt them out to strangers.

Praise the Lord!

Progress was being made, at least with the owner. Blanton Collier was speaking softly in Modell's ear, telling Modell to be *positive*, be *optimistic*, but don't make *predictions*.

And, remarkably, Modell took Collier's advice.

He did speak out on other matters. In *The Sporting News*, he dis-cussed the decline in baseball attendance compared to the rise in foot-ball's popularity: "Cleveland isn't the only place where [baseball] atten-dance is down. The Yankees have a great championship team, but they are losing attendance, yet the [NFL] Giants play in the same stadium and it is sold out. Football fills the public demand for a contact sport with speed, drama, emotion, and above all, action."

Joan Ryan noticed that her husband, Frank, had a special feeling about the season. Usually, they rented a home in suburban Lyndhurst until December 20, which was right after the final regular season game. This time, Ryan insisted on a lease into January of 1965, to make sure they had a place to live during the playoffs. As Joan Ryan wrote in the *Plain Dealer*, "We have to win or forfeit a precious half-month's rent!"

Game 1: Browns 27, Washington 13

The Browns opened in Washington, in a steady rain that reduced the field to mud by the end of the game. It also helped the Browns, as Washington fumbled four times. The game ended with Frank Ryan kneeling in the slop that was once the baseball infield.

Ryan was just happy it was over. Three of his passes had been picked off. His statistics were miserable: eight of 19 passes and one touchdown, a 23-yard strike to Gary Collins.

The defense won this game with their four fumble recoveries. Jim Brown and Ernie Green both had good days running the ball and combined for three TDs to bail out Ryan. Sensing that Ryan's confidence could use a boost, Collier said the quarterback "showed true genius" with the play-calling late in the game.

This also was the first game in the NFL career of future Hall of Famer Paul Warfield. He did not catch a pass.

Browns record: 1-0-0

Game 2: Browns 33, St. Louis 33

The team opened at home against St. Louis, and Modell was not happy. The game was not a sellout. Modell couldn't understand it. His team had a 10-4 record last year, St. Louis was strong at 9-5. What did people want? The *Plain Dealer's* Chuck Heaton went with Modell's line, writing a column that asked, "What About a Save the Browns Movement?"

The newspapers had been full of stories about saving the Indians, who'd had yet another miserable year at the gate and were being romanced to move to Seattle. Like Modell, Heaton thought the Browns should have had over 80,000 for their opener.

In his column, Heaton quoted a fan as saying, "Wouldn't surprise me a bit if the Browns were looking for greener pastures."

Heaton replied, "Hogwash. Art Modell knows he has a good thing. Aren't the fans behind him? Haven't the newspapers given the team great coverage?"

Heaton also wrote, "Mr. Modell is a trifle concerned. Tickets have been moving a little slow for this one. It will be well under the 81,000 who saw the Giants open here two years ago. Might be only 70,000."

Right there, someone should stop and say, *only 70,000?* That's 70,000 fans. That is a lot of people, more than nearly any other NFL team would draw. Why would Modell ever think of moving, be it in 1964 or 1994? But already, that was in the back of the minds of some fans.

On the morning of the game, there were still over 20,000 seats on sale at the Stadium. By kickoff, there were 76,954 fans in the stands— so Modell didn't exactly have to sell pencils on Public Square to pay the bills that week.

The most interesting part of this game came in the fourth quarter. The Browns were losing, 30–26. There were only 90 seconds left in the game. The Browns had the ball on the St. Louis 45-yard line. It was fourth down and 19 yards to go.

Collier sent Clifton McNeil in from the bench. He was carrying a play. As he approached the huddle, he saw Gary Collins wave him off the field. McNeil froze. Collins waved again. Not knowing what to do, the rookie receiver finally just ran back to the bench. The play call was never delivered. The players had already decided on what they would do and they weren't interested in consulting the coaches.

Somewhere, Paul Brown was watching and probably on the verge of a stroke. What do you mean, the players sent the play back to the bench?

Ryan dropped back to pass, Collins bolted for the goal line. Two defenders covered him, yet he fought them both off and caught the ball on the 2-yard line. Then Jim Brown scored the TD, putting the Browns ahead, 33–30.

But the defense didn't hold, and St. Louis came back to tie the game with a field goal in the final minute.

Little was said about Ryan and Collins's ignoring Collier's play—at least in the media. Collier and Ryan talked about it privately and said everyone was on the same page, and that was that.

Ernie Green was ejected in the second quarter for punching defensive back Pat Fischer. Future Hall of Famer Leroy Kelly appeared in the backfield for the first time in his pro career. Ryan was not ready to trust Kelly, who carried the ball just once the entire second half. But Paul Warfield finally caught a pass, covering 40 yards and a touchdown.

Browns record: 1-0-1

Game 3: Browns 28, Philadelphia 20

Want to know the difference between 1964 and today? Listen to this lead on a Chuck Heaton story the week the Browns were to play in Philadelphia: "Frank Ryan was outside tossing around a football with neighborhood kids when we called."

1. Would a quarterback today be outside playing with neighbor kids during the regular season?

2. If he were, would he actually come inside to talk to a reporter on the telephone?

Ryan did both. The subject of Heaton's call was Ryan's slow start. In fact, both men had been taken to task in the *Plain Dealer* letters column, where the relentless Ted Stepien wrote again, "You have written excuses, Mr. Heaton, for Frank Ryan's poor average. A .250 hitter in baseball after five years never progresses beyond .250. You should know this."

That didn't stop Ryan from insisting he was just fine, and Heaton reaffirming his faith in both Ryan and the Browns.

The game in Philadelphia was a sellout, but at Philadelphia's old Franklin Field, a sellout was 60,671. Compare that to the pregame 70,000 Modell thought was "disappointing" in Cleveland only the week before. If Modell had only 60,000, he would have been ready to jump into Lake Erie.

Anyway, that crowd in Philadelphia saw Ryan throw three touchdown passes, including a 40-yarder to Jim Brown.

In this game, Browns offensive coordinator Dub Jones sent in a running play from the sidelines. Interestingly, Jones said, "Frank has the option of not using it if he believes something else has a better chance of working." Apparently this was the compromise struck from the week before, when McNeil was sent in with a play but waved back to the bench before he even reached the huddle. Now, Ryan would allow the plays to come in, but view them as suggestions.

Anyway, Ryan took a pass on the running play from the bench, and instead threw a 12-yard TD pass to Collins.

As Chuck Heaton wrote, "The age of democracy has come to the Browns."

Both the players and coaches knew it was wise to keep the owner happy. They named a running play for Jim Brown "The Modell Burst," and the running back scored on the play. In the press box at Franklin

Field, Modell stood, cheered, and yelled, "The Modell Burst, I love that play! Way to run, Jim boy."

If you thought Modell was bad, consider a fellow named Jerry Wolman. He bought the Eagles for $5.5 million at the start of the 1964 season. About three times a week, he went to practice with his team and ran pass patterns against the defensive backs. You can be sure the Eagles players gave him plenty of room to get open and catch the ball.

Browns record: 2-0-1

Game 4: Browns 27, Dallas 6

As the Browns were preparing to face Dallas before 72,072 fans, the Indians finished the 1964 season with a crowd of 6,347. The Tribe's final record was 79-83, and their total home attendance for sixty-five dates was 653,293—10,051 per game.

In 1964, the Browns, with only eight home dates, would outdraw the Indians 658,878 to 653,293. Now you know why Art Modell believed he owned Cleveland in the middle 1960s, and why he had such problems coping with the rise of the Tribe in the middle 1990s.

On this, the fourth week of the season, the Browns put together their best game thus far. The defense destroyed the young Cowboys. The Dallas kicker was Dick Van Raaphorst, the neighbor of Lou Groza's who kicked at Ohio State. Van Raaphorst went to training camp with the Browns to challenge Groza, but was awestruck by Groza's presence and was cut. He signed with Dallas. But the Browns destroyed the rookie, blocking two of his field goals. He also had an extra point blocked.

Frank Ryan threw three TD passes, including a 40-yarder to Paul Warfield. Gary Collins also caught a TD pass.

In this game, the Browns lost defensive tackle Bob Gain for the season when he broke his leg. Ross Fichtner suffered a serious concussion and was out for several weeks. Bobby Franklin filled in at safety for Fichtner, and Jim Kanicki played in place of Gain.

Browns record: 3-0-1

Game 5: Pittsburgh 23, Browns 7

The Browns faced Pittsburgh and Steelers fullback John Henry Johnson. Like Jim Brown, Johnson was a punishing runner who seemed to take as much delight in the contact of the game as he did in carrying the ball. "There are too many people in this league who would like to see Johnson carried off the field on a stretcher," Jim Brown wrote in his book, *Off My Chest*. "This uncharitable attitude stems from hard-blocking John Henry's tendency to break things. Like jaws and cheek-bones, noses and teeth."

The Browns were a two-touchdown favorite in this game, and 80,530 fans showed up expecting to take utter delight in watching the Steelers being embarrassed. Instead, John Henry Johnson ran for three touch-downs and a career-high 200 yards. Not bad for a thirty-five-year-old fullback who was supposed to have been on his last, battered legs. Guess he hurt the Browns a lot more than they hurt him.

Pittsburgh used a strange formation, a six-man defensive front line. Neither the Browns' coaches nor Ryan could figure out how to counter it. Ryan was only 13 for 29 passing, and Jim Brown had only 59 yards rushing—but Ryan gave him the ball just eight times. So Ryan didn't pass well, and he failed to use Jim Brown. That was why fans were screaming for Jim Ninowski by the end of the game.

Pittsburgh was always a bitter memory for Ninowski. He had been the Browns' starter during the first half of the 1962 season until he suffered a broken collarbone against the Steelers. Ryan took over. Two years later, Ninowski was healthy but had started only one game (15 for 28 passing in 1963). Some fans believed that in the Browns' first five games, Ryan had played well only twice—against Dallas and Philadelphia. They wanted Ninowski.

Browns record: 3-1-1

Game 6: Browns 20, Dallas 16

You know this was 1964, long before political correctness ruled the day. The *Plain Dealer* billed the Browns game in Dallas as the "Battle of the Cripples" because both teams had several players injured.

It was another rough day for Frank Ryan, who was 9 for 20, passing for only 95 yards. But Collier's fingerprints were on the game plan, and the plan was to give the ball to Jim Brown. No more of those afternoons where Brown had only eight carries; Brown ran for 188 yards in 20 carries.

But the Browns were losing in this game, 16–13, with six minutes left. That was when Bernie Parrish picked off a pass and ran it back for a 54 yard TD, giving the Browns the 20–16 victory.

Earlier in the fourth quarter, Ninowski was warming up on the side-lines as Collier gave serious consideration to benching Ryan in favor of the backup. But Collier believed in Ryan. He knew Ryan's confidence could be shaky. He wanted to win this game, but he didn't want to lose Ryan to self-doubt for the rest of the season.

So he stayed with Ryan, and Parrish bailed him out. Later, Ryan would thank Parrish "for saving my job." The Browns were tied for first place, but not playing like a championship team.

Browns record: 4-1-1

Game 7: Browns 42, New York 20

In 1963, the Giants were the Eastern Conference champions. A year later, they were an old team in a rebuilding mode with a 1-4-1 record. But the Browns were not sure of that as they approached the midpoint of the 1964 season. All they knew was that the Giants were a team that had driven Paul Brown to distraction. They were a team that knew how to beat the Cleveland Browns, even on the Giants' worst days. In their last meeting, the Giants crushed the Browns, 33–6, in 1963.

The Browns, and especially Ryan, also knew they had to find a way to play better. Collier was happy that Jim Brown was back in the middle of the offense. He liked how rookie Walter Roberts was leading the NFL in kickoff returns with a 36.2 yard average. Against the Giants, Leroy Kelly would return a punt 68 yards for a touchdown. Collier also was pleased with Dick Modzelewski, who was acquired from the Giants to be a backup at defensive tackle, though injuries combined with Modzelewski's fine performance forced the coach to start the veteran.

In this game, at home before a crowd of 81,050, Bernie Parrish had another key interception late in the first half to stop a Giants drive. Still, the Browns went into the dressing room trailing, 7–6, at the half.

The defense set the tone for this game. Two of the Browns' TDs were set up by fumble recoveries, two more by interceptions. They needed the defense, because the Browns' lead was only 14–13 after three quarters. Then they exploded for 28 points in the final period to finally put the game away.

In this game, the Age of Democracy continued as Collins caught a nine-yard pass from Ryan. "It was a play Frank drew up in the infield dirt," Collins said. "We were in the huddle. He knelt down. He drew an X for me, an O for [defensive back] Erich Barnes of the Giants. Then he drew the pattern he wanted me to run."

Browns record: 5-1-1

Game 8: Browns 30, Pittsburgh 17

This time, in Pittsburgh, the Browns were not confused by the Steelers' six defenders on the defensive line and one linebacker.

They remembered to give the ball to Jim Brown, who ran for 149 yards.

They even gave it to Ernie Green, who ran for 86 yards in 17 carries. Green also scored two touchdowns and was awarded the game ball.

Part of the reason for the emphasis on the running game was Collier. The other factor was that both Collins and Warfield had sore hamstring muscles and didn't practice that week.

"Blanton came in on Wednesday and had about twenty running plays on the blackboard," Warfield said. "We had more running plays than that, but these were the twenty that Blanton thought would work best for that particular week. Then Blanton would ask Jim Brown, 'Okay, Jim, which of these do you like?' Jim would pick maybe five or seven. He'd tell Blanton why he liked those plays as opposed to some of the others—and then we'd really work on those plays during practice."

None of this had ever happened in the Paul Brown regime.

Nor would the huddles have been the same.

"We had a lot of discourse," Ryan recalled. "The linemen would tell me when they thought they had their men set up for a certain play. They made play suggestions. So did Jim Brown. So did the coaches. The receivers told me when they were open and what patterns worked best."

Often, Ryan moderated in the huddle. He was like a president who had a boisterous cabinet. Everyone felt free to brainstorm, but in the end, he made the decision.

"The important thing was the freedom I felt," recalled Ernie Green. "I could tell Frank that the linebackers weren't covering me, or whatever. He'd really listen. He didn't always take your suggestions, but he did it often enough to make you want to keep looking for plays that would work."

"Frank was a smart guy with a Ph.D., but he never acted like he was superior," Warfield said. "He'd ask our advice."

That is another reason Collier wanted to keep Ryan as the quarter-back—the players liked and trusted him. Ryan was not a screamer, but he had the perfect temperament to lead this team.

"I remember one day when Frank and Jim Brown disagreed in the huddle," Monte Clark said. "He told Jim to watch out for something, and Jim said, 'I'm standing back here with you. I can see things just fine.' Frank didn't press the issue, but he did get this message across to Jim without making Jim feel as if he were challenged. And Frank also didn't see a need to challenge Jim, when Jim seemed to dismiss what he had to say. It was a fine line, but Frank walked it so well."

Browns record: 6-1-1

Game 9: Browns 34, Washington 24

The Browns always had Monday off, and Frank Ryan spent that day with his family at the Cleveland Zoo. "That was the only place where I found a group of Clevelanders who weren't criticizing me," he said. Ryan added that his wife said her favorite player was Bernie Parrish, because the defensive back's key interceptions helped the Browns win games and helped Ryan keep his starting job.

Monday night, Ryan spoke to a group of advanced science and math students at Lakewood High. No, the subject was not football, it was science, math, and the pursuit of infinite numbers. Suddenly, Frank Ryan was making it cool to be smart in math and science, said one student.

Meanwhile, Joan Ryan, Nancy (wife of Galen) Fiss, Carolyn (wife of Paul) Wiggin, and Carol (wife of Bernie) Parrish were getting together every Wednesday night at the Parrish home, where they worked on individual art projects.

Ryan teaching math? The wives painting? Do we ever hear stories like these today in the NFL?

The Browns played the Redskins that week, and the most interesting play was when Jim Brown took a handoff from Ryan . . . and Brown dropped back to pass, and threw a 13-yard spiral to Gary Collins for a touchdown.

While this game was played on November 8, it was sunny and nearly

70 degrees at the Stadium. Several writers referred to it as "Modell weather," which pleased the fans and helped the owner's gate receipts. The 76,385 fans saw Ryan hit Paul Warfield with a 62-yard bomb for a score. Ernie Green scored on a 21-yard run as the Browns dominated the game.

Browns record: 7-1-1

Game 10: Browns 37, Detroit 21

Heading into this game, Art Modell was unhappy with Cleveland Stadium. The Browns drew 83,064 fans to watch their team clobber the Lions; it was the largest crowd in Browns history, but Modell was concerned because so many of his customers had to sit behind poles and didn't have a clear view of the game.

"What can I do?" he told the *Plain Dealer*'s Hal Lebovitz. "When I first came here [1961], we sold 16,846 season tickets. This year [1964], it is 32,488. Fans are realizing that the surest way to see the team is to buy the whole schedule. If we win the title, I wouldn't be surprised if we had over 40,000 season tickets sold in 1965."

The Browns did win the title, and they sold close to 41,000 season tickets. While he complained about the condition of the Stadium, he loved having those 80,000 seats, especially when the team was winning and there was "Modell weather" to entice a few more fans down to the lakefront.

Modell had a way of keeping himself in the news. During this season, he donated $15,000 to the American Cancer Society in memory of Ernie Davis, who had died of leukemia before the 1963 season. He hinted he might buy the financially troubled Indians, although no one was sure where he'd find the money. He made a bid to bring the National Basketball Association to Cleveland, but that didn't pan out, either.

Modell watched his team play from the press box, "with two packs of cigarettes and some antacid tablets," wrote Chuck Heaton. He tried not to cheer, but he'd scream when things went well, moan with the disappointments. He tried not to second-guess, and did a better job of that than during the Paul Brown era. By the end of every game, his tie was hanging long and loose from his neck. His hair was mussed. His shirt was sweat-stained and stuck to his back. The two cigarette packs were empty.

"Back to the padded cell for another week," he said after the Browns beat the Lions.

Jim Brown ran for 147 yards and two touchdowns. Walter Beach intercepted two passes, running one of them back 65 yards for a TD. Lou Groza had broken his nose the week before trying to make a tackle on kickoff coverage, but he was back on the field and kicking field goals of 37, 38, and 47 yards.

With four games left, the Browns (8-1-1) had a two-and-a-half-game lead over St. Louis (5-3-2) in the Eastern Conference.

Browns record: 8-1-1

Game 11: Green Bay 28, Browns 21

The Browns went to Green Bay with a chance to wrap up the conference title.

Instead, Jim Brown gained only eight yards on five carries in the second half. He even fumbled twice.

Frank Ryan threw two interceptions.

Bernie Parrish said he made some mistakes in his defensive calls that allowed Packers receivers to be open.

It was a nightmare, a Packers victory, and the St. Louis Cardinals crushed Philadelphia 38–13 to cut the Browns lead to one and a half games.

Browns record: 8-2-1

Game 12: Browns 38, Philadelphia 24

When most fans think of 1964, they assume that the Browns just rolled to the title. They don't remember that Frank Ryan nearly lost his job. They don't remember that key players such as Ross Fichtner, Frank Parker, and Bob Gain suffered major injuries.

But the Browns had to win several important games down the stretch, and this home game was one of them. The Browns responded by crushing the Eagles in front of 79,289 fans. They had a 21-3 lead at the half, one of the most entertaining plays being Jim Houston's 44-yard interception return for a TD. The linebacker made several fakes and quick cuts, demonstrating why several Browns coaches insisted he could be the second best athlete on the team, after Jim Brown.

Tight end John Brewer, known for his excellent blocking but questionable receiving skills, caught two TD passes. Rookie Sid Williams blocked a punt and fell on the ball in the end zone for a score. With 133 yards rushing, Jim Brown gained more yards on the ground than the entire Philadelphia team.

Browns record: 9-2-1

Game 13: St. Louis 28, Browns 19

If the Browns were to win in St. Louis, it would mean their first conference title since 1957. That year, they clinched by watching Pittsburgh beat the New York Giants on TV. The Browns were in a Detroit hotel, waiting to play the Lions the following afternoon in what turned out to be nothing more than an academic exercise to complete the schedule.

This time, they could win the title on the field.

A sellout crowd of 32,801 was on hand in St. Louis. Yes, Art Modell, the Cardinals played in a stadium that held only 32,801. The Cardinals were right behind the Browns in the standings, yet this was their first sellout of the season. In four games in St. Louis, the Browns had never lost. They were a four-point favorite in this game.

"The Cleveland Browns ordered four cases of champagne to be delivered to the Bel Air Motel in St. Louis on Saturday night," wrote Ed Shrake in *Sports Illustrated*. "The bottles were stacked in a refrigerator to await what the Browns hoped would be a barrage of popping corks, spewing wine and gay laughter on a Sunday afternoon. A taxi was ready to rush the champagne [from the hotel] to the Browns' locker room at Busch Stadium the moment the Browns were sure of victory. Fortunately, someone in the Cleveland organization had the discretion to order the champagne on consignment. By Sunday night the four cases were on their way back to the liquor store."

The defense gagged up 317 yards. Frank Ryan had only one TD pass, while two of his throws were picked off. The only thing that kept them reasonably close was Lou Groza's four field goals.

It looked like there would be no championship.

Or, as Don Robertson wrote in the *Plain Dealer*, "So color the Browns black. Hang crepe. Play the pipe slowly and bang the drum slowly. The Eye was watery. Hearts were heavy. Ah, but there's always next week. The Browns are playing the New York Giants, and the Giants are in last place. . . . so hold your breath. Cross your fingers. The enemy has won a battle, but we can win the war."

Browns record: 9-3-1

Game 14: Browns 52, New York 20

The Browns had to win in New York. If not, St. Louis was headed to the title game against Baltimore.

"If Y. A. Tittle can beat the Browns, we'll vote him a share of the championship money," Cardinals defensive end Joe Robb said.

Tittle was the Giants' great, aging quarterback. On so many afternoons, he had frustrated the Browns.

"After what we had been through in the past [with late-season collapses and losses to New York], it was hard not to think, 'Here we go again,'" recalled Galen Fiss. "We really had to regroup, and Blanton brought us together."

During the 1964 season, the Browns practiced at crumbling League Park, which had been the home of the Indians until the 1940s, when they began playing most of their games at the Stadium.

"Babe Ruth once played there," center John Morrow recalled. "But that didn't make it a good place to practice in 1964. The offense met on one side of the field under the old bleachers, the defense on the other side. The concrete was cracking. There was only one toilet for over fifty guys. If it rained, the ceiling leaked. It was a dungeon. There were no real lockers, just hooks on the wall to hang your clothes."

"Paul Brown used to tell us that we were the class of the NFL, yet we trained at that dump," Paul Wiggin recalled. "The neighborhood was deteriorating. I once saw a knife fight in front of the park. Rats roamed those old bleachers and the locker room."

"You never left anything at that park overnight, or you'd show up the next day and discover those big, old, ugly rats had gnawed on it," recalled Gene Hickerson.

"If you hung your helmet up, you had better check inside before you put it on your head," Monte Clark said. "Rats liked to hide in there. The whole place should have been condemned."

Yet the Browns seldom complained about it.

Collier made a couple of crucial decisions.

He did not show any of the film from the loss at St. Louis. He knew the team was already in a negative frame of mind and didn't need to replay the debacle from the week before. Instead, he put together films of what the team and individual players had done right in other games during the season. This was a time to stress the positive.

But he did not ignore the newspaper stories, where several St. Louis players said the Browns would be "the laugh champs" because they would have "backed in" to the title by beating the Giants, who had a miserable 2-9-2 record. He wanted the players to hear those charges, to be angry.

"For our last practice before the New York game, Blanton took us to the Stadium instead of League Park," Paul Warfield recalled. "We pulled up to the Stadium, and there was a sign that read: NEXT GAME, BALTIMORE COLTS, DECEMBER 27. That sign made me feel very confident."

The next day, the Browns flew to New York for the game at Yankee Stadium. Collier gave a brief pregame talk. After reviewing the basic Xs and Os, he simply told the team, "You know what you have to do out there today."

Early in the game, Dick Modzelewski crashed through the Giants' line and sacked Tittle. Modzelewski was playing with a vengeance, still angry that the Giants had traded him.

He looked at the bald, creaky Tittle in the dirt and said, "You ought to retire."

Tittle stared up at his old teammate's fiery eyes and said, "Tell me about it. Maybe you're right."

It would be Tittle's last game as a pro, and he'd always remember it for the wrong reasons. The Browns embarrassed his Giants.

Ryan was brilliant, completing 12 of 13 passes for 202 yards. Of those 12 completions, five went for TDs. He threw two TD passes to Warfield, and one each to Collins, Green, and Jim Brown. Ryan even ran 12 yards for a TD. It was the best game of his NFL career.

This time, there was no champagne on ice in the dressing room. But by the time the team was on its charter plane, the champagne had arrived from a liquor store in Newark. The players drank it all and ate filet mignon. Over 5,000 fans greeted them at the Cleveland airport.

That same day, Otto Graham said he never intended for the Browns to trade Jim Brown. He just believed that Brown's blocking left much to be desired, and he thought some public criticism would inspire the fullback. While Brown never admitted it, something had changed because, in the words of Collier, "Jim not only was a great running back, but he was an excellent blocker, too."

The Browns beat the Giants on a Saturday. The next day, Frank Ryan tried to watch the Baltimore Colts game on TV to do a little scouting for the championship game. He lasted about a quarter, and fell into a very sound, satisfying sleep. There would be plenty of time for preparation. After all, the NFL championship game—the only playoff game in these pre–wild card, pre–Super Bowl, pre-hype days—was two weeks away.

PREPARING FOR
THE COLTS

A few days before the Browns were to meet the Baltimore Colts in the title game, Art Modell ran into Colts owner Carroll Rosenbloom.

"I hope you don't embarrass us," Modell said.

"We'll try not to," said the Colts owner.

Modell was livid. He was just trying to be gracious to one of the league's veteran owners.

"The guy looked at me as if there was no doubt his team would win," Modell said. "In fact, his attitude was that if they wanted to embarrass us, they could."

Maybe Modell was right. Or maybe he was just hyper and reading too much into the exchange. Why should Rosenbloom be polite to a young upstart such as Modell if Rosenbloom really believed that his team would blow out the Browns? This much was certain: No one outside northern Ohio gave the Browns much chance. Even many of those who were Browns fans and/or admirers of the team and Blanton Collier had their doubts.

"Art told me that in his private moments, he worried the team might get beaten by 20 points," said Kevin Byrne, former Browns vice president of public relations. Modell wasn't alone.

As Bob August wrote in the *Cleveland Press*, "I think I hear a ticking, I think it comes from the Colts and they will explode and win a title at the Stadium."

"It wasn't that I lacked respect for the Browns," August said thirty years later. "It's just that the Colts appeared to be the superior team."

The *New York Times* saw it that way, too. Arthur Daley wrote, "Nothing ruffles Johnny Unitas. If the Browns blitz him, that will just give him room to manipulate. . . . The Colts just have too many weapons for the Browns . . . so this Grandstand Quarterback picks Baltimore to win. The choice is made without hesitation."

Tom Melody wrote in the *Akron Beacon Journal,* "It is unreasonable to imagine the Browns emerging triumphant." The story ran under the headline: "Browns Fans Face Long, 'Colt' Afternoon." Melody believed that the quarterbacks would settle the issue. While he conceded that when Frank Ryan was hot he was as good as anyone in the league, he had every reason to wonder if Ryan would be on top of his game, and every reason to believe Unitas would be in his usual All-Pro form. The difference, wrote Melody, was that Ryan had nineteen interceptions in the regular season. Unitas had "a mere six."

Only Chuck Heaton of the Cleveland *Plain Dealer* picked the Browns to win. But he was just staying with his preseason choice, the only notable sportswriter in the country to insist that the Browns would be playing for the title. During the 1964 season, Heaton had picked the Browns to win every single week.

The Browns' march to greatness was his story, and he had every reason to stick to it. Before the championship game, he wrote, "There seems to be a feeling about town that young coach Don Shula has assembled a squad of supermen. They are believed to be capable of running the Browns right into Lake Erie." Heaton told the Browns fans to keep the faith, and once again predicted the team would beat Baltimore.

But most other sportswriters followed the lead of *Sports Illustrated's* Ed Shrake, who wrote, "It is yawningly conceded that the Eastern Conference champion Cleveland will be playing merely for the dubious pleasure of being thrashed by Baltimore on December 27. There are at least three teams in the West that are superior to any in the East. To be realistic about it, the championship game of 1964 has already been played. Baltimore won it in October by beating Green Bay for the second time."

There was every reason for *Sports Illustrated* to support the Colts. The magazine had held a coronation for the team four games into the regular season, when it ran this story about the Colts: "The Making of a New Pro Dynasty."

Just to prove that we haven't just invented Rushing to Judgment in the 1990s, consider how *Sports Illustrated* hyped the Colts. Their record was 3-1 when the Dynasty story ran. The previous season, the Colts were 8-6. Yes, Baltimore was the NFL champion in 1958 and 1959, but from 1960 to 1963, the Colts' record was 29-25.

Granted, there were reasons to love the Colts early in 1964. Reasons like Unitas, who was the best quarterback of his era, and maybe any era.

The last time the two teams played, Baltimore crushed the Browns, 36-14. Jim Brown had his worst day as a pro with only 14 yards rushing in 11 carries. That game was played in 1962 during the waning days of Paul Brown's regime.

Jimmy Orr and Raymond Berry were two top wide receivers. John Mackey was one of the best tight ends of his time. And all three of these men had Unitas throwing them the ball.

Lenny Moore had a monster season at running back, setting an NFL record with 19 touchdowns.

The defensive line was strong. Gino Marchetti was talked out of retirement—he owned a chain of hamburger joints named Gino's in Maryland—and returned to anchor the defensive line along with Ordell Braase. Marchetti was thirty-seven, three years older than head coach Don Shula.

Yes, Shula was a reason to like the Colts, too. Only thirty-four and already proclaimed a genius, Shula had played for the Browns and Paul Brown from 1951 to 1955. He played another season for Baltimore, and was released by Washington in 1957, deemed too slow to be a defensive back. He spent two years as an assistant to Blanton Collier at Kentucky. Two weeks before the game, Collier said, "Don Shula knows a lot more about coaching than his years would indicate. I never knew a player with as fine a football mind. He always thought about coaching, even when he was playing. So I'd say he's had the experience of a man in the profession for ten years."

So the Colts had the Player of the Year in Unitas and the Coach of the Year in Shula, at least according to the sportswriters who did the voting for the Associated Press during the final week of the regular season.

Browns fans were upset. They couldn't understand how anyone but Jim Brown could be the MVP. They also thought Collier deserved more than three of the twenty-nine Coach of the Year votes. Unitas outpolled Jim Brown, 32-8.

But the Colts had a 12-2 record, and their second loss came after they had already wrapped up the Western Conference title. (Despite the Colts' superior record, the game would be held in Cleveland because the home field for the title game alternated between Eastern and Western Conference champions.) They set an NFL record by scoring 54 touchdowns. They not only led the NFL in scoring, but their defense allowed the fewest points.

"What I remember about going against the Colts was that they had all these great names," Paul Warfield said. "Now when I think about it, it seems like the Colts team has more players in the Hall of Fame than we do from our roster."

Warfield, Lou Groza, Leroy Kelly, and Jim Brown are the only members of the 1964 Browns in the Hall of Fame. But Groza was purely a kicker by then, and Kelly played only on special teams.

The Colts had six: Unitas, Mackey, Moore, Marchetti, Raymond Berry, and Jim Parker.

So those are the facts.

The greatest area of concern was the Browns' defense.

They had allowed 293 points, which was the fifth fewest in the league. That's not too bad. But the Browns' "Bend but don't break" approach meant that no NFL defense coughed up more total yards. The Browns allowed 20 more first downs than any other team in the league.

The Browns' defense also had the fewest quarterback sacks in the league, yet gave up the most first downs on the ground. This is a real contradiction; if a team isn't rushing the passer to create quarterback sacks, it should be sitting back a bit, stopping the running attack.

Statistics showed that the Browns did neither.

There seemed no way they could keep the Colts out of the end zone, and the only hope was that Cleveland's offense would simply outscore Baltimore, winning one of those 42–35 games.

"Going into the game, Baltimore thought they could do anything they wanted with us," recalled defensive lineman Dick Modzelewski. "They figured they could run when they needed to, and then throw against us at will. During those two weeks of practice, we kept reading, 'You're gonna lose, you're gonna lose.' A team in that position can either go along with that and say, 'Yeah, we're gonna lose, all right.' Or a team can pull together and show the world how wrong it can be. We got tired of hearing it and simply said, 'We're gonna win this damn game and shut everyone up.'"

Or as Warfield said, "While the Colts had all these great players in the primes of their careers, we also knew that any team with Jim Brown can beat anyone. Then there was Blanton Collier; we knew that no one could prepare a team for a game like Blanton, and he had two weeks to do it."

When you talk to the Browns players now, they will tell you that the Colts were anywhere from 14 to 17 point favorites. To them, it seemed that way.

But the spot was only seven points. The Colts were supposed to win by a touchdown.

Here is how the world was for NFL coaches in 1964:

Before the title game, the Browns and Colts exchanged five game films. Remember, this was before videotape and VCRs. It was when there was one NFL game a week on television, and that was Sunday afternoon. Teams such as the Browns and Colts would have paid no attention to each other, since they were not scheduled to play during the regular season.

Grainy black and white game films were the key scouting tools. Shula and Collier each picked out five of their team's game films, and then made a trade. Sure, Collier called his NFL friends who had played the Colts and picked their brains. Shula did the same, asking advice and insights from his friends who had watched the Browns.

But in the end, the game plans would come from those five films.

You give Blanton Collier a film projector, a quart of ice cream, and some time, and he'll come up with a Picasso of a game plan. That's what Collier did in those first few days after his team beat the New York Giants to earn the right to play the Colts. He holed up in his den at his Aurora home. He sat in his favorite chair, a quart of vanilla ice cream in his lap. In one hand, he held a spoon; in the other, he had the switch to play and replay the film of the Colts.

Collier's wife, Forman, noticed that after the first night of solitary study, her husband was in a very good mood. Collier was not one to act as if coaching a football team was a matter of life and death. He really did put his family first. He never completely forgave himself for the ordeal his wife endured from the angry boosters during his final days at Kentucky.

But Forman Collier loved her husband and she really did like football—although for the life of her, she would never understand why the game made people so crazy. She could look at her husband. He was right in the middle of the swirl, taking the heat from fans and owners—yet he never lost his head. She knew better than to ask many questions when her husband was watching those films over and over, but she also knew that things were going well. He was intense but not worried. Yes, one night she kissed him good night and awoke the next morning to find him still in the study, still going over those films, an empty ice cream carton nearby. He had been awake all night, but he wasn't tired at all. He was in a good mood. She made him biscuits and gravy for breakfast.

The more Collier watched the Colts, the more he was convinced his team would win. Baltimore was a good team. They had some great players. On certain Sundays, they could even be a great team.

But they weren't unbeatable. They weren't the next pro dynasty. In certain spots, they were very vulnerable.

"I hated it when people said my team couldn't do something," Collier said. "And so did my players. The more we prepared for the Colts, the more we became convinced that they couldn't beat us. It was the feeling of confidence."

Collier, his coaches, and his assistants knew exactly what the Colts and everyone else had forgotten—in 1964, the Browns had the best team in football.

Yes, Unitas was a better quarterback, but when Frank Ryan was right, he could pass with Unitas or anyone else.

Lenny Moore may have scored 19 touchdowns, but there has never been a runner to compare with Jim Brown.

Raymond Berry and Jimmy Orr were fine receivers, but so were Paul Warfield and Gary Collins.

The Colts had a great defensive line with Gino Marchetti and Ordell Braase, but Collier believed that his offensive line was very underrated, that it was the best in all of football. He just knew that his linemen could contain Baltimore's pass rush.

Defense was where the game would be decided—defense, especially in the secondary.

Collier stared at films of each Colts player, breaking down their strengths and weaknesses. Never forget that it was Collier who invented this technique, an individual scouting report featuring a player's every tendency. He did it at the request of Paul Brown, and Collier's technique was the norm by 1964. Yes, Don Shula was doing the same thing; he had learned it from Collier. But at the age of thirty-four, Shula was no Collier.

Armed with his notes and film reels, Collier and his assistants began tutoring individual players.

In the final weeks of the regular season, Collier began talking to his team about Zero Defects. Its origin was the U.S. Defense Department, which had designed an "error-free plan" to cut down on the malfunction of missiles. The authors of the plan insisted to Defense Department employees: DO IT RIGHT THE FIRST TIME.

Collier seized those phrases.

ZERO DEFECTS.

DO IT RIGHT THE FIRST TIME.

That had been his approach to football ever since he began working for Paul Brown. It was Paul Brown's philosophy, only now Collier had something else besides Xs and Os to put on the blackboard.

ZERO DEFECTS.

DO IT RIGHT THE FIRST TIME.

That was what it would take to beat the Baltimore Colts.

———————

The softest spot in the Browns' offensive line was supposed to be right tackle, where Monte Clark was matched up against Gino Marchetti. The assumption was that Marchetti would simply toss Clark aside and live in the Browns' backfield all afternoon. After all, Marchetti was a Hall of Fame caliber end, while Clark was a journeyman tackle.

"Gino rushed the passer on every single down," Clark said. "I mean, *every time,* he was coming at the quarterback. He could be physically punishing, but he didn't just run you over. Sometimes he went around you. He was quicker than he looked. But most of all, he was relentless."

Marchetti was thirty-seven years old, but still had surprising speed for a man who was 6′4″ and 245 pounds. Usually, Marchetti was taller than the opposing offensive tackle, but not this time; Clark was 6′6″, 255 pounds.

As Clark watched films of Marchetti, he noticed two things:

1. Marchetti usually began with a head-and-shoulders fake. He

made it appear that he was going to rush right with the fake, then cut back to the left.

2. Just as he delivered the fake, he'd smack your helmet. The idea was to get you off balance. Between the fakes and the slaps, you could lose your footing—and then you'd lose Marchetti.

Clark's strategy was simple.

JUST STAND THERE.

Let Marchetti fake away.

DON'T MOVE.

And when Marchetti went for the helmet slap, he ran into trouble with Clark. Remember that Clark was two inches taller than Marchetti. The defensive end liked to whack down on a tackle's head, using his hand like a hammer to the helmet. But if Clark just stood there, if he didn't bend or bite on the fakes, Marchetti had to swing *up* to hit him, and that created a very soft blow to the head.

Clark was an outstanding student at Southern California and would later coach in the NFL. In 1964, he was twenty-seven and already knew the value of film study and preparation. For two weeks, he lived with Gino Marchetti, both on the screen and in his head. He knew Marchetti's fakes from watching the films. He pictured how he'd react, how he'd use his height to frustrate one of the greatest defensive ends to ever play the game.

By game time, Clark was ready. He knew what he'd do, and he planned to DO IT RIGHT THE FIRST TIME.

———————

Dick Schafrath was the Browns' left offensive tackle.

His man was Ordell Braase, the Colts' star defensive end.

Think about this: Ordell Braase was only 6´3˝ and 230 pounds.

"The man was tough and he was quick," Schafrath said. "I was stronger [6´3˝, 240 pounds], so I didn't worry too much about him on running plays. I knew that I could take him, one-on-one. But passing plays, where I had to back up—especially at the Stadium in December where I knew the turf would be wet and I could slip—that worried me. I was fast, but Braase was just as quick."

Schafrath found that he couldn't study film during the practices and meetings, so he stopped over at Collier's home for a few nights, sitting up in the study with the coach.

Collier ate his ice cream. He ran film of Braase over and over. "He's left-handed," Collier said. "Remember that."

Most linemen (like everyone else) are right-handed, which meant their first moves were usually to their right. Not Braase. He went left.

Sometimes, it looked like he'd go right, but he almost always went left. Don't go for the fake to the right.

Schafrath had never played against Braase. Like Marchetti, Braase liked to head-slap, which was a legal play in 1964. Whack, bang the helmet, stagger the lineman, shove him out of the way and sack the quarterback.

Remember, the head-slap would come from the left.

"My way of dealing with that was to punch him under his chest pad," Schafrath said.

Because Schafrath was an inch taller than Braase, the defensive end had to reach up for the head-slap. That made his chest vulnerable.

"Just as you felt him hit your head, you dug your fist into his chest," Schafrath said. "Listen, those slaps would get your head spinning. So you had to lock on to him, and I did that with the punch. Then he couldn't get around me."

And if Schafrath hit Braase just right, he could knock some of the wind out of the Colts star.

"I got him with my right hand," Schafrath said. "It was an inside punch, starting at his waist and going right up into his chest. I saw myself doing that as I watched the films, and come game time, it worked just as I thought it would."

Veteran defensive tackle Dick Modzelewski was matched up against Colts offensive guard Alex Sandusky. These two warriors had been dueling for years. There were no secrets, and usually Modzelewski held his own against Sandusky. Modzelewski didn't need films to see Sandusky's moves. All he had to do was close his eyes and the reel began in his head. Collier knew this as well.

So he asked Modzelewski to do more than just prepare for Sandusky. He wanted Modzelewski to help young Jim Kanicki find a way to handle Jim Parker.

A perennial All-Pro selection, Parker was huge for this era, 6´4˝ and 275 pounds. He was a left guard, and he had opened holes all year for Lenny Moore. Usually, Parker had a size advantage, as he was the largest left guard in the NFL.

Or as Gary Collins said, "Parker's arm is bigger than my chest."

Kanicki was 6´4˝, 270 pounds—almost the same as Parker. But Kanicki had just turned twenty-three. He had played little in college, and this was his first year as a starter in the pros. Collier did not plan to start Kanicki, but veteran Bob Gain had been injured all season.

The Colts believed that Parker would overpower Kanicki. Then they could establish their running attack. Once that happened, Unitas would have all day to throw.

Collier didn't ask Modzelewski or Kanicki to sack Unitas. He just wanted them TO HOLD YOUR GROUND.

He told them to PLAY THE RUN.

If they could hold the middle, then Paul Wiggin and Bill Glass could unload from the defensive ends, putting pressure on Unitas.

Modzelewski and Kanicki spent hours together, watching films of Parker. There were no secret moves.

"The key was that Jim was just as big and strong as Parker, and Parker was not used to facing someone with that size," Modzelewski said. "If we could get Jim to match him physically—and give Jim the confidence to do that—Parker could be in for a real surprise."

Sports Illustrated wrote, "It is unreasonable to assume that Kanicki would be able to defeat an all-pro like Jim Parker."

The manager of a grocery store spotted Kanicki stocking up in the meat department. He told the young lineman, "I just read a story that said the Colts were gonna run at you every time they needed five yards."

Kanicki was a nice farm kid from Michigan. His teammates wanted him to get meaner. If Kanicki was in the right frame of mind, Modzelewski was convinced the kid lineman could engage Parker in a wrestling match, stand him straight up, and maybe even throw him down. Modzelewski knew this much: Parker would not be able to go right through his protégé.

"I told Jim that it was good how everyone thought we were the underdogs," said Modzelewski. "I told him that it would work to his advantage that everyone thought Parker would kill him, because he and I knew better. We were going to surprise some people. A lot of guys underestimated Jim, they didn't know how determined he was to become a damn good football player. And on that Sunday, he let it be known."

Another regular visitor to Collier's study was Bernie Parrish.

Raymond Berry and Jimmy Orr and John Mackey were maybe the three best receivers in the league.

Mackey was a great tight end, but the Browns were sure they could control him. Jim Houston would handle most of the coverage; Houston was a linebacker, but many Browns believed he was the team's second best athlete (in terms of combining speed and strength) after Jim Brown.

Yes, Houston would handle Mackey. The more film Collier and Parrish watched, the more they were convinced of that. In situations where Houston couldn't cover Mackey, Ross Fichtner would—and Fichtner was tougher than a bucket of rusty nails. As it turned out, Fichtner covered Mackey more than Houston, and shut him down.

But what about Orr? What about Berry?

Collier knew that they were both savvy receivers, but not quick. They ran precision patterns, and they seemed to catch the ball at just the right moment.

"They were timing plays," Parrish said. "Sometimes, Unitas threw the ball even before those guys looked back at the quarterback. They'd run their pattern, turn—and the ball would be there. It was all scripted, a timing play."

The more films Parrish watched, the more he wondered something.

"All of those guys who covered Orr and Berry kept dropping off and giving them a lot of room," he said. "Why? It's one thing if the receiver is fast and was going to beat you deep. Then you had better give him room, or he'd beat your ass but good. But that wasn't Orr or Berry. They weren't going to just run past you. Yet teams kept playing them that way."

As they watched the films, Parrish kept saying, "Let's smother these guys. Let's get right up on them, right at the line of scrimmage, and bump them a little. Let's screw up their timing."

That became the plan.

Walter Beach would cover Berry, Parrish would take Orr.

Safeties Ross Fichtner and Larry Benz would have to cover deep, in case Berry or Orr broke away from the cornerbacks.

This was a major change in strategy for the Browns. Defensive coordinator Howard Brinker believed in the Bend, Don't Break defense. He would give up short yardage plays, especially passes, to prevent a bomb that turns a game around. That meant the corner-backs usually played off the receivers, giving up those short passes that Orr and Berry loved.

According to Parrish, he argued with Brinker the morning of the game about this strategy, and Brinker still wasn't sure it was the best tactic. Collier knew that the way to upset Unitas (and buy more time for his pass rush) was to cover Unitas's primary receiver. Make him take another look for the open man—this would give the defense a chance to harass him.

Parrish called it "clamping."

In an interview the night before the game, Unitas said on TV that he expected the Browns' secondary to play back because they didn't have the speed to cover the Colts' receivers.

Safety Ross Fichtner saw that. So did Parrish.

They agreed. They had to clamp 'em.

Walter Beach liked the idea. He could handle Berry, he was sure. He had watched films for two weeks. Most receivers gave you one fake, then made their moves. Berry usually used two fakes, sometimes three. Beach believed he was quicker and stronger than Berry.

As Beach watched the films, he noticed something else: Berry could fake with his head, his shoulders, his feet, even his eyes. But not his waist. Wherever Berry's waist went, so went Berry.

Yes, Beach said, he could play Berry tight.

Clamping would work, he agreed.

And clamping became the heart of the defense that was the first to shut out the Colts in thirty-one games.

As for the Browns' offense, they knew they'd score.

They knew that the only way to really cover Paul Warfield and Gary Collins was to double-team them, and the Colts couldn't double-team both of them. They both were too quick to be shut down by clamping.

Collins or Warfield, one of them was going to have a big day.

Then there was Jim Brown. No one would stop him. He led the league with 1,446 yards rushing, an average of 103 yards per game.

If Clark and Schafrath handled Marchetti and Braase, Ryan would have plenty of time to throw. While Unitas deserved all the headlines, the facts were that in 1964 it was Frank Ryan who led the NFL in touchdown passes with 25.

In fact, eleven days before the game, Ryan told reporters, "We have more offense than the Colts."

"Our offense had great practices," Schafrath said. "Gary Collins kept telling me, 'We're going to win.' He was telling me that a couple of times every day. Finally, I said, 'Gary, just shut up about it. If we are going to win, we're going to have a big party after the game.' Gary told me to book the band and buy the drinks, because he had no doubt—we'd win."

Two days before the game, Blanton Collier was talking with Hal Lebovitz.

"Hal, we have covered everything," he said. "We are prepared. We are going to win."

Lebovitz remembered thinking how rare it was for any coach to say that, especially a man who was as careful about details as Collier.

"At that point, I sensed something special was about to happen," said Lebovitz.

THE GAME OF THEIR LIVES

The afternoon before the championship game, Dick Schafrath had to get out.

He couldn't stay at the hotel any longer. He couldn't look at the walls. He couldn't walk the halls, not for another second.

So the Browns' offensive tackle decided to go to a movie, a matinee. He knew that the team would attend a movie that night, but he didn't care. He had to get out of the hotel.

Thirty years later, Schafrath could not remember which Cleveland movie house he picked, or the title of the movie.

"All I remember was that it had already started," he said. "There were only about five people in the whole place. The usher took me to a row, and I sat down."

Schafrath noticed someone a few seats away, in the same row. He stared hard in the dark. Immediately, he knew who it was . . . but it couldn't be . . . but the man was looking right at him.

Yes, it was *him.*

Schafrath had been looking at films of this man for two weeks. He had been dreaming about him. Now, he wanted to get away from this guy for just a few hours, and there he was, ten feet away.

"Hey, Dick, how ya doin'?" asked Ordell Braase.

Schafrath looked at him. He thought about how Braase planned to head-slap him. He thought about how he was going to punch Braase right under his chest. He remembered to watch out for Braase's left hand. The man was left-handed.

"How ya doin', Ordell?" said Schafrath.

Then Schafrath got up and moved to the opposite end of the movie theater. Braase stood, and found a seat as far as he could from Scha-frath.

The Browns stayed at the old Pick-Carter Hotel, which was about a half-mile walk from the Stadium. In the middle 1960s, it was one of the best Cleveland had to offer. It was where Paul Brown had his Browns stay the night before Sunday home games—and it was where Blanton Collier kept the team.

Every player had a roommate, even Jim Brown.

The greatest running back of any era stayed with offensive guard John Wooten. Brown arrived that gloomy December Saturday after-noon, the day after Christmas, wearing a black overcoat and carrying an attaché case. These and other details of Jim Brown's movements during the championship weekend come from Hal Lebovitz, the leg-endary *Plain Dealer* columnist who shadowed Brown for two days as he researched what became a wonderful piece for *Sport Magazine*.

Jim Brown believed in dressing well when in public, and that meant a business suit and tie. On this day, Brown wore a black suit coat, black tie, white shirt, white suspenders, and black pants. He looked like he'd just come from a board meeting at Pepsi, for which he was a company spokesman.

Brown and Wooten stayed in room 1012, on the hotel's tenth floor. They went into the dining room for a team meal, which was fruit cock-tail, steak, potatoes, green beans, and ice cream. Most of the players had watched the American Football League championship game on TV that afternoon as Buffalo beat San Diego, 20–7. The Bills' quarterback was future vice presidential candidate Jack Kemp, and the Browns thought he called a very shrewd game.

After the team meal, the players went to a movie. This was when downtown Cleveland was the most popular place in town to see a movie, and there were six grand theaters on Euclid and Prospect Avenues. Usually, the players went off in three or four groups, based upon which movie they wanted to see.

"Hey, Jim," said veteran linebacker Galen Fiss. "Let's all go to the same movie."

That was fine with Brown.

Fiss said that most of the players wanted to see *Sex and the Single*

Girl, which was at the Allen Theater. Brown asked Wooten if he had an opinion. He thought Fiss had a good idea, and thirty-six players walked into the Allen. On the way, Brown looked at the gray skies. He was sure it was going to rain, snow, or something. It was windy. The temperature was in the high 30s. But so far, it was dry.

"Let's keep the weather just like this," Brown told Wooten.

The two men then talked about the first play of the game. The plan was for Brown to run a sweep. Brown said that maybe they should let Ernie Green run the ball, that the Colts would be looking for Brown to carry it.

They watched the movie, which ended at 8:40 p.m. The players returned to the Pick-Carter. Brown wanted to watch a TV special on the team, called *The Browns Spectacular,* so he went to his room. Brown bought a copy of *Variety* at the gift shop on the way to the elevator. He had already made a few movies and loved to keep up with the news and gossip from Hollywood. As Brown tried to watch the TV show, the phone kept ringing. Sometimes, it was a friend who wanted tickets. But five times the same drunk called, telling Brown how the Colts were "going to kick your ass."

Deciding to get away from the phone, Brown and Wooten went down to the snack bar, which was next to the hotel. Brown wanted to listen to the Temptations on the jukebox.

"But a bunch of Colts fans were staying at our hotel, if you can believe that," recalled John Wooten. "About fifteen of them carried musical instruments. They saw us in the snack bar, and they came up to us and played taps right in front of our faces. Jim didn't say a word. He just got up and left, and I followed him. When we got away from those people, he turned to me and said, 'We are going to kick the crap outta them.' That was all he said."

––––––––––

Frank Ryan held a meeting in his room for the offensive linemen. He also invited Jim Brown, but Brown declined.

"John, just tell them my idea for the first play," said Brown, meaning to let Ernie Green carry the ball.

Wooten and Schafrath gave Ryan several ideas about the offense. Every player in the room believed that the Browns needed to come out and establish the running game first. When Wooten came back to room

1012, he saw Brown reading an early edition of the *Plain Dealer*. He saw an article where Chuck Heaton had picked the Browns to win.

"Wonder if this is a 'What have I got to lose' prediction, or if Chuck really means it?" Brown asked Wooten.

Wooten shrugged.

In their room, Galen Fiss was trying to sleep and Bernie Parrish was pacing.

"Bernie could be like a terrier," Fiss said. "Very nervous, doing a lot of talking."

Fiss was a Bob Dole–like Kansan, a man who believed in the brevity of language. They were an intriguing pair.

"If nothing else," Parrish told Fiss, "at least we know that on this team, we don't have a bunch of guys who are stupid enough to go out chasing women the night before a big game."

Over and over, he told Fiss how smart the team was, and how that would carry the day. He also was worried that defensive coordinator Howard Brinker would not like the idea of the defensive backs tightly covering the Colts' wide receivers.

One player who was not in his room was Jim Ninowski.

"I was in the hospital," said the backup quarterback. "In the two weeks before the Colts game, I had lost fifteen pounds. It was some kind of virus, and I couldn't shake it. They had me on an IV, just trying to get some fluids in my system."

Frank Ryan had played the last few games on a tender right ankle. Ryan never received due credit for his durability. The man had missed only one game in his first six years as a pro, and that was when a linebacker named Bill Pellington had separated Ryan's shoulder. It happened in the second-to-last game of the 1961 season. Joan Ryan said it was nearly a month before Ryan could use both hands to tie his own shoes.

Who would be the middle linebacker for Baltimore in the 1964 championship game? The same Bill Pellington.

So Blanton Collier and offensive coordinator Dub Jones were worried when Ninowski was rushed to the hospital. They were told that Ninowski was dehydrated, and there was no way he could play on Sunday.

Who would be the quarterback if Ryan were hurt?

"Most of the guys didn't even know that Nino went to the hospital," safety Ross Fichtner recalled. "They made no announcement, but one of the coaches told me that they were worried about his life. But they didn't want to upset the team by telling them."

Collier wanted to keep everything positive. Ninowski was one of the most popular players because he had handled playing behind Ryan with such grace. He was talented enough to start for most teams (and some players also believed that he was a better quarterback than Ryan), but Ninowski never complained and he strongly supported Ryan.

So now what? What if Ryan went down?

Collier and Dub Jones asked Fichtner to see them after the team dinner on Saturday night. They told him about Ninowski's illness. They said he had been a good quarterback at Purdue, and they were sure he could handle the team in an emergency.

"Ross, we want to go over the offensive game plan with you tonight," Collier said.

"Blanton, I can't do it," he said. "I've got enough to worry about on defense, and with John Mackey. If something happens, I can take a snap. I can hand off to Jim Brown. I can flip the ball to Jim Brown. I can run some rollouts to the right or to the left."

Fichtner had suffered a serious concussion earlier in the season. He still had headaches that brought tears to his eyes. He felt as if his left eye "would bounce" when he ran.

He was on overload. He'd played defense ever since coming to the Browns in 1960. He could not learn the entire offense in one night before the championship game.

"Blanton, if you need me, I can help out," he said. "But don't ask me to memorize the entire game plan. I think I'll do better if there were an emergency and you just threw me in there, where I didn't have a lot of time to think about it."

Collier looked at this gritty safety, who he knew came back faster from the concussion than most men would. He just nodded, and sent Fichtner on his way.

Meanwhile, Art Modell had a problem.

Over 130,000 fans had sent in requests for tickets to the championship game.

In 1964, the prices for the Colts-Browns title game were $10 and $8. The Browns averaged nearly 80,000 fans during the regular season. Modell had 45,000 season ticket holders; they received tickets to the championship game, too.

That left 85,000 fans wanting the remaining 35,000 tickets.

This meant there were sure to be unhappy fans. To make people even more unhappy, Modell refused to have the game televised in Cleveland, because he wanted to make sure it was a sellout. The last thing young Arthur B. Modell wanted to happen was for the country to see his team in a championship game—and for there to be empty seats! Think how that would look! And suppose he agreed to let the game be on TV? What if some of his loyal fans decided to save the eight bucks and stay home?

Furthermore, even after it was obvious that Modell could have sold 130,000 tickets for his 80,000-seat stadium, he still refused to put the game on TV—at least not live. He agreed to have it televised, but *thirty hours later.* Sunday's championship game would be seen Monday night in Cleveland.

Fans hated him more for that than they did for firing Paul Brown.

The TV blackout covered seventy-five miles, meaning towns such as Erie, Pennsylvania, Buffalo, New York, and Toledo, Ohio, could carry the game. Never before had so many Clevelanders booked motel rooms in Erie, Toledo, and Buffalo. For those who lost Modell's "ticket lottery," or however he decided to sell his tickets, there was a new game—find a motel far enough away from Cleveland that had the game on TV. The *Plain Dealer's* Chuck Heaton even had this note in his column three days before the game: "Space in three Erie motels—the Niagara, the Downtowner, and Scott's Motel—is still available for those wanting to watch the game on TV."

The Associated Press reported that Clevelanders had reserved 180 motel rooms in Toledo for the game, "and even though the guests don't plan to spend the night, they will be charged the regular room rate."

The Cleveland City Council passed a resolution asking Modell to change his mind and televise the game. "It would be an expression of gratitude on the part of the league and the Browns for this support."

Modell declined, this time saying it would be unfair to those who had already bought tickets if he were to televise the game.

Huh? How is it unfair to those who already have tickets to allow fans who don't to watch it on TV? Did Modell believe that people were so petty that they'd say, "Look at that! I paid eight bucks for a ticket because I didn't think it would be on TV, and now I just could have stayed home and saved the money"?

Even in 1964, with actions such as these Modell demonstrated a fundamental misunderstanding of the mentality of the Browns fan. Instead of following the lead of the City Council, he issued the statement, "Under no circumstances will the game be televised in the area," and he meant to keep any theater or anyone else who planned to bring in the signal from showing the game to the public. Anyway, 336 TV stations across the country did carry the game. CBS paid $1.8 million for the rights to the game, which was a huge increase from the $75,000 paid by the DuMont TV network to carry the Browns-Rams title game in 1951. But it still wasn't shown in Cleveland.

Modell then put 5,000 standing-room-only tickets on sale at $6 each.

"Anybody who wants to stand can still get a space," said Browns spokesman Marsh Samuel. "Anyone who wants to sit down—well, he's out of luck."

Nice attitude.

Anyway, most of the fans who were rejected when they mailed in for seats were appalled with Modell's hard-line attitude about TV and refused to bite on the standing room tickets. He sold only half of them.

While all the debate about tickets was taking place, the Indians were threatening to move, possibly to Seattle. Among other things, Tribe president Gabe Paul said that most people had moved to the suburbs, so they didn't want to travel downtown for baseball games at the Stadium.

New York Mets manager Casey Stengel heard Paul's remarks, then read about the scramble for football tickets. Stengel said, "Well, I guess all the fans moved back to town for football season."

Jim Brown awoke at 7:30 on Sunday morning when the phone rang. It was the wakeup call, the same call that every player received on game day. John Wooten got out of bed first. Brown asked him what the weather was like, fearing the answer. Outside the window, Wooten didn't see the sun, just a sea of gray clouds. No snow, but the wind howled. Wooten dressed and went to church. Brown tried to go back to sleep. When Wooten returned to the room, he talked of a strong wind. It wasn't snowing, but it *felt* like snow.

"Better snow than rain," said Brown.

The weather was a huge issue, at least among the fans and the reporters. Snow was predicted. It had snowed on and off during the week. Modell ordered groundskeeper Harold Bossard to hook up heaters, and he had twelve of them around the field. The ground had frozen early in the week, and Bossard wanted to thaw it out. The twelve heaters supposedly raised the field temperature to 30 degrees. They swallowed 3,000 gallons of gas during the week. But nothing could help the dirt part of the baseball infield, which was near the end zone. Bossard tried to drive a metal stake into the dirt; when he belted it with a hammer, the stake bent.

The Colts were experimenting with surgical gloves to keep their hands warm. This was long before the days of players wearing golf gloves to help their grip; most of them just cheated a bit and put sticky pine tar on their hands, but the weather was too cold for that to work.

Collier told his players to bring tennis shoes, their regular cleat football shoes, and soccer shoes with rubber cleats to the game. The plan was for them to try the various shoes out during warmups and pick the ones that give the best traction.

The newspapers had fun with the weather, especially the *Cleveland Press.*

Bob Sudyk wrote, "The gray concrete and steel in late December gives the Stadium all the cheery warmth of a fog-shrouded castle in Transylvania." He also interviewed a Rev. Henry F. Brinkenhauer, who had spent a year in Antarctica. His advice? Wiggle your toes and walk around so your feet don't freeze.

Cleveland Press medical writer Ed Seitz asked city health commissioner J. Glen Smith if drinking would help fight cold. But Dr. Smith said no way. As Seitz wrote, "Even an occasional 'medicinal dose' of Old Panther juice—say one shot per quarter—could ripen you for pneumonia." Seitz said that Smith worried that fans would ignore his advice and "Too many will fall flat on their faces at the Stadium. . . ." Dr. Smith said to drink coffee and hot chocolate instead. He also said, "This might be one time when women would be better off wearing slacks in public." Remember, this is when men wore suits, ties, and hats to games—and women wore dresses.

———————————

The Browns players met in the dining room of the Pick-Carter for breakfast. Jim Brown had a steak, cooked medium well, tomato juice, and eggs for breakfast. Wooten was surprised. Usually, Brown didn't like eggs. But on this Sunday, Jim Brown just said, "I feel like eggs."

Some players such as Bernie Parrish had nothing at all, nothing but coffee.

"Too nervous to eat," Parrish said.

Of course, the last thing coffee does is calm anyone's nerves. But this was 1964, back when no one understood what coffee and caffeine did to your nervous system. It was when most American adults began the day with a cup of java and an unfiltered cigarette at breakfast, and when breakfast was bacon and eggs—no one had even heard of cholesterol.

Parrish's roommate, Galen Fiss, had plenty of steak and eggs.

"How can you eat that?" asked Parrish.

"We're not going to eat again until tonight," he said. "I'm hungry."

After breakfast, Fiss and Parrish went to Leo Murphy's room. The Browns' trainer marked the door with a white cross he made out of athletic tape.

"With that cross on the door, it was like he was Father Murphy, hearing confessions," Parrish said. "He was a psychologist. By the fifth week of the season, everyone was playing with some kind of an injury, but Leo had a way of getting you out there to play. Most of us were taking novocaine or some other painkilling shots. I was playing with Morton's Neuroma on the ball of my foot. The doctors never quite figured it out. For four years, I took a novocaine shot in the ball of my foot on game day. If I didn't, I could barely walk and the thing just hurt like hell."

Fiss had separated his left shoulder while in college, and it never fully healed. Before each game, Murphy shaved the hair off Fiss's left shoulder, then he taped it up. Fiss also was playing with a broken thumb on his left hand. Murphy taped the hand up, too.

"I really think that Galen kept getting that hand taped long after the thumb healed," Parrish said. "He broke it clotheslining somebody earlier in the year. They made one of those temporary casts, and Galen used it to club people."

"The cast did have its benefits," Fiss admitted. "Slap people upside the head with that cast, you really get their attention. In practice, I'd make a real pest out of myself, whacking people in the head with my cast. For games, we had to cover it with rubber and the officials inspected it, but it still was like a club. The cast went from my knuckles to about two thirds of the way to my elbow. The darn thing probably weighted two or three pounds, and by the time you swing your hand and land one, it's going to have an effect."

So Murphy had plenty to do this Sunday morning, be it with Parrish's foot, Fiss's shoulder and hand, or Jim Brown, who wanted his ankles taped just so. The trainer spent hours cutting hair and taping body parts. By the time he was ready to go to the Stadium, you could barely see the carpet for all the hair and pieces of tape.

Dick Schafrath ran into Art Modell in the hotel lobby.

"Art, we're having a party after the game," Schafrath said.

"Really?" asked Modell.

"We're winning the game, and you're paying for the party," Schafrath said.

"Who told you that?" asked Modell.

"Gary Collins did," Schafrath said.

"Okay," Modell said. "You win, and you've got a deal."

The cold weather didn't bother Gary Collins.

"It's because of my body temperature," he said.

Really?

"My hands are never cold," he said. "My feet don't freeze."

Why not?

"My temperature usually is between 96.8 and 97.2," he said. "I believe that gave me an advantage that day."

By ten in the morning, Jim Brown was back in his hotel room. Wooten had gone back to bed and somehow managed to fall asleep. Brown stared out the window. He knew it would snow, and it did. Not a lot of snow, just little flakes swirling in the wind.

As they walked into the hotel lobby, they ran into more Colts fans. They wanted the players' autographs. After Wooten and Brown signed, some Colts fans followed them out the door.

"You guys are nothin' but Laugh Champs," said one.

"Marchetti will rub your face in the dirt," said another.

Brown and Wooten didn't say a word. Because the hotel was only a half mile from the Stadium, there was no team bus; players either walked, took a cab, or used their cars. Brown drove his Cadillac. Wooten could see him squeezing the wheel harder than normal. The man was seething about the Colts fans.

When Brown and Wooten arrived, all the other players were there. That was Brown's tradition—being the last one to walk into the dressing room. He hated the waiting.

The Browns' other running back had been in the dressing room for a while. In fact, Ernie Green was lying on the floor—asleep!

"I could hardly sleep the night before a game," Green said. "But in the locker room, I'd just get on the floor, close my eyes and I was gone. I think it might have been my escape mechanism, thinking that, 'I'll go to sleep and when I wake up, everything will be over.'"

Paul Warfield was on the field. He was always one of the first to arrive for the game. He liked to go on the field, by himself, walking through his patterns, feeling the turf under his feet.

Monte Clark had injured his knee during the 1963 season. It still hurt. Clark refused to take any painkillers. He thought the tape would be enough support, if only he could get it taped just right.

He put the tape on, took it off. On . . . off . . . on . . . he ripped it off and threw the tape on the floor.

"I tried it five different ways and it never felt right," he said. "I kept thinking about how I had to go against Marchetti, and I needed my quickness. I decided that this was the biggest game in my life, and if leaving that tape off gave me just a little more mobility, I wanted that edge."

The happiest man in the dressing room was Ross Fichtner.

"That was when Jim Ninowski walked in," he said. "Nino was looking kind of green. You could tell he was still sick, but he said he was ready to play—and I didn't have to worry about Ryan getting hurt and me ending up at quarterback."

Ninowski was surprised at how well he felt when he awoke in the hospital that morning. Okay, he didn't feel great, but he was still alive and there was a championship game to be played. He checked himself out of the hospital and reported to work at the Stadium.

When he warmed up on the sidelines, his passes had their usual zip.

"I was throwing really well," Ninowski said. "Dub Jones watched me and said, 'We ought to put you in the hospital more often.'"

Schafrath had secured a field pass for his uncle, who had a movie camera.

"I want you to film our warmups, get everything on film that you can because we are going to make history today," he told his uncle.

Jim Brown sat in front of his locker, appearing to read a game program. He had no idea what the story said. He was just staring at the words.

When it was time to get dressed, Brown put on a thermal undershirt. He pulled his No. 32 jersey over it. He wore his football pants very tight with no hip pads, because he believed they hindered his mobility.

Game time was supposed to be 1:30 p.m., but it would actually be closer to 2 p.m. About 1 p.m., Collier called the team together.

"It's time for us to go out there and loosen up," the coach said. "Really, there is nothing else for me to say. You know what you have to do."

Then team captain Galen Fiss said, "There is no point in making speeches. Let's say our prayer."

Then Fiss led the team in the Lord's Prayer.

If anyone was looking for a pep talk or words of wisdom before this game, that was the extent of it. Collier believed the team was as prepared as any he had ever coached, and nothing else needed to be said. Fiss believed that it never was a bad idea to ask the Lord for help and to keep everyone free of injury.

With that, the players headed to the field. They jogged and loosened up.

At 1:37 p.m., the Browns' offensive unit was introduced. Rookie Paul Warfield didn't wait to hear the first name, he just ran out of the dugout.

The crowd roared.

The announcer said, "Starting at center for the Browns, John Morrow."

This turned out to be the only mistake the Browns made all day.

Brown was the final player introduced.

"I always worried that one day I'd run out of the dugout, through the goal post, and fall flat on my face," Brown told Hal Lebovitz.

But that would never happen. Not to Jim Brown. Certainly not on this day.

The best description of the weather came from Red Smith of the *New York Herald Tribune:* "The skies were a sullen gray, heavy with their freight of unspilled snow. The field was a spongy carpet of uprooted turf and the barren infield. The official game-time temperature was 32, but the wind of 20 mph kicked up white caps on Lake Erie and bit deep into the bones of the 79,554 customers."

The Browns won the coin toss and elected to receive. Walter Roberts took the kick and carried it to the Browns' 21-yard line. Now was time for the first play, the play that was supposed to be Jim Brown on a sweep, and then was changed to Ernie Green. In fact, no play was discussed as long as this one by the coaches and players.

Frank Ryan faked a handoff to Jim Brown into the line, then pitched the ball to Green, who was supposed to run a sweep.

Green gained two yards.

So much for planning. And so much for the Browns' offense in the first half. They tried to establish the running game, and all they established was that the Colts were ready to step on Jim Brown after he was down. They kicked him in the ribs. They tried to gouge his eyes.

Someone stepped on his left hand, and for a moment, Brown swore it was broken. But he didn't think of leaving the game, not even for one play. Jim Brown wouldn't sit out a practice, much less a championship game. So the hand hurt. The hand was numb. He wanted the ball.

That was the attitude of the entire team.

Monte Clark was fighting off Marchetti's head slaps. He was keeping Marchetti off Ryan's back, playing the great Colts end to a draw.

When Ordell Braase went to slap Schafrath in the helmet, Schafrath countered with a punch to the chest.

Galen Fiss was clubbing people with his cast.

Bernie Parrish and Walter Beach had their noses nearly inside the face masks of the Colts receivers, that was how close they played Jimmy Orr and Raymond Berry.

Warfield was double-teamed. Collins was open, and was telling Ryan that. But the quarterback kept the ball on the ground.

Nothing much happened—for either team.

Johnny Unitas didn't like any of it. Not the wind. Not the swirling snow. Not the turf that was soft in some places, hard and slippery as ice in other spots. Nor could he understand why Walter Beach and Bernie Parrish were playing so tight on the Baltimore receivers.

And Kanicki. What was going on there? Was Parker going to block this kid, or what?

Before the game, Collier and Dick Modzelewski reminded Kanicki of the plan—just get out there and fight Parker. That's right, fight him, like two big bears wrestling. Don't try to run him over. Don't try to slip past him. Grab him. Make it hand-to-hand combat, and throw the big guy down.

This was exactly what Kanicki did.

And Modzelewski was playing more like twenty-three than thirty-three.

Unitas couldn't believe it. That old man and the kid were getting in his face. Where was the blocking?

Finally, the Colts put together a semblance of a drive. They set up for a field goal at the Browns' 19-yard line, but Bob Boyd fumbled a snap from center. Walter Beach tackled him, and the threat was over.

To this day, the Browns players tell you about the hit Galen Fiss put on Lenny Moore.

Remember that Fiss was no kid. He was thirty-three, had a successful insurance agency back in Kansas, and even gave some thought to retiring before the 1964 season. But when camp drew near, Fiss wanted to play again. He needed to play again. He loved it.

Yes, his left shoulder killed him from the separation ten years ago. Then he had that broken left thumb. He was a linebacker, and sometimes it seemed as though he was just getting tired.

Browns players were always amazed to see Fiss trudging through the locker room in bedroom slippers.

A linebacker in bedroom slippers?

Yes, and a linebacker who was pounding everyone in sight with that cast on his left hand. In the middle of the second quarter, Unitas threw a screen pass to Lenny Moore. Granted, the Colts were only on their 30-yard line, but it appeared that Fiss was all that stood between Moore and the goal line. Moore caught the ball, and Fiss knew the defensive scheme. He knew he had to make the tackle, and he knew that Moore was very adept at breaking arm tackles.

So this linebacker who was partial to comfy bedroom slippers turned himself into a human cannonball. He rolled into Moore, cutting the Colt's legs right out from underneath him.

It was a five-yard loss.

It brought the nearly 80,000 to their feet, many of whom were sipping on Old Panther Juice, despite warnings from the Cleveland Department of Health—and they decided to have a drink on good old Galen.

At halftime, the score was 0–0.

"I remember all the out-of-town writers complaining about how boring it was," said Bob August of the *Cleveland Press*. "But I was absolutely astonished at what I was watching. Unitas and the Colts couldn't do a thing with the Browns' defense. Nothing. And I knew that Cleveland's offense would eventually break through."

August's reading of the scribes was correct. As Red Smith wrote, "The first half ended without a score. Never had so many paid so dearly—$10, $8 and $6 a ticket—and suffered sorely to see so little."

The score may have been tied, but the Colts went into the dressing room stunned, like a heavyweight who had been knocked to the canvas twice in the first round by a powder puff.

"When the score was 0–0 at the half, I thought we had won the game," said John Wooten. "Everyone talked about our no-name defense and how they were overmatched, but Kanicki, Fiss, Beach, Parrish, Modzelewski—these guys were dominating the game. At halftime, we on offense promised them that we'd take care of business."

Collier was surprised to find himself spending more time with the offense at halftime. The coach had every reason to assume that he'd have to make some defensive adjustments, but the Colts did nothing, and if the cow ain't sick, you don't call the vet.

So the coach asked the players for input on the offense.

"They're stacking it up pretty well inside," said Jim Brown. "It might be time to throw the ball more."

Warfield said he was double-teamed. Collins said that all there was between him and the goal line was little Bob Boyd, and he could beat Boyd anytime he wanted. Ryan sat there, taking it all in.

Meanwhile, Bernie Parrish was pacing, wired. Finally, he drawled, "Hey, offense, are y'all ever gonna get into the game, or do we have to do *all* the work?"

———————

Halftime was not going well for Art Modell.

He had flown in the Florida A&M band, which was known more for its high stepping and flashy formations than it was for its music.

"I agreed to pay them $18,000 plus expenses," Modell said. "I was bragging to [Commissioner] Pete Rozelle about how he had never seen a band move across the field like this."

But the 180-piece all-male band just walked on the field and played.

"Art, when will they do something?" asked Rozelle.

"Soon," Modell said. "Very soon."

But they never did.

"The only thing that moved was the tuba player's stomach," Modell said. Afterward, Modell asked the band director why they deviated from their usual style. "I saw you guys in the Orange Bowl and you were all over the field," Modell said. "It was a great show."

The band director said his band wanted to be known for more than their marching, "because we have an excellent music school, too."

A disgusted Modell could do nothing but sit in his box and sip a little Old Panther Juice.

———————

Lou Groza opened the second half by kicking the ball completely out of the end zone. Four times on this day, the forty-three-year-old kicker would do that—put a toe to a ball that went at least 70 yards.

The Colts' first drive yielded nothing, and a short punt gave the Browns the ball on the Baltimore 47. The Cleveland offense picked up a first down, then stalled. Onto the field waddled Groza, his ample stomach hanging over his football pants. His field goal attempt would be 43 yards. He had the 20 mile-per-hour wind at his back.

The snap was good. So was the hold. So was the kick.

Years later, Groza didn't recall feeling any extra pressure. He said that if he did everything right, the kick would be good—simple as that.

"Those things are like hitting a home run in baseball," he said. "The minute you connect, you know."

Finally, the Browns had scored.

———————

Baltimore again could do nothing on offense. The Browns got the ball back on their own 31-yard line. Finally, they put together a real drive, the first key play being a sweep in which Jim Brown gained 46 yards. On the play, Ernie Green first knocked Ordell Braase flat with a block, then Green scrambled to his feet, ran downfield, and blocked linebacker Bill Pellington.

"That play really got us going," Green said. "We finally broke Jim loose, and we knew we were going to be all right."

Now it was time to see if Collins was as open as he claimed. Collins was supposed to run a pattern toward the sidelines, but noticed that Bob Boyd was covering him in that direction. So Collins broke the other way, dashing straight for the goal post. The offensive line gave Ryan plenty of time, especially with Clark and Schafrath holding off the head-slaps of Marchetti and Braase.

Ryan saw Collins break the pattern and create his own as he headed to the goal post. This was when the posts were located right on the goal line, not 10 yards behind at the back of the end zone as they are today.

Collins was wide open.

All Ryan had to do was get him the ball.

Ryan laid the ball out nicely, and then winced. The ball and Collins were both heading directly for the goal posts.

"Five times that year, I had my passes hit the goal post," he said.

Not this time. The ball went under the post and into Collins's arms. Browns, 10–0.

———

Again, the Colts did nothing.

Again, Ryan found Collins, this time for a 43-yard TD pass.

"That play was called Hook & Go," recalled Ryan, thirty years later.

A hook pass is when a receiver runs about 10 yards, then hooks (or turns) back to the quarterback to catch a pass. A Hook & Go meant that Collins would fake the hook, freeze the defensive back, then run straight for the goal line.

"Gary was so wide open, I had buck fever," said Ryan. "There was no one within 20 yards of him. I had the wind at my back. It surprises you when a receiver is that wide open, but it happens occasionally. I just had to make sure I got him the ball, because Gary could have caught it and walked into the end zone."

Buck fever is when a hunter has a deer in his sights and he hitches, missing an easy shot.

Ryan didn't miss. Collins didn't walk, but he indeed could have.

"When I faked, Bobby Boyd slipped and fell," Collins said. "When that ball was in the air, I kept thinking that if I dropped it, I had better catch a jet right out of Cleveland right now."

He didn't.

Browns, 17–0.

———

In the fourth quarter, it was Ryan & Collins again, this time for 51 yards. This time, Boyd was all over Collins, and he actually got a finger on the pass—but the ball bounced right into Collins's arms.

Browns, 24–0.

Ryan saw it differently.

"Gary was such a strong guy that he'd fight a defensive back for the ball," he said. "You could throw it up there, and Gary would just take it right out of the other man's arms."

Collins had a huge size advantage over Boyd. The Browns' receiver was 6´3˝, 215 pounds while Boyd was 5´10˝, 190 pounds.

It was curious that the Colts never adjusted to help Boyd. They continued to double-team Warfield, who caught only one pass all day. They left Collins to Boyd, who was an All-Pro defensive back but was clearly unable to handle Collins.

"When a receiver and quarterback have a day like that, we call it Pitch & Catch," Warfield said. "That was Frank Ryan to Gary Collins."

The Browns' final score was a 10-yard field goal by Groza. At the age of 43, Groza was the oldest man in the NFL in 1964.

Final score: Browns 27, Colts 0.

You look at the numbers from that game, and they are astounding.

Johnny Unitas was only 12 of 20, passing for 89 yards with two interceptions. Raymond Berry caught three meaningless passes, as Walter Beach blanketed him. Jimmy Orr did little damage to Bernie Parrish. Jim Houston and Ross Fichtner took turns shutting down John Mackey.

By the end of the day, Jim Parker had learned to spell K-A-N-I-C-K-I, a guy *Sports Illustrated* reported "looks very much like an enormous baby with soft, pink cheeks and what looks like baby fat still on his 270-pound body."

Thirty years later, one Cleveland player after another tells you that Kanicki "played the game of his life" that day.

Galen Fiss had several bone-rattling tackles.

"We weren't supposed to even be on the field with their offense," Fiss said. "That is why the shutout meant so much to us, why we never let up even after our offense had blown the game open."

The Browns had no champagne in the dressing room. Apparently, Modell didn't want to get stuck with it after his experience in the regular season, waiting for the Browns to clinch the title.

Nor did they have any special championship hats or shirts, as you always see today in a winner's locker room.

But they had each other.

They had Jim Brown saying, "This is the biggest thrill of my life."

They had Blanton Collier hugging Brown and whispering, "Jim, thank you for your leadership."

They had Galen Fiss in his bedroom slippers.

They had Bernie Parrish telling the world how his defense shut down the Colts.

They had Frank Ryan and Gary Collins talking about the three touchdown passes.

They had Lou Groza puffing on a victory cigar.

They had Art Modell embarrassing himself on national TV. The Browns owner had celebrated each of Collins's TDs with some Old Panther Juice, and it took its toll. "I went on TV and I was slurring my words," he said. "I've always regretted that."

Meanwhile, many of the fans had followed Modell's lead. With 26 seconds left, they'd stormed the field and torn down the goal posts.

As Don Robertson wrote in the *Plain Dealer*, "This was a real teeth-clicker of a day. . . . Never let it be said that a pro football fan doesn't know how to keep himself warm. They brought blankets. They brought woolly hats. They brought face masks. And a great many of them brought anti-freeze, and after the game you could find many empty bottles of that anti-freeze . . . and about 1,500 of these characters swarmed on the field and hauled down the goal posts. . . . There were 200 police on duty and they did as good a job as expected, but it would have taken a thousand of them to repulse these Goal Post Nuts. The miracle was that no one was killed."

In the Colts' dressing room, there was nothing but silence and regret. When someone did speak, it was to compliment the Browns and to wonder what happened.

"We had zero points on the scoreboard and I wasn't satisfied with anyone," said Don Shula, looking dazed, as if someone had just smacked him in the face with a frying pan.

Unitas had no explanation for the outcome or his struggles. "All he said was that the defensive backs played his receivers tight, the linebackers made the perfect drops right into the passing lane, and the Browns had a strong rush," said Bob August. "I had never seen a great player perform so against his usual form as Unitas did that day."

Six times, a befuddled Unitas ran with the ball—this from a quarterback who hated to run the ball. But when he dropped back to pass, his initial receivers were covered and the rush was coming, so he ran for his life.

Unitas could have used the wind as an excuse, but he saw that it didn't bother Ryan. Nor did the cold weather hurt Collins.

"They just beat us in every conceivable way," said Shula.

Or as Don Robertson also wrote, "It was so quiet in Baltimore, you could hear a tear drop."

It was a tough afternoon for the sportswriters who had picked the Colts to romp. Most gave Cleveland its due, as Bill Boni wrote in the *St. Paul Pioneer Press:* "Rarely have so many experts been so wrong by so wide a margin."

But Arthur Daley wrote in the *New York Times,* "This was hardly a game that will move glowingly into the memory books. It will be remembered here in Cleveland, but everywhere else this unbelievably dull finale will be dropped into the File & Forget folder."

Browns defensive end Paul Wiggin best expressed the feeling of his teammates that day.

"If you were to ask me what was the greatest feeling in my life, it was winning that championship," Wiggin said thirty years later. "I don't wear jewelry. I don't wear my wedding ring. But for years, I wore that championship ring. My wife asked me why, and I tried to tell her that for one moment in my life, nothing has ever meant as much to me as that championship. It only lasted a short time, but to have that feeling about being the best in the world . . ."

Wiggin paused, searching for the right words.

"As I walked out of the Stadium that day, there was a telephone pole," Wiggin recalled. "I wanted to climb up that pole and just yell to the whole city of Cleveland that I was a part of the best football team in the world—and I know that the city would have understood what I was talking about. We had a group of guys from Georgia, California—you name it. White guys, black guys, it didn't matter. Nothing mattered except on that one day, we came together and did something very special. I have spent a lot of years in pro football trying to duplicate that feeling, and I never have."

POSTGAME

The party was at the Sheraton Hotel on Public Square.

Most of the players walked from the Stadium to the hotel. They walked past Lake Erie, its angry gray waters making them wonder if the lake was a Colts fan. They walked through the swirling snow, which never did stick. It was like the same flakes were just being tossed about by the wind all afternoon.

It was about 5:30 p.m. when most of the Browns players walked outside the Stadium. It was getting dark on that December 27, but none of them noticed. It had been gray all day. And besides, they were the champions of the world.

And, as we now know, they were the last champions of the team we grew up with as the Cleveland Browns.

They had no way of knowing that. Most of them were young, in their late twenties. Most of them had the swagger of great athletes, or professional athletes who thought they were great. This was just the beginning. So you can excuse them for not seeing the garbage whirling in the air or the empty bottles of beer and Old Panther Juice rattling around the empty streets.

It was cold, the temperature dropping into the 20s, but they didn't feel it, not when they were embraced in what truly was a glow of victory. As Paul Wiggin said, they wanted to climb a telephone pole and shout to the world. Look at us. Look at what we did. Remember, there might never be another day like this.

For most of them, there wasn't.

But there was still a party, a party organized by the players—not scripted by the NFL or the front office.

"The rookies like Walter Roberts and Leroy Kelly did most of the work, lining things up," said John Wooten. "Veterans like [linebacker] Vince Costello helped, too."

That night, Gene Hickerson came up to Frank Ryan and gave the quarterback a huge bear hug.

"Let's see, we have the greatest running back in the world," Hickerson said. "We have the greatest offensive line in the world. We have the best receivers in the world. And our quarterback, well, you could say that he is adequate."

The two men laughed.

"Guess we surprised them," said Hickerson. "Mr. Don Shula and them Baltimore Colts thought we weren't even gonna show up."

More laughter.

There were jokes about Colts linebacker Bill Pellington, who predicted that Baltimore would win, 24–7.

There was talk about what the Browns saw in the eyes of the Colts.

"They couldn't believe what was happening," said Galen Fiss. "They had that look of, 'What the hell is going on here?' And they had no idea how to stop us."

There were stories of the day that Jim Houston was asked to give a pep talk. An insurance man when he wasn't playing linebacker, Houston was supposed to provide inspiration.

"By then, everything that could be said had already been said," Houston recalled. "So I got up and started talking about 'Individual Reliability,' and one of the guys yelled, 'What's that, a new insurance company?' That was the end of my pep talk."

The players said they were worried about Houston launching into a discussion of whole versus term life coverage.

In the empty Browns dressing room, young Casey Coleman was helping equipment manager Morrie Kono clean up. He spotted a pair of spikes in the trash near Jim Brown's locker. Coleman dug them out, and discovered the shoes belonged to Brown.

"It wasn't like today when players had ten or twenty pairs of shoes and these huge contracts with shoe companies," Coleman said. "Most guys bought their own shoes and wore them until they wore out. Jim had only two pairs, one for practice and one for games."

After the season, he tossed away his game shoes—they had more than enough mileage on them after rushing for 1,446 yards and catching 36 passes for another 340 yards.

"I took those shoes home and I still have them," Coleman said, thirty years later.

Today, a superstar would never throw away his spikes after a championship game. Heck, he might wear four different pairs, one in each quarter, so he could sell them for thousands of dollars on the Home Shopping Network.

Jim Brown did not head immediately to the party. Instead, he returned to his home in Shaker Heights. As he came to the front door, he saw a huge plastic Santa, placed there by his wife, Sue. He opened the front door to find about a dozen friends and relatives, along with a huge Christmas tree and gifts everywhere for his three children.

A bottle of champagne was opened.

Jim Brown never drank or smoked. He prized his body too much for that. But on this night, two days after Christmas, he had a glass of champagne. Then he asked his wife to accompany him downtown to the party at the Sheraton.

When he walked into the Gold Room at the Sheraton, the players and their wives grew silent. Then they stood and applauded.

"No applause ever meant as much to me as that from those guys," Brown said.

The Browns were celebrating for another reason besides the championship.

The winners received $8,027. The loser's share was $5,000.

Most of these guys were making between $10,000 and $15,000, so the $8,027 meant a lot—enough so that several players will tell you that exact figure ($8,027) over thirty years later.

As Ernie Green said, "I took that money and bought a home in Shaker Heights."

"I used it to buy the farmland outside Ashtabula that I live on today," said Jim Kanicki.

"I bought part ownership in a radio station in Ashland, Ohio," Fichtner recalled. "And I still own it."

It was even a bigger day for Gary Collins's wallet. In addition to the $8,027, he was voted the MVP of the game by *Sport Magazine*. He caught five passes (three for TDs) and was awarded a Corvette.

"The book value was $3,900," Collins said. "It was a three-speed convertible. All it cost me was the $274 in sales tax."

The car was a step up for Collins. He and Dick Schafrath lived near each other in suburban Aurora, and they often rode to practice together in Schafrath's Volkswagen Bug.

"It had no heater or defroster," Schafrath said. "When it snowed, one of us had to roll down the window, hang our head out, and try to scrape the ice off the window."

So the Corvette would upgrade their transportation.

"I blew it," said Collins. "I kept it for only two years, then sold it. A few years ago, I was telling my son about the car. He put a trace on it and found some guy in Arizona had it, and the asking price was $51,000."

Tom Melody didn't attend the party. The Akron sportswriter had to write his story, and when he returned home, he found his wife in tears.

"All of these Browns fans were calling my house and threatening to do terrible things to my body because I had picked the Colts," Melody said. "The one guy who upset my wife most said that he knew where we lived, and he planned to burn our house down—and he sounded serious."

Lucky for Melody, the guy also was probably drunk, but it made for an uneasy night in the Melody household.

Ross Fichtner had more on his mind than John Mackey, Jim Ninowski's health, and a championship ring that last Sunday in December of 1964. His wife, Lynda, was about to give birth to their second child. Lynda Kay Beck Fichtner was a former Miss Ohio, and she insisted upon going to the game.

"My father found a spot in the parking lot where he could get out in a hurry," Fichtner recalled. "But she held up just fine."

In fact, Fichtner was even able to stop by the party that night.

"The baby came two days later, on December 29," he said.

Tamara Lynn was seven pounds, two ounces.

"She came just in time for me to use her as a tax deduction for 1964," Fichtner said. "I've always thanked her for that."

———————

After stopping at the Sheraton in downtown Cleveland, Dick Modzelewski collared Jim Kanicki and said, "Let's go somewhere quiet and get something to eat." During and after the game, Modzelewski felt twenty-three years old. Suddenly, he felt fifty-three.

"After the cheering and hullabaloos were over, I just sat down and it was like all the energy drained right out of me," he said. "I was exhausted. I said to myself, 'Jesus, Mary, and Joseph, we won this thing.' No one gave us a chance, and we played the game of our lives. But then the bruises started to hurt, and I could barely move."

He wasn't in the mood for a long, rowdy party.

"I drove Kanicki out to a Holiday Inn in Eastlake," Modzelewski recalled. "We walked into the dining room, and guess who was sitting there? Don Shula. I couldn't believe it. But Don was from Painesville, which was near there. He was eating with some relatives. We stopped over to say hello, and poor Don had the look of absolute dejection. You had to feel bad for the guy."

———————

When Art Modell awoke on December 28, he had a huge bill from the Sheraton for his team's party. His head also told him that he'd had too much to drink the night before, but he never felt better.

"This was a vindication for me," he said. "We had to win after I fired Paul Brown. If things had gone sour those first few years, they would have run me right out of town."

Instead, Modell was being toasted.

Yes, some fans were still unhappy about Paul Brown's dismissal, although they said little in the wake of what the team did in 1963, and especially 1964. More fans were upset with Modell's TV blackout and his handling of the championship tickets.

When the game finally was televised in Cleveland—on Monday night, thirty hours after it ended—over 70 percent of the households in the Cleveland area watched it, nearly all of them from start to finish.

Modell picked up the *Cleveland Press* and saw himself called "the courageous yet modest Browns owner" on the editorial page, of all places! The fascinating thing was that courageous and modest was exactly how Modell saw himself back in 1964, although Browns fans would eventually have a much different opinion.

The only disappointment for the Browns on the day they beat the Colts came after the game. Frank Ryan had a football in his locker, a special ball that was awarded to him after he threw five touchdown passes in the Browns' 52–20 victory at New York that clinched the Eastern Conference Title. The game ball was signed by the entire team.

While Ryan was giving interviews following the victory over Baltimore, someone stole the ball out of his locker.

As his wife, Joan Ryan, wrote in her *Plain Dealer* column, "Frank was crestfallen. The ball means so much to him. . . . He considers it a tribute from his teammates."

The stolen ball was reported on TV news shows and in newspapers across the country. Just as it sometimes works today on *America's Most Wanted,* a policeman in Syracuse, New York, received a call from a man who said he knew of a teenage boy who had a ball just like the one they talked about on TV.

Sergeant Alfred Disaola knocked on the door of the sixteen-year-old boy and discovered the ball among "several unorthodox sports trophies," according to wire reports. The kid was ahead of his time, in terms of the memorabilia craze. He reportedly had a phony press credential to the New York Yankees' dressing room, and had stolen Roger Maris's bat. He also had swiped a helmet from the Syracuse dressing room after a Syracuse-Pitt football game.

The ball was mailed to the Ryan household in Houston.

It was a rough week for *Sports Illustrated* following the Browns victory. The magazine had prepared a cover featuring Don Shula and Johnny Unitas, assuming the Colts would win. It was in full color. Following the upset, they quickly had to replace it with a black and white photo of Frank Ryan.

A few days after the championship game, Ernie Green was driving south to visit his relatives in Columbus, Georgia. He stopped at a diner in Tennessee.

"It was a real greasy spoon," Green recalled. "I just wanted a sandwich. I sat there and sat there, but no one would wait on me."

Then Green realized what was happening.

"It didn't matter that I was the starting halfback for the best football team in the world," he said. "I was a black man in the South in 1964 and that was all that mattered to some people."

Green angrily walked out, and then sought out a "black restaurant" where he'd be served.

Perhaps the most meaningful postgame story came from Hal Lebovitz.

"You know what Jim Brown did right before he went to bed the night of the game?" Lebovitz asked. "He called Western Union and sent a telegram—not to Blanton, but to his wife, Forman Collier. He thanked Mrs. Collier for allowing her husband to spend so much time with the team. To me, nothing could have been more thoughtful than that."

And the morning after the game, that telegram arrived for Forman Collier at their home in Aurora. It was something that Blanton and Forman cherished for the rest of their lives.

Paul Brown (right) may well have forgotten that football coaches could be fired—until the arrival of Art Modell. (Diamond Images)

Unlike his predecessor, Blanton Collier had no problems with Art Modell looking over his shoulder.
(Diamond Images)

Blanton Collier's willingness to solicit Jim Brown's views was a big factor in his gaining the star's confidence and trust. (Cleveland Browns)

The Browns at practice—basic football in very humble surroundings. (CSU)

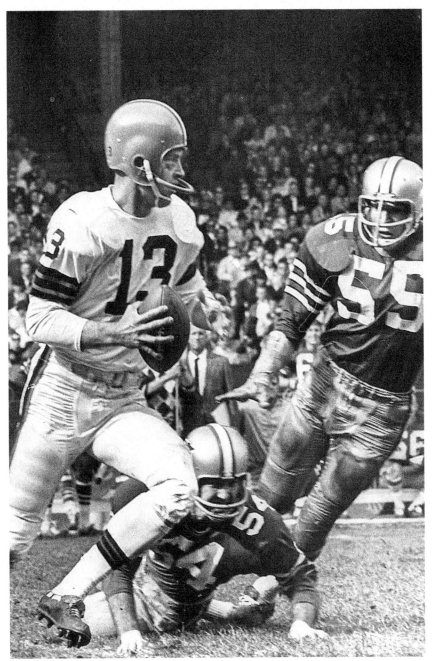
Frank Ryan: QB, Ph.D., math wizard, winner. (CSU)

Browns legend Lou "The Toe" Groza was lured out of retirement in one of Modell's best moves. (Cleveland Browns)

"The senior partner," Jim Brown was perhaps the greatest running back of all time. (CSU)

A true gentleman, Blanton Collier loved talking Xs and Os–to players, coaches, and reporters. (Cleveland Browns)

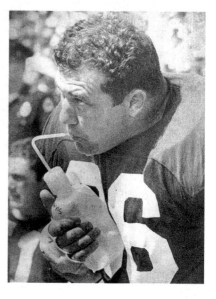

Backup quarterback Jim Ninowski. On many Sundays he was the most popular man in Cleveland. (CSU)

Gene Hickerson, one of the best offensive guards ever to play the game. (Cleveland Browns)

Bernie Parrish—star defensive back, team rebel. (CSU)

Blanton Collier and Frank Ryan discussing a little strategy during a timeout. Few fans knew that Collier wore hearing aids and had trouble with crowd noise.

(Diamond Images)

Gary Collins—a big game player, and not afraid to sweat. (CSU)

Dick "Little Mo" Modzelewski, the rock of Cleveland's defensive line, came from the Giants to show the Browns what it takes to be champion. (CSU)

Bill Glass—still holds the Browns sack record; he's now a prison minister.
(Cleveland Browns)

Dick Schafrath and Jim Brown discussing yet another way to exploit an opponent's defensive scheme. (Cleveland Browns)

The Browns defensive backfield (left to right: Bob Franklin, Ross Fichtner, Larry Benz, Bernie Parrish) was considered the weakest part of the team but played surprising well in big games. (Cleveland Browns)

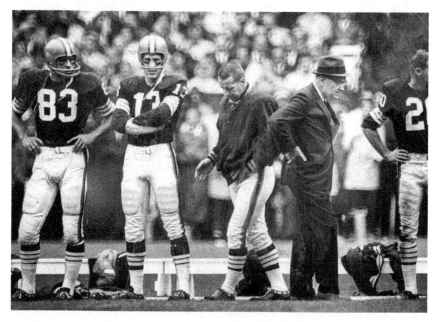

"Collier had tremendous concentration and was able to compensate for his hearing loss with his other senses. Even though he wore glasses, he had excellent eyesight. He could just feel the game. He caught all the details," said defensive end Bill Glass. (CSU)

The public knew Jim Kanicki as "Smokey the Bear," but to his teammates he was "Baby Huey." (Cleveland Browns)

Galen Fiss, perhaps the most underrated player on the team. (Cleveland Browns)

Ernie Green, Jim Brown's backfield mate, was more than capable of running the sweep behind the blocking of guards Gene Hickerson, #66, and John Wooten, #60. (CSU)

Leroy Kelly, the rookie running back and kick returner who would later replace Jim Brown and forge a Hall of Fame career of his own. (CSU)

Lou Groza boots a field goal against the N.Y. Giants. "The Toe" had a big belly but even a bigger heart. (CSU)

The other star of Cleveland's feared receiving corps: rookie wide receiver Paul Warfield, a step ahead of the defender and with a perfect read on the ball. (CSU)

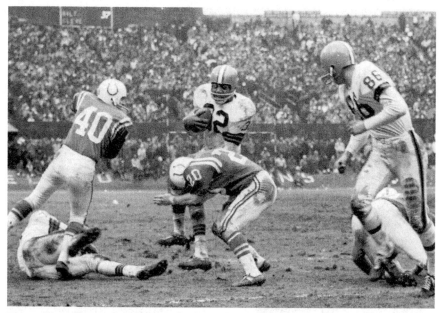

It usually took more than one guy to bring down Jim Brown. (Diamond Images)

Johnny Unitas being hounded by Jim Kanicki and Dick Modzelewski in the championship game against the Baltimore Colts. The Browns defense won this game.
(Diamond Images)

1964 championship post-game—fans rush the field in celebration. (Diamond Images)

Frank Ryan, the last quarterback to lead the Browns to a title, still loved by
Browns fans. (CSU)

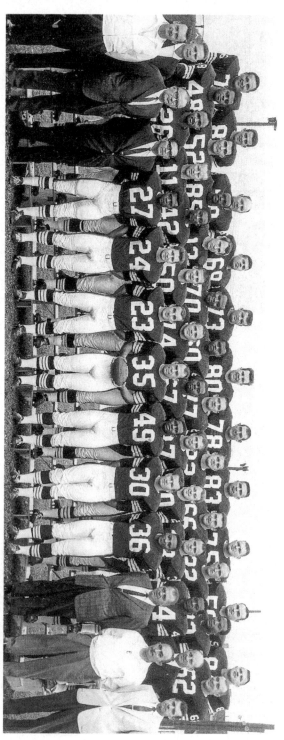

Front Row (left to right): Leo Murphy, trainer; Blanton Collier, head coach; Fritz Heisler, offensive line coach; Walter Roberts, 27; Bobby Franklin, 24; Larry Benz, 23; Galen Fiss, 35; Walter Beach, 49; Bernie Parrish, 30; Charley Scales, 36; Nick Skorich, defensive line coach; Morrie Kono, equipment manager; Eddie Ulinski, linebacker coach.

Second Row: William "Dub" Jones, offensive backs and ends coach; Dave Raimey, 26; Jim Ninowski, 11; Paul Warfield, 42; Vince Costello, 50; Dick Modzelewski, 74; Sidney Williams, 67; Tom Hutchinson, 87; Ross Fichtner, 20; Stan Sczurek, 38; Leroy Kelly, 44; Howard Brinkner, defensive coach.

Third Row: Ernie Green, 48; Mike Lucci, 52; Clifton McNeil, 85; Frank Ryan, 13; John Brown, 70; John Wooten, 60; Dick Schafrath, 77; Jim Houston, 82; Gene Hickerson, 66; Lowell Caylor, 22; Jim Brown, 32; Dale Memmelaar, 62.

Back Row: Lou Groza, 76; Gary Collins, 86; Bob Gain, 79; Jim Kanicki, 69; Monte Clark, 73; Bill Glass, 80; Frank Parker, 78; Johnny Brewer, 83; Roger Shoale, 75; John Morrow, 56; Paul Wiggin, 84. (Cleveland Browns)

FOREVER
BROWN

JIM BROWN

You ask Jim Brown about the 1964 championship game, and he tells you about the touchdown he didn't score. You're surprised; you don't even remember the play he's talking about, but thirty years later, he still can't forget it.

"We had the ball near the goal line," he said. "I was trying to pound the ball in. Remember, this was when the goal posts were right on the goal line. I reached out with my left hand, grabbed the goal post, and was trying to pull myself over the pile of bodies and across the goal line."

What was wrong with that?

"Dumb," Brown roared. "How dumb could I be? If I could touch the goal post, that meant I could get my arm across the goal line."

So?

"So why didn't I just put the football in my left hand and reach out with it?" he said. "Instead of grabbing the goal post, I'd have put the ball across the line and had a touchdown."

But the Browns won, 27–0, right?

"I know," he said. "That was my biggest thrill in football, winning that championship. But I can't help myself. I think about these things."

What things?

"There was another play early in the game," he said. "I could have gone for a long gain, maybe all the way. I had great blocking in front of me. Gene [Hickerson] and John [Wooten] were knocking people on their ass. But I slowed down, and then I cut the wrong way."

Even the greatest running back in the world can make a mistake.

"They caught me from behind," said Brown, shaking his head and still not believing it some thirty years later.

"*They caught me from behind,*" he repeated a little louder.

You have a feeling that Jim Brown would rather have his right foot whacked off with a chainsaw than to be caught from behind.

"The mistakes I made on those two plays could have been critical," he said. "What I remember most from my career is my mistakes, because I agonized over them,"

As you listen to Brown, you begin to realize why Vince Lombardi called this man "the greatest football player I've ever seen." Yes, the physical tools were there: The forty-seven-inch chest. The thirty-two-inch waist. The muscled legs like pistons and the arms like jackhammers.

"The first time I saw Jim Brown was during training camp at Hiram College," Kevin Byrne recalled. "He was walking down the stairs and had this big radio box under his arm. I was just a little kid. He was 6′2″ and 230 pounds, bigger than some linemen back then. He had this huge head, a massive chest, and an itty-bitty waist. His wrists were wider than my biceps."

"The man's hands—huge," Leroy Kelly recalled. "He'd carry that football in one hand, run while holding it out from his body as if it were a loaf of bread. But when you got a look at those hands, you saw that they were all scarred and bruised. We didn't wear gloves back then like they do now. His hands took a beating from hitting all the helmets and being stepped on with those cleats. Yet somehow, those fingers were strong enough to hold the ball."

"When I was with Detroit, I tried to tackle Jim Brown," Bill Glass said. "He had the ball out in one arm. As I closed in on him, he took his free arm and dropped it straight down on my helmet. He bashed me with his forearm, and it was like being hit with a lead pipe. I mean it, visualize a long, straight, lead pipe. No bend in the elbow. He just dropped it down on your head. I've never seen a running back do that before or since. It gave you a headache. Some of the biggest, toughest guys in the NFL got pretty scared when they saw Jim swinging that arm of his. Jim Brown could knock you senseless."

In 1963 Jim Brown rushed for more yards than all but two NFL teams. That is why Washington's Jim Steffen once said, "The best way to tackle Jim Brown is to hold on and wait for help."

But there was more to Brown than strength and size.

"My game was to try and beat you mentally," he said. "If someone was close to my talent, I still should have the mental edge over him. I went into every game thinking, 'I am not going to make a mistake.' Paul Brown said that if you make the fewest mistakes, you win. He drilled that into us and I adopted that. The only things from the past I dwelled on were my mistakes, so I wouldn't make them again."

That is getting closer to the essence of Jim Brown.

This is a man who not only played in every game, but never missed a practice. Toward the end of his career, he'd tell Blanton Collier that his legs or something else were hurting. Collier would think that Brown wanted a day off—but no, all Brown wanted to do was apologize in advance, telling the coach that he would not go hard on every single play in practice.

Then Brown would insist that Collier not say a word.

"Jim just wanted me to know that he wasn't loafing," Collier once said. "Even Art Modell didn't know how much he was hurting."

Modell recalled that in 1963, Brown had a broken big toe on his right foot.

"I took him aside and told him that he had to do something with that foot," Modell said. "I told Jim that I wanted him to see a doctor."

"Art," said Brown. "I know it's fractured. If I have an X-ray, all it will show is that the toe is fractured. I'll still have to play with it."

Modell smiled at the memory.

"He just took a painkiller shot and played," Modell said. "I never even remember Jim Brown taking himself out, not for one single play. There may have been games where the coaches took him out for a play, but Jim never asked to go out."

In 1963, playing on a broken toe, Jim Brown set an NFL record by rushing for 1,863 yards in fourteen games.

Brown believed that was part of his job, to play all the time.

"Now, I see these guys run the ball a couple of times, raise their hands and want to rest . . . " Brown said, shaking his head. He couldn't finish the sentence, almost as if he were offended by what pro football has become.

Obviously, Brown did need medical treatment for the bruises, breaks, and cuts. He'd meet trainer Leo Murphy at 6:30 on Monday mornings, because he knew that no one else would be in the dressing room.

"In 1962, Jim had a left wrist that was so badly sprained that he couldn't even tie his own shoes," recalled his roommate, John Wooten. "I always believed that was why 1962 was Jim's worst year. He used his left hand as a club to fight off tacklers, but he couldn't use the arm that much in 1962. That year, Jim could only carry the ball with his right hand, which also hindered his running. [Equipment manager] Morrie Kono would come over and tie Jim's shoes for him that season, but he made sure to do it when no one was watching. Jim never wanted his teammates to know he was hurting. I promised him I'd never say a word, and I never did until after he retired."

Why the secrecy?

"Everything is mental," Brown said. "If you are always in the trainer's room, always getting rubbed down, you get too comfortable. I liked to stay close to the nitty-gritty. If you were a marked man like I was, then your attitude was you had to be tough. You had to take the pain. If you broke your toe and you could still walk, you played. To be the kind of runner I wanted to be, you needed a strong mind."

But why not tell your teammates that you're less than one hundred percent?

"I didn't want them to know something was wrong with me," he said. "That might bother them, because they counted on me. I also didn't want my teammates going to the Pro Bowl and telling their friends on other teams that Jim Brown is always in the training room. I wanted them to say, 'That guy never goes into the training room. Man, he's crazy.' It was like I held my breath for the nine years that I played. I didn't want to make a mistake. I didn't want anyone to see I was hurt."

He carried the image even further.

"He is the easiest man for equipment I've ever seen," Morrie Kono once said. "He doesn't want any pads inside his uniform. At the start of the season, I hand him his stuff and that is it. He never asks for anything. On a cold day, I hand him a coat, but I don't even know if he wants it. He never asks for one. He never takes a sip of water during the game. He never says he's hurt. He never complains."

The only concession Brown made to the physical demands of football was his hesitant, almost painful walks back to the huddle after he carried the ball. You would have sworn he was a man headed to his deathbed.

"If someone did lay a good hit on him and he felt it, the slow walk gave him time to catch his breath and get his senses back," said Wooten. "But he never wanted the defense to know that they put a good hit on him. So if he walked the same slow walk to the huddle every time after every carry, they'd just think that was Jim Brown walking like he always did." Or as Brown said, "The defense is always looking for a sign of weakness. You can't give it to them. You have to do things the same way, every time. So that's why I never varied how I went back to the huddle."

Brown seldom complained to officials (another sign of weakness, he believed), yet he was on the wrong end of cheap shots virtually every Sunday. He was elbowed and kicked while at the bottom of a pile. Some men tried to step on his hands or feet when no one was looking. Most players would have cocked their fists and responded in anger. But not Brown. He was in only two brawls during his career. The first was when he was a rookie, and he vowed never to do that again. The second was toward the end, when he felt a couple of Dallas players were trying to injure Browns quarterback Frank Ryan.

Early in his career, some defenders tried to bring him down by the face mask, an illegal and dangerous tactic that could lead to a broken neck. Brown had a way of dealing with that—stick your fingers into his helmet, he'd bite them. Word got around that if you liked your fingers, keep them away from Jim Brown's mouth.

"You know, I used to beat myself up," he said.

How so?

"When I was playing, it might be a Wednesday night and I was walking down a street," he said. "I was into visualization. In my mind, I'd see how a play should have been run, and how I missed the hole. People would walk by me and hear I was talking to myself. I wanted perfection."

His opponents had another name for him.

"Superman," said Dick Modzelewski. "When I played for the New York Giants, we called him that. Once I got a standing ovation in Yankee Stadium just for tackling him. The Browns ran a draw play. I reached out and got my hand caught in Jim's shoulder pads, behind his neck. I couldn't get it out. Then Gene Hickerson threw me to the ground, and in the process, I took Jim down with me. It looked like I brought him down with one hand, and the crowd couldn't believe it, so they gave me an ovation."

Modzelewski will never forget the first time he faced Brown.

"Jim was in the middle of this pack of guys," he said. "It was like he was dragging about eight of us forward. Really, eight of us had at least one hand on him, and *we couldn't bring him down*. He *just kept moving*. I was thinking, 'How can he be dragging us forward?' I'd never seen a runner like that. For a while, I thought he used some kind of powder on his Rayon pants, so our hands would slip off. Once, in a pileup, I spit on my hands and rubbed them on his pants to check for powder. But there wasn't any."

———————

Superman was born on St. Simons Island, a Georgia coastal town about halfway between Savannah and Jacksonville, Florida.

Jim Brown loved the island, the security that comes from a warm sea breeze, the familiarity of the salt in the air, the bright sun overhead, the pure white sand underfoot. St. Simons Island was palm trees, and it was small farmers tilling fields with plows pulled by horses.

"It was another world," Jim Brown said recently.

When Jim was two years old, his mother moved to Long Island, where she worked as a maid in Great Neck. Jim stayed behind with his grandmother, Myrtle Powell, his aunt, Bertha Powell, and his great-grandmother, Nora Petersen.

Brown's father was Swinton "Sweet Sue" Brown, a wanderer and a gambler who separated from his mother not long after Jim was born.

"Sue was a huge man who had been a good football player over in Brunswick [Georgia]," Brown wrote in his book, *Off My Chest*. "He had boxed professionally around Georgia. . . . He was said to be impossible to dislike. It just happened that he had a weakness for dice and cards."

Swinton "Sweet Sue" Brown also went north to seek his fortune.

Despite growing up without either parent, Brown was happy. He had a grandmother, a great-grandmother, and an aunt to spoil and watch over him. He was dressed neatly, taught to wash and be polite. He went to the Baptist church every Sunday. He played with both white and black children, the favorite activity being to dig for crabs.

"Sea Island was real close," Brown said. "It was a resort for rich white people. This was the 1940s, so Jim Crow was in full force. I was vaguely aware that there were certain places that I couldn't go, but it didn't bother me. There were stores and other businesses for blacks. We had our own churches, our own social lives. I went to a two-room schoolhouse where one teacher handled all the elementary grades. All the kids were black. But it never occurred to me that anything was wrong.

We had our own self-contained community and it was a very good way to grow up."

When Brown was eight, his mother sent for him. She had a live-in job as a domestic, and was given a small apartment. Brown moved to Manhasset, New York. The year was 1944.

"I'm always amused when people say that I am anti-white," Brown said. "When I moved to New York, instead of running into a racist world, I was embraced by a white community. Two of my biggest supporters and best friends ever are white men—Ed Walsh and Kenneth Malloy."

Walsh was a local high school coach. Malloy was a Manhasset businessman who liked sports and helping young people. Some would say that these men latched on to Brown because he was a great athlete, and "great" may not even do him justice.

In three years at Manhasset High, he earned thirteen varsity letters in five different sports.

As a senior basketball player, he averaged 38 points per game and set a Long Island single-game scoring record with 55 points.

As a senior football player, he averaged 15 yards per carry. That's right, 15 yards each time he touched the ball.

He played only one year of baseball, did well, but quit because he found the game boring. Yet he received a letter from the New York Yankees inviting him to try out—and the letter was signed by Casey Stengel.

In track, he set several records.

"But these men looked at me as much as a person as an athlete," Brown said. "They kept telling me to use sports to get an education. They told me that I was smart, and to prove it, they gave me an IQ test. I scored high, and they said, 'Look, that shows you can think.' They convinced me to run for chief justice of the student body during my senior year."

Jim Brown graduated with a B average.

Walsh was the football coach, a gentle, quiet man who loved to spend time talking strategy with Brown after practice. Yes, this was the same approach that Blanton Collier would use ten years later, and part of the reason Brown so loved Collier was that the Browns coach reminded him of Ed Walsh.

Ken Malloy was a Syracuse alumnus. Another friend of Brown's was Dr. Ray Collins, who was the superintendent of the Manhasset public schools. As the college offers poured in, Walsh, Malloy, and Dr. Collins would help Brown with the decision. Walsh favored Ohio State; the football coach was impressed with Woody Hayes, and he believed that Hayes not only would develop Brown as a player, but also as a student.

Dr. Collins had taught at Syracuse. Malloy graduated from there. They contacted the school and told the football department about Brown. Syracuse never scouted him. In fact, Syracuse was not among the forty-five schools to offer Brown a scholarship. Yet Dr. Collins and Malloy were convinced that Syracuse was the best place for Brown.

Jim just didn't know. No one from his family had attended college. He respected Ed Walsh's opinion, but he also had never been to the Midwest, and Ohio State sounded a million miles away.

Malloy kept talking Syracuse, insisting it was only a three-hour drive. (Six hours is more like it.) Brown could even come home on weekends. His friends could drive up and visit him.

Brown thought that Malloy had convinced Syracuse to give him an athletic scholarship. Instead, Malloy and forty-three of his friends chipped in and paid for Brown's first year of school, hoping Syracuse would come to its senses and give him a scholarship.

When Brown arrived at Syracuse, he found a very white world. He was the only black in the entire football program. He heard stories of a player named Marion Farris, who was the previous black football player. In *Off My Chest,* Brown said that he was told that Farris dated white students, had an altercation with a coach, and was supposed to be a very bad guy. Over and over he was told, "Don't be like Marion Farris." It didn't take Brown long to realize that Farris may have gotten a very bad rap, that maybe these charges were trumped up to run him off.

Even worse for Brown was that the football coaches took little interest in him. You have to wonder exactly what these men were thinking. Here is a kid who was the greatest high school football player in the history of Long Island. He walks on to their campus at 6′2″ and 210 pounds of muscle. He didn't even use up a scholarship.

You'd think the coaches would have spent every night for a month on their knees, giving thanks to the Almighty for the great gift they had been presented. Instead, they seldom played him. They hardly spoke to him. They seemed to be trying to make him quit the team.

Brown would have left, except that in the spring a sympathetic track coach took him in and gave him a scholarship. When Brown went out for football as a sophomore, he was fifth string on the depth chart at halfback. One coach told him that he'd never be a good running back, and that he belonged on the line.

Again, what was in the water up there in Syracuse?

Brown didn't start until there were three games left in his sophomore season, and that only happened because two running backs had been injured. The game was against Colgate, and he ran for 151 yards. He never sat again.

In college, Brown played football, basketball, lacrosse, and ran track. Some insisted his best sport was really lacrosse. On one day during his senior year, Brown scored the winning goal in a lacrosse game, then went over to the track meet and won the high jump and the discus throw.

He didn't play basketball as a senior, but he was drafted by the NBA's Syracuse Nationals.

In his senior year, he was the MVP of the football Cotton Bowl and the North-South lacrosse all-star game. In addition to being a running back, Brown played safety on defense and was the team's placekicker.

In 1957, the Browns had the sixth pick in the draft.

This was one of those times it was lucky the Browns were not drafting higher. Otto Graham had retired after the 1955 season, and Paul Brown was in the market for a quarterback. He loved Jim Brown, he really did; he was sure that Jim Brown would be a star. He knew Jim Brown could do almost everything on the football field—everything but play quarterback.

He needed a quarterback. And there were two quarterbacks he liked: Len Dawson and John Brodie. If either was available, he'd have to draft a quarterback.

But by the time Cleveland's turn came, Dawson and Brodie were gone. So were Ron Kramer, Jon Arnett, and Paul Hornung. Paul Brown was sad/happy. Sad that he would not get his quarterback, but almost astonished that Jim Brown was still available. How could the first five teams not see that Jim Brown was the best athlete in the draft? Maybe the best in any draft.

When Paul Brown's turn came, he never hesitated. He picked Jim Brown, and then thought, "I can get a quarterback from somewhere else."

Of course, Paul Brown didn't tell the young running back all this. He still had to sign Jim Brown, and the only thing that bothered Paul Brown as much as losing was spending money, especially on rookies. So he talked about Jim Brown working in slowly, and how Ed [brother of Dick] Modzelewski was a very fine fullback, and Jim could be his backup.

Finally, Jim Brown agreed to a $15,000 contract—a $3,000 bonus and a $12,000 first-year salary.

"This was back when they had the college all-star game in the fall, right during NFL training camps," Brown said. "I went to the game in Chicago, and I hardly played. I was really upset because the game was on national TV, and I had a lot of friends and family watching— and they wouldn't play me. After that game, I was so upset that I just jumped in my car and drove all the way to Hiram, all night. I got there in the early morning, and I went straight to practice. I hadn't slept and could hardly keep my eyes open. The first thing they did was line me up with all the other running backs to run the 40-yard dash. Even though I was dead tired, I won that."

"After one day of practice with Jim, my brother [Ed] told me, 'Well, I've just become a backup,'" said Dick Modzelewski.

Jim Brown's first exhibition game was against Pittsburgh in the Akron Rubber Bowl.

"We ran a draw play," he recalled. "And I broke free for a long run and a touchdown."

When Jim Brown came back to the bench, Paul Brown quietly walked over to him.

"You're my fullback," said the coach.

Then he walked away.

But over and over, Brown heard those words in his head: "You're my fullback . . . You're my fullback."

That was it.

First game, one good run.

You're my fullback.

That was in 1957, and forty years later, they have stayed with Jim Brown.

"Those words," Brown said. "I'll never forget them. He told me that I was his fullback, and then never said another word about it."

———

The Browns had a running back the likes of which no one had ever seen.

Players talked about his power, his unrelenting will to carry a thousand pounds of bodies with him for a few extra yards.

But there was also the grace, the intelligence.

"I never ran out of bounds [to avoid a tackle]," Brown said.

What he'd do was dash to the sidelines, stop dead, check the defender, then almost *tiptoe* around him, cutting in an unimaginable direction. That is what many tacklers recall, Jim Brown refusing to take the easy route and go out of bounds in order not to be hit . . . Jim Brown stopping quicker than a snap of the fingers . . . Jim Brown almost on his tiptoes, suddenly taking a couple of dainty steps to change his direction, then exploding around you.

"Everyone thinks that Jim just ran over people," said Bill Glass. "But his moves and his balance were the keys to his running. That's why it was so hard for one defender to bring him down—he made it almost impossible for you to get a clean shot at him."

Brown liked to take a handoff and bang into the line in a semi-crouch; he thought it was better for his balance. So was carrying the ball with one hand. He also loved the freedom to pick his own holes, to run in a different direction than where the play was designed to take him.

"The great thing was that we had men on our line who'd block once, then get up and keep blocking," Brown said. "I knew if I got past the line of scrimmage, those linemen were out there somewhere, blocking downfield. That gave me even more incentive."

"Jim never said much to the offensive linemen," recalled center John Morrow. "But we knew that he appreciated us, and we were honored to block for the guy. The first time we ran a flip [a sweep around end] with Jim, I was out in front looking for someone to block. I heard a noise, like someone was breathing right down my neck. It was Jim, he would almost run right up your back so that when you made your block, he could slip right around the defender. Now, I find it amazing that I heard his breathing, with all the crowd noise and everything else going on during a game—but I could hear him and feel him right behind me."

Line coach Fritz Heisler seldom mentioned Jim Brown's name. He would just tell his offensive lineman, "The Running Back likes the blocking to do this . . . " It was always "The Running Back," just as White House staffers say, "The President wants . . . "

"Blanton Collier would say, 'Just get Jim to the line of scrimmage,'" recalled John Wooten. "Then Blanton said that Jim could do the rest. Jim just ran so hard, and expected others to do that. When Paul Warfield was a rookie, he caught a pass and sort of doubled back and lost a few yards as he ran the ball. Jim was furious. In the huddle, he told Paul to know where the first-down marker was, 'and you had a first down when you caught the ball.' Then he told Warfield to 'quit dancing, and get the first down if you don't have it. Run straight ahead.' Jim was more than a great running back, he was a leader."

Warfield joined the Browns in 1964. "I grew up in Warren, Ohio," he said. "I watched Jim on TV. At school, I'd sit there and cheer for Jim with fifteen other guys while we watched Browns games. I tried to be cool when I was around him, but I was in complete awe of the guy."

Warfield mentioned how he drew Brown's anger. It was before an exhibition game. Warfield was injured and did not suit up. He was joking with some players in the dressing room.

Brown approached him, scowled, and said something to the effect of, "Some of us have a game to play today."

Warfield remembered he wanted to crawl under a chair and never be seen again.

If you think Brown was intimidating to opponents, you should talk to some of his teammates.

"Other than John Wooten, Jim was not close to a lot of people on the team," recalled Bill Glass. "He was very aloof, very proud. If you were nice to him, he was nice to you. We got along very well. But Jim had a way of putting some distance between himself and most people."

"Jim had the locker next to mine," said Jim Kanicki. "He didn't say very much to me or most of the guys. Even when he did talk to you, he really didn't look you in the eye. He sort of looked over your shoulder.

What I did like about Jim was that he was turned off by phony people. We had a good relationship because I was always straight with him. He hated people who put on an act."

Or as John Morrow said, "Jim and I had a very professional relationship. We didn't talk that much. He talked more to my wife. He'd see her at the airport and right away, they'd get into an interesting conversation."

Michael Heaton, son of longtime *Plain Dealer* football writer Chuck Heaton, will never forget an act of kindness from Jim Brown. Michael was seven years old, hanging around the Browns' training camp in Hiram. Brown saw the bored youngster throwing stones in the parking lot. Brown was heading to nearby Garrettsville, and asked Michael to come along. He asked Michael about school, his father, and what interested him. In Garrettsville, they walked around for a while, and he bought the kid some comic books and a grape soda. Then he took Michael back to Hiram. Jim Brown didn't do it to score any points with Chuck Heaton, who already was a Browns supporter. Jim Brown never did much of anything unless he wanted to, and there is a side of Jim Brown that is very nice to little kids.

His teammates said Brown never was any sort of problem on the team. Rather, "We liked him so much because he not only was a great player, but he never acted like anything was wrong—even when things were going wrong," said Kanicki. "We drew strength from him."

But there were days when Jim Brown was just in a rotten mood, days when it was wise to give him plenty of room.

"He could be a moody, brooding guy," said Tom Melody. "One day at practice, Jim ran a sweep and kept running it out of bounds—he ran right over Nick Skorich. He made no effort to get out of Nick's way, he just ran down the assistant coach. When you watched practice and Jim came toward the sidelines where you were standing, you knew you had better get out of his way."

As his career came to a close, Brown often spoke out on racial matters. In his book, Brown said that he would counsel young black players "Not to try to clown and win friendships . . . don't seek false friendships by being something the white man wants you to be. He expects you to be jolly and laughing. When he wants to talk foolishness, he comes to you. When he wants to talk seriously, he goes to a white man. . . . Let the white man know that you are interested in the same thing that he is—

getting ahead, having a nice life, a home, a family. Then if he accepts you on that basis, you are headed in the right direction."

When Jim Brown scored a touchdown, there was no celebration, no TD dance. He once said that a player should act like he had been in the end zone before. He also did not want people to see black athletes as children. To him, football was a business, and you should treat it as such. Brown said that too many white players assumed their black teammates were just out to party and chase women. He said that black players had to break the stereotype of being able to compete with whites on the field, but not being as smart as whites in other areas. He talked about how the Browns had an odd number of black players one year, and rather than have one of the black players and one of the white players room together, the front office kept the color line intact by giving the "extra" black player a private room. He insisted that Black Muslims were "not terrorists. They are a religion. They believe blacks should beware of the white man."

Today, most of this sounds like common sense and relatively tame. In 1964, many thought Jim Brown was a radical. On September 22, 1964, a crackpot phoned a Cleveland radio station and said he planned to bomb Jim Brown's home because Brown was on the air discussing his views on race. Police guarded Brown's home for a few days.

Even after he retired, Brown continued to urge blacks to conduct themselves with pride and dignity. His gospel was that of "green power."

As he told *The National* (the defunct sports daily) in 1991, "Blacks have been on a wild goose chase for 30 years. Instead of civil rights, they should have been pursuing economic rights—the right to rebuild their own communities, the right to pursue their own fiscal destiny. . . . Integration as a goal was the worst kind of joke. . . . We should have been saying, 'No, we'll stay in our own neighborhoods, but we'll take your liberal money. We'll use it to build our own schools and hospitals and live in our own tidy neighborhoods like the Koreans and Jews do. . . . Whenever anyone starts talking to me about Mother Africa, I just laugh in their face. I've been to Africa, and you don't want to live there. It's hot, it's backward and there ain't no McDonald's."

"Most people don't want to rock the boat," Brown said recently. "But this country was founded by people wanting to rock the boat. What was the Boston Tea Party? What did George Washington do when his army went out to fight with frozen feet and no food and the Continental

Congress didn't back them? Those guys stood up and said, 'Hell, we ain't backing down from what is right.' They just decided they were not going to be ruled by a king anymore. That is the spirit of this country." And Jim Brown tells you that always was and still is his spirit.

Art Modell had to know that.

And if you want to know why Jim Brown retired at the end of the 1965 season—still in his prime at the age of twenty-nine—you have to blame Modell.

Brown had made a few movies, mostly Westerns. He had a three-picture deal with Paramount Studios.

After the 1965 season (when Brown again led the NFL in rushing with 1,544 yards), he flew to London to begin filming *The Dirty Dozen*. Training camp for the 1966 season opened, and Brown wasn't there. Modell was under the impression that Brown planned to play one more season.

"After 1965, I told Art that I was leaving, but if he needed me, I might consider coming back," Brown said.

Modell definitely needed Jim Brown.

"The movie was taking longer to finish than they thought," Brown said. "Art was putting out all these statements about how he had to fine me if I didn't show up in camp. I told Art, 'Hey, you have a one-way contract. I only get paid if I play. I'm not guaranteed any money.' How could he fine me when I wasn't even being paid?"

Art Modell didn't like questions such as that, even by a man he used to call "my senior partner." Nor did he like the idea that Jim Brown would rather make a movie than spend a month in training camp in rural Hiram, Ohio. Most of all, Art Modell hated the thought that Jim Brown was somehow challenging his authority.

By God, Art Modell fired Paul Brown and won . . . and if he had to, he'd win without Jim Brown, too.

At least that seemed to be his attitude, even if he never said as much.

"A key thing was that Art was pressuring Jim to come back *right now*," recalled Hal Lebovitz. "I think Jim was kind of angry at Art for pushing him. He thought he had a career in the movies, and he said, 'Fine, that's it, I quit.'"

Modell was threatening to fine Brown about $1,500 for each week of training camp he missed. Modell was upset because he had been unable to reach Brown by phone and was convinced Brown was ignoring his messages.

"There was discussion (in 1966) that maybe Jim was just dodging training camp," said Bill Glass. "But I think Jim stopped playing because he was at the height of his game. He wanted to be remembered as the greatest. And his movie career was going well."

"You just don't give Jim Brown an ultimatum like Art Modell did," Jim Kanicki said. "Jim was not going to back down to Art Modell or anyone else. I remember there being a team meeting where Blanton Collier and Art told us that Jim had retired. But most of us didn't believe it. We thought Jim would be back a few weeks before the season."

The more Modell made noise, the more Brown refused to listen. On July 14, 1966, a letter arrived at Hal Lebovitz's office at the *Plain Dealer*. It was from Brown, and he gave Lebovitz the exclusive scoop that he was retiring. Brown was the first black athlete to cross over and make mainstream Hollywood movies. In 1964, he starred in a feature called *Rio Conchos*, where "he is beaten by bandits, tortured by Indians, dragged by a horse and trapped in a burning building and he refused to use a stunt man," according to United Press International.

Today, Jim Brown sort of indicates that he would have retired regardless of what Modell did or said, but at other times, he has said the "arm-twisting" was a factor in his decision to quit. Certainly his teammates would not have cared if Brown had missed most of training camp to finish his movie, especially since the players knew Brown's work ethic. They also were aware that 1966 would have been his final season.

Many years later, Modell admitted "I may have acted hastily [with Brown] in 1966. If I had told him to just forget training camp and show up when he could, I think he would have returned. But it wasn't fair to the coaches and players [for Brown to miss camp]."

But was it fair to take away one last chance to play with Jim Brown, maybe one last chance for a title? That's the question Art Modell doesn't want to answer.

Modell and Brown did reconcile, and Brown served as a $50,000-a-year "advisor" to the team in the 1990s. He had some brushes with the law, although he was never convicted of anything. In 1965, Brown was charged with assault and battery on an 18-year-old girl. He was found not guilty by a Cleveland jury. In 1985, he was charged with rape and assault on a 33-year-old teacher. The charges were dropped. A woman named Eva Bohn-Chin was found unconscious on the ground below the balcony at Brown's home in Los Angeles. He was charged with assault, but that charge also was dropped.

His movie career fizzled by the 1980s. His main interest today is an organization called Amer-I-Can, where Brown and his associates work with hard-core gang members and ex-convicts. He has had some success with people whom others have long written off. He does some speaking, and is both riveting and inspirational. It's hard to know if Jim Brown is ever really happy, but he seems content with his life and his mission working with black males on the edge.

And as the years pass, Jim Brown seems to enjoy being Jim Brown. "You know what makes me feel the best about that?" he asked. "It's when I meet a middle-aged man, and he introduces me to his son. He talks about how I was a part of his life, a part he loves to remember. I've had three generations—grandfathers, fathers, and sons in front of me, telling me how the Cleveland Browns were a bridge from one generation to the next, and how they liked watching me play. That is very special to me, hearing those words."

DICK MODZELEWSKI

Everything about Dick Modzelewski was square.

His head.

His shoulders.

His trunk.

His crew cut.

Even his legs.

One big, immovable block of human granite. When the Browns players saw Modzelewski in their dressing room for the first time, they suddenly knew why they couldn't shove this guy out of the way.

The Great Wall of China never bends, right?

That is what Art Modell and Blanton Collier had in mind when they traded for Modzelewski in the spring of 1964. They wanted a human boulder, a man who would be the Rock of Gibraltar of the defensive line. They didn't care that Modzelewski was thirty-three, and an "old thirty-three" according to the New York Giants. They didn't care that the Giants believed it was wise to trade Modzelewski a year too early rather than a year too late. They didn't care that the man called "Little Mo" was supposed to be too small, a 6-foot, 250-pound defensive tackle. All they knew was that for six years, Modzelewski's New York Giants were playing for NFL championships and the Browns were not. Word was the Browns were a soft team, especially on defense.

No one ever said that about Modzelewski.

He was the son of a coal miner, and grew up near Pittsburgh. Modzelewski often talked about his father spending thirty-five years in a coal mine, a helmet with a light perched on his head. His father was a coal loader, a man who often stood in water up to his waist as he shoveled coal into a cart. Furthermore, the man seldom could stand up, because the mines were only five feet high. So he spent thirty-five years underground, crouching, in water, working nearly until he dropped.

He told his sons that they had to do the right things in school, they had to become college men. Whatever they did, do it aboveground. Do it in an office where you dress nice and you don't have to worry about the roof caving in.

Modzelewski had an older brother named Ed, who attended Maryland and played five years [1955–59] as a fullback with the Browns. By 1964, Ed "Big Mo" Modzelewski was out of football, living in Cleveland and running a classy restaurant named Mo & Junior's. The family owned the place. Oldest brother Joe was a chef and Ed managed it. Dick worked the room during the off-season, when he lived in Cleveland despite playing for the New York Giants.

"I'd see Art Modell in the restaurant and he'd tell me that he was going to trade for me," Modzelewski said. "I'd tell Art, 'Please, don't do it. I love New York.' And it was true. I fully intended to finish my career with the Giants."

Remember that Art Modell grew up in New York, and grew up a Giants fan. Allie Sherman, Sam Huff, and that tough defensive line—those were Modell's guys.

"People used to tell me that I deserved more attention when I played for the Giants," Modzelewski said. "I didn't care. Just being on the same defensive line with Rosie Grier, Jim Katcavage, and Andy Robustelli meant that I got a lot of publicity. Of course, we had Sam Huff as our middle linebacker, and he was the first pro football player ever to make the cover of *Time* magazine. We made defense popular when no one in the NFL thought about defense. We were the first real Fearsome Foursome, and the fans would start with that 'DE-FENSE, DE-FENSE!' chant. We'd go out and shut people down. It got to the point where even our offense would say, 'Get an interception and go all the way, we need this game.' It was impossible for me to ever believe that they would break us up."

Especially after the 1963 season, when the Giants had an 11–3 record and went to the championship game, losing 14–10 to Chicago.

"We had won three straight conference titles and I'd been to six championship games in eight years," Modzelewski said. "Who'd want to leave that?"

One day after the 1963 season, Sam Huff was passing through Cleveland. He stopped at Mo & Junior's for dinner. The phone rang. It was New York coach Allie Sherman.

"He told Sam that he had been traded to the Washington Redskins, right there in my restaurant," Modzelewski said. "I knew if they could trade Sam Huff, they'd trade anyone. And three weeks later, Sherman called me at the restaurant to say I'd been traded to the Browns."

Modzelewski had been traded before; his first two years were spent with the Redskins. But New York was home, even if he didn't live there. Wellington Mara was his friend, even if Mara was also the Giants' owner and a businessman. But Modzelewski's family was thrilled; Dick could stay in Cleveland all year, help out at the restaurant. Besides, playing for the Browns would be good for business.

"I considered retiring, I really did," he said.

But he saw that Sherman was intent on breaking up the Giants, getting younger. Other veterans were traded or released. New York's Fearsome Foursome was no more. All New York wanted was young blood. The Giants took Bob Crespino for Modzelewski. Crespino had been one of Paul Brown's few draft blunders, their No. 1 choice in 1961; a tight end out of Mississippi, he caught only six passes in three years with the Browns.

Modzelewski saw the deal for what it was—a dump job, and he was kicked out the door.

"A few weeks after the trade, I went to see Modell about my contract," he said. "I was still so mad about the trade, I could hardly talk.

"I told him, 'Give me a blank contract.'

"Modell did.

"I signed it and shoved it back at him, 'Write in whatever you want.'

"Then I stormed out the door. Modell always said he paid me more than he intended because I did that. But frankly, I was so mad, I didn't care. I think he gave me $17,500, which was more than I made in New York."

Blanton Collier was overjoyed to have Modzelewski. This was his kind of player—experienced, smart, steady. He knew that Modzelewski would do more than just clog the middle of the defensive line. Little Mo was a man who loved people, a natural leader; he had other players over to his house and restaurant, and the Modzelewski brothers would cook up Polish dishes such as pierogi and stuffed cabbage. He sang Polish folk songs. He talked about his father, the coal miner. ("One day, he was listening to one of our games on the radio and peeling potatoes. He got so mad that he threw away the potatoes and boiled the peels.")

He also told stories of Sam Huff and the great Giants defense. He was on a team that had consistently beaten the Browns for the Eastern Conference title in the late 1950s and early 1960s.

Modzelewski had earned respect.

And despite the rumors from New York that he was breaking down physically, he played. Every Sunday, Little Mo was there. When the Browns acquired him, he had played in 138 consecutive games, the longest streak in the NFL at that time.

"He is just a solid man and a solid player," said Giants lineman Andy Robustelli. "What he does is not spectacular, but it was important to us. He never resented that the other linemen got the publicity."

When the Browns opened training camp in 1964, Modzelewski was there. He told the players of a speech that Robustelli would give each year at the opening of training camp: "Men, we start winning the division title right now. I'll pause ten seconds so anyone who doesn't agree can get out now."

When Modzelewski said it, none of the Browns moved.

Collier's original plan was to use Modzelewski as a backup to veterans Bob Gain and Frank Parker. He also thought Modzelewski could teach Jim Kanicki about life on the line. But early in the season, Gain and

Parker were both injured, and that left Modzelewski and Kanicki as the starters, with little depth behind them.

"Mo came to our team with this great, upbeat attitude," recalled Galen Fiss. "He had all this experience with the Giants, but was such a delightful man who loved to talk and made time for everyone. He fit in immediately."

"I'll never forget how quickly the guys accepted me," Modzelewski said. "I also found out that it was a lot more fun to be on the same team with Jim Brown because you didn't have to tackle him."

While most of the Browns players had their own reason for wanting to win a championship—namely, proving they could do it without Paul Brown—that didn't matter to Modzelewski. "I wasn't around for that [Brown's firing] and I had tremendous respect for Paul Brown," he said. "I wanted to show the Giants how wrong they were to get rid of me. I'll tell you, Sam Huff, myself, and the rest used to talk about how the Giants traded us in 1964, then won only two games and allowed 399 points. Yes, 399 points, the most any team gave up that year."

Modzelewski loved it when the Browns beat New York, 42–20, in their first meeting, then destroyed the Giants, 52–20, in the final regular season game. That was at Yankee Stadium, and it sent the Browns to the championship game while the Giants finished the year at 2-10-2.

Before that game, he said he had zeroed in on New York quarterback Y.A. Tittle: "I love that bald-headed old buzzard, but I wanted to see him flat on his back."

Which is where Tittle spent much of that afternoon.

Modzelewski didn't have many sacks in 1964. His job was to occupy the offensive linemen.

"The linebackers were always on our butts to keep those linemen off their backs," he said.

The Browns players were impressed at how this thirty-three-year-old man just kept coming on every play. Because he was so square, he didn't even look his full height of 6 feet. As the season ground down, he also lost weight and was under 240 pounds by the championship game.

But the offensive line just couldn't move Little Mo out of the way. Usually, it took two men to block him, and that left room for the defensive ends and linebackers to make critical tackles.

"Being traded to the Browns was the best thing that ever could have happened to me," he said. "The fans were great to me. I had a good off-season job. I used to be a beer distributor and made about $75 a week by going to all the local bars and selling them cases of beer. When I was traded to Cleveland, I got a PR job with Phillip Morris where they paid me $200 a week to make appearances, and they gave me a new car to drive and a nice expense account. It was a great way to end a playing career."

The coal miner's son was very practical; with the bonus for winning the 1964 title, Dottie Modzelewski took her husband's cash and bought a stove, washer, and dryer.

Modzelewski retired after the 1966 season. He later served as line coach with the Browns (and head coach for one game in 1977). He also was an assistant in New York, with the Cincinnati Bengals, and retired in 1990 after being a line coach with the Detroit Lions.

Modzelewski lives on the ocean in New Bern, North Carolina.

"I quit at the age of fifty-nine," he said. "The game had changed so much over the years. I got tired of guys having a little bump and saying they couldn't play—guys making $500,000. That same guy had his agent telling him, 'Don't play. Don't take any chances. You want to play a long time and make a lot of money, right? Then take the day off.' That just didn't happen in my day. Heck, I remember Sam Huff telling me how he went to [Giants owner] Wellington Mara to ask for a guaranteed contract, and Mara threw Huff out of the office. I mean, when I played with the Browns, you were too ashamed to say you were hurt and couldn't play. I'd guess that is why most of us are limping today."

Modzelewski has had back surgery. His left ankle swells up most days. His shoulders are very sore. That's the price you pay for being square, for refusing to buckle no matter how often you were hit.

"The most I made was $21,500 in my final year with the Browns," he said. "That was for a guy who played fourteen years and 180 consecutive games. I used to tell my wife, 'All this pain wouldn't bother me now if I'd made a million bucks.' But you know what? I exercise a little and I stretch. I take two drinks a day and I look at the ocean. And I'd do it all over again. Every play, every minute. Yes, I would. Lord, I loved it so much."

LOU GROZA

Lou Groza meets you at the door, wearing a shy smile and a nice blue tie. His steps are small, slow but certain—souvenirs of two hip replacement operations and twenty-one years of pro football.

Groza lives in a comfortable house in Berea, the same house for the last thirty-four years. That tells you a lot about the man.

So does this: "I hate controversy."

And this: "My parents always told me to treat people how I was treated and to look people in the eye when you shake their hands. I took that to heart."

And this: "When the Browns moved, I felt like I lost a close relative. I was so upset that I couldn't even talk to anyone the day it happened. I now know why it happened, but I still don't understand why. I just know it still hurts."

No one played for the Browns longer than Groza. Most fans remember him as "The Toe," who kicked for the team for twenty-one years and was the only player to have been on all eight of their championship teams. He also was an offensive tackle from 1946 to 1959.

"I'd block some guy, he'd step on my foot—then I'd have to get out of the mud and go kick a field goal on the next play," he said. "I wore my square-toed kicking shoe even when I was playing tackle."

Groza was 6′3″ and weighed more or less 250 pounds (well, probably more than 250) when he played for the Browns. Most of us remember him approaching the ball—taking exactly two and a half steps each time, every time—and booming the ball through the goal posts.

We also remember a healthy gut hanging over his football pants.

"I tried to watch my weight when I played," Groza said, laughing. "And I just kept watching it. Believe it or not, I was the smallest of the four boys in our family. My father weighed over 300 pounds."

Groza was born in 1924. He is from the generation that grew up during the Depression, fought the last great war to keep America safe, then set out to make life better for their children.

Groza will tell you about Martins Ferry, an Ohio River town near Wheeling, West Virginia. He'll tell you how smoke in the air and soot on the windows were good signs.

"That meant money and that meant jobs," he said.

He was born above Groza's Tavern on Main Street. His father had emigrated from Hungary at age twelve. He worked in the coal mines, where he earned the nickname "Big Spot." That came from the day when one of the company mules near the mines kicked him in the eye, creating a huge shiner.

"My father's brother also worked in the coal mines," Groza said. "There was a cave-in, and his brother ended up with brain damage. It was so bad that they had to put him in an institution. That was it for my father in the mines. He was determined to spend the rest of his life working aboveground."

So he opened a pool hall, then the tavern. Groza remembers his mother making six pies every day to sell at the tavern.

Groza said his father's tavern was an orderly place partly because his father was all of 300 pounds—and partly because he had a pistol behind the bar, even though he never had to use it.

"Our family never really left that tavern because it was open almost all the time," he said. "Each of us had chores and we did them. My father never tolerated much nonsense."

He learned his kicking from older brother Frank, and he practiced booting footballs between telephone poles and over power lines. They played pickup games at a place called Mill Field, near the steel mills. There was ash in the air, but no one much cared. Afterward, they swam in the Ohio River.

"No one talked about pollution," he said. "We knew the river was dirty, but no one worried much about it."

Groza still loves that town on the Ohio River, and while most of the mills have closed, the spirit of the place remains. The Wheeling, West Virginia area (which includes Martins Ferry, Ohio) was rated among the country's ten safest places in terms of violent crime by the FBI in 1994.

"Last time I went to Martins Ferry, the bar was gone," Groza said. "It was just an empty lot. But on the corner near the bar, I found the curb where I had carved my initials, and they were still there."

So were the lessons from his parents, lessons that pushed him to study hard, to attend college and become somebody. So Lou Groza, All-State football player, All-State basketball player, member of the National Honor Society, and the kid his friends called "Big Chief," earned a scholarship to play football for Paul Brown at Ohio State.

"My high school coach had played at Ohio State," he said. "He introduced me to Paul Brown, who said, 'The best we can do is give you a
scholarship and a job loading trucks for $50 a month.' So I worked at
Davis Baby Beef, loading trucks along with Bill Willis, who later played
with me on the Browns. Until I went to college in Columbus, the far-
thest I had been away from home was a weekend trip to see relatives in
Cleveland. I went to college with one suit on my back, and just enough
clothes to fill one bag—that was all I owned."

As you listen to Groza, you realize that he loves football. But it wasn't
the game that shaped him. It was life on the Ohio River, and his time
in the Pacific.

That's because after a year at Ohio State, he was drafted into the U.S.
Army. The year was 1943.

Groza said his time in the Pacific was no big deal. He said millions
of men have stories like his. You went out and did your duty—that was
nothing special. All of that might be true, but those of us from later
generations still need to hear what these men did in that war. Their
stories are important, because they tell us so much about our country's
history. Groza was a "surgical technician," which means he helped the
first level of doctors, guys in tents only a few miles behind the front
lines. His first stop was Leyte, in the Philippines, and then Okinawa.

"I remember getting out of a [landing craft] on the beach at Leyte,"
he said. "It was the first time I saw combat. A guy about ten feet from
me was shot. It about took his face off. Then another soldier went over
and took money out of his wallet."

Groza stared at the man robbing the dead. "The guy said, 'Well, he
won't need it anymore,'" Groza said, shaking his head. "That shows you
how brutal it can be."

Then Groza found it could be worse.

"After one of the battles, they put me in charge of one of the details
to dig up the bodies that had been buried on the beach so we could put
them in boxes and send them home," he said. "That was worse than the
battle itself."

Groza often paused as he talked about his war. Just when you thought
he was finished, something else came to mind.

"My job was to get guys ready for surgery," he said. "It was always dirty and muddy over there. Guys would be wounded and brought to us caked with mud. I'd wash them down, especially around the wound, so that the doctor could operate. Then I'd do anything else the doctor wanted. One day, a friend of mine showed up at the hospital. He said he was jumping into a hole when he was shot through the cheek and the bullet went right out of his mouth. He sort of laughed about it. Then he told me that I was lucky I wasn't on the front lines. If they put me up there, I'd be such a big target that there was no way they'd miss me."

Groza spent nearly two years in the Pacific. He was to have been part of the invasion of the Japanese mainland. Those who criticize Harry Truman's decision to drop the atomic bomb never talked to men such as Groza.

"If you were there, you know he did the right thing," he said. "That saved a lot of lives, both Japanese and American. You have no idea how fierce the fighting was over there."

Was he ever wounded?

"Nah," he said. "Just a terrible case of roundworm. I got it while taking a shower. Made me sick as a dog."

Paul Brown began sending Groza letters and a contract to sign with the Cleveland franchise in the new All-American Football Conference. Groza signed for $7,500—"very good money for 1946," he said. "I went to my first pro training camp in army fatigues and carrying all my clothes in a duffle bag."

He played tackle and kicked for the Browns in the late summer and fall, then went to Ohio State in the winter. He was an All-Pro football player in Cleveland and an honors student at Ohio State, earning a degree in business in 1949.

"None of us thought football would be anything but a job for a few years," he said. "We all figured we'd have to get real jobs. That's why I sold insurance."

In Groza's study there is a gold shoe, the one he used to kick the winning field goal in the 1950 championship game. He said he never felt special pressure on that or any kick. He says the key was his four-step approach to kicking: stance, approach, contact, follow-through. He shows you a football and how he aimed for a spot near the middle of the ball, "on the seams, just under the center part."

Groza was a fixture with the Browns from 1946 to 1967 (although he sat out the 1960 season with an injury and was presumed to be retired.) "Lou was the Browns to me," said John Morrow. "When I was traded to Cleveland, I was assigned to be Lou's roommate. I showed up at Hiram for training camp. Those rooms were so small, and it was sticky hot in August. One bed was by the window, one by the wall. I took the bed by the window, leaving my bags on it. I left the room for a second, and returned to find Lou standing there, staring at the bed. He wanted to know who the hell I was to take his bed by the window. That was the only time we ever had a disagreement."

The other Browns players love Groza, who was the consummate teammate and family man. Paul Brown even called Groza "My Louie" when referring to him in private.

"After some of those two-a-day practices at Hiram, Lou would grill some steaks," Morrow remembered. "Afterward, we'd go for a ride in the countryside. I had an Olds 98 convertible, and we'd light up a couple of good cigars. It was great to sit there in that car, the farms going by on a warm summer night, with a good cigar. Later that night, Lou would sneak into Frank Ryan's room. Ryan was a heavy sleeper, and Lou would take that stinky cigar butt and leave it by Frank's pillow so Frank would wake up in the morning and smell it."

"Lou is special to me," said Jim Kanicki. "When I joined the Browns in 1963, Lou was old enough to be my father, but he'd kick off, then run 40 yards down the field and tackle someone. Because he was just a kicker then, he had time for practical jokes, like putting a dead rat in someone's shoe or hot powder in someone's jock."

But in 1964, the Browns brought in Dick Van Raaphorst to compete with Groza for the kicking job in training camp. He had grown up down the street from Groza in the Cleveland suburb of Berea. Groza had tutored him in high school. While Van Raaphorst set some kicking records at Ohio State, he wasn't prepared for the first day of camp.

"Lou and the kid were kicking at the same time," Tom Melody recalled. "Instead of starting someplace easy like the 20-yard line, Lou said, 'Let's begin at the 40.' Lou boomed it through the uprights. Then he moved back to the 45-yard line, and boomed another field goal. After two kicks, the kid was broken mentally. Lou was already old and fat in 1964, but he was a legend. To a kid like Van Raaphorst, Lou *was* placekicking."

As famous as Groza was for his kicking and his cigars, he was the veteran who invited rookies to dinner and helped them find apartments. He and his wife, Jackie, were known as the Browns' First Family. All the while, he kept selling insurance, something he does to this day.

Groza is now in the Hall of Fame. The days of tackles who kick are over, and straight-on kickers such as Groza are extinct.

"I don't know why all the kids kick soccer-style," he said. "They kick the ball with the side of their foot, which is supposed to give them better control. I don't know, I never tried it. I'll tell you, I always thought of myself more as a tackle than a kicker, at least until I couldn't play tackle anymore."

Groza played twenty-one years with the Browns, "and I signed twenty-one contracts, all for one year," he said. "My top salary was $50,000 in my last season [1967]."

He is a man who has been married since 1950, and who, along with his wife, Jackie, raised four children. *Sport Magazine* once wrote: "Lou Groza doesn't break training, punch referees or insult reporters. As a result, he only gets his name in the paper when he kicks."

Just a kicker? No, Lou Groza was so much more than that.

PAUL WARFIELD

To understand Paul Warfield, you need to know about his family.

You've heard that Warfield was one of the classiest people ever to wear a Browns uniform. You talk to him for five minutes, and you realize that he is as graceful in person as he was as a Hall of Fame wide receiver.

Then you listen to the story of how Warfield became a member of the Cleveland Browns, and you realize that you're hearing the story of millions of black families after the Depression.

It starts with his father, Dryden Warfield.

"He was always very prominent in the Baptist Church," Warfield said. "He was a deacon until he was eighty-two years old. During the week, he worked the swing shift at Republic Steel in Warren, Ohio. That meant he was always rotating shifts—one week it was days, the next afternoons, and then overnight. So sometimes, we didn't see him much during the week. But on weekends we did, and we spent a lot of time with him in church."

Today, most people would scream and file grievances if they had to work changing shifts like Dryden Warfield. But Dryden Warfield knew the steel mills were a good deal, even if it meant sleep never came easy. Just when you got used to sleeping at night, you had to work when it was dark and then try to find a way to keep the sunlight out of your bedroom windows.

But that was fine with Dryden Warfield, who grew up in Guthrie, Kentucky, near the Kentucky-Tennessee border. It was a place where blacks felt the walls of history closing in. The Civil War and Reconstruction seemed to have missed Southern towns such as Guthrie. Jim Crow ruled. It wasn't just "separate but equal" for blacks, it was a way of life that amounted to legal slavery.

"The only future for my father was sharecropping, just as his parents had done," Warfield said. "It really was no future, because you never were going to earn enough money to own your own farm."

But sharecropping was all blacks knew in Guthrie, at least until Dryden's brother joined the Merchant Marines. He traveled across the country. He saw that everywhere was not like Guthrie, that those factories and smokestacks in the North meant jobs, money, and some semblance of dignity, even for blacks. When his military duty was finished he followed the smoke to the steel mills in Pittsburgh. There blacks worked next to whites, and because of the union, blacks earned as much as whites. The work was hard, long, and dirty. But it was also an honest job, a job with health benefits and a pension.

Today all this is a given, blacks and whites working together in a factory. But in the 1940s, it seemed like a miracle to the blacks from the South—even if they were painfully aware that nearly all the foremen and union bosses were white. They believed the door of opportunity had been cracked open, and it was time for them to knock it down and take their place in the same room with mostly white men.

"My uncle wrote my father and said there was a steel mill outside Warren, Ohio, that was hiring," Warfield said. "He was going to work there, and he told my father to join him. My dad immediately left for Warren."

Dryden Warfield made the pilgrimage north. He had no idea what he'd find in Warren; he had never even heard of it until his brother's letter. But he pinpointed the town on a map, scraped together enough money for a bus ticket, and he was gone.

"You can look at all the towns between Cleveland and Pittsburgh that we now call the rust belt," Warfield said. "Places such as Youngstown, Canton, Warren, and Sharon, Pennsylvania—all of them were built around the steel industry and nearly all of the black families living in those areas came from the South to work in those mills. There were good jobs for the black male heads of families, jobs that meant their children would always have decent clothes, shelter, and food. We were never wealthy. But because of the mills, we were never poor, either."

Paul Warfield was born in 1942 in Warren.

He grew up with church, with people who went to work, and with sports. But his mother was nervous about football, worried about her only son being turned into a pretzel. She looked at him in junior high and thought, "Paul is just so skinny."

Baseball was a good game for her son. So was basketball. Track, too. Not football.

"I played all those other sports in junior high," Warfield said. "But during football season, I delivered newspapers. When I was in the ninth grade, I wanted to play football so much, but my mother still wouldn't allow it. I went to my father, and he talked her into it. In my first practice, they handed me a pair of shoulder pads and I didn't even know how to put them on. And once I did get them on, I couldn't figure out how you were supposed to wear those pads and catch a football, too."

He figured it out.

The first time he carried the ball in a game was in his sophomore year. He went 50 yards for a touchdown.

"I had just moved up to the varsity, and they didn't even have my name on the program," Warfield said. "I heard the public address announcer say, 'That was a 50-yard scoring run by . . .' He stopped, because no one knew my name."

It wasn't long before everyone at Warren Harding High knew Warfield's name. By his junior year, he was a star running back. In his senior year, every major college in the country wanted him, not only because he was a great running back, but because he was also an excellent student and a model citizen.

"Woody Hayes came to my house and convinced my parents that Ohio State was the only place for me," Warfield said. "He was a great salesman. He told my parents that he would personally look out for my welfare and guarantee that I'd get a good education. That impressed them, how he promised I'd go to class and do my work. He hardly mentioned football. My parents left the decision up to me, but I really didn't want to go to school very far from home. Woody had made such an impression on my parents that it seemed like the right place to go."

Over thirty years later, Warfield still likes the decision.

"In terms of football, Ohio State played a grind-it-out style, which was not best for me," he said. "But Woody Hayes really did care about education. I liked and trusted the man, and I got a degree in education and a minor in physical education. Woody Hayes's father was a school superintendent. He felt his primary job with us was to make sure we got a degree, not to prepare us for the NFL. He was dead serious about us being good people and representing the school and ourselves well. There was nothing phony about Woody Hayes."

And Paul Warfield is the kind of player who made Hayes proud.

Even a year after he was fired as the Browns coach, Paul Brown still had an eye for talent and he still was sending players to the Browns.

Right before the 1964 draft, this letter arrived at Art Modell's office.

"Dear Mr. Modell,

"My recommendation for this year is that the Browns draft Paul Warfield high up and they draft him as a defensive back."

Paul Brown was still being paid $82,500 annually by Modell. He agreed to act as a "superscout," occasionally checking out games at Ohio State and reporting on games he saw on TV.

Paul Brown loved Ohio State players, and he was enamored with Paul Warfield. Modell took the letter to Blanton Collier; Collier was very familiar with Warfield.

"I like him, too," Collier said. "But I think his future may be as a receiver."

It was hard to know what Paul Warfield should play, but it was clear that this young man was a terrific football player. At Ohio State, Woody

Hayes used Warfield as a running back and a defensive back. What Hayes really wanted was Warfield on the field, and in his senior year no member of the Buckeyes played more minutes than Warfield.

Warfield was 6-foot and 180 pounds. In high school, he set Ohio records in the 100-yard dash, the 180-yard hurdles, and the long jump. He was a premier sprinter in college during the spring, then starred for Woody Hayes in the fall. At Ohio State, he caught 39 passes in his career, and carried the ball 191 times.

Maybe that was why Paul Brown envisioned Warfield as a defensive back. Or perhaps Brown was aware that the team's weakest spot was the secondary, with Bernie Parrish being the only reliable veteran.

As time has passed, some members of the Browns organization have tried to imply that Paul Brown's judgment about Warfield was wrong because he wanted Warfield on defense. Actually, it made a lot of sense. Furthermore, Paul Brown's main point was that Warfield would be a tremendous player almost regardless of position, and the Browns had better not squander a chance to draft him.

They didn't.

"We didn't know it at the time, but the Browns had just signed the most gifted football player I'd ever see," recalled Tom Melody. "He was like the Michael Jordan of receivers. He'd just glide through his patterns. You'd swear his feet weren't even touching the ground. He was so smooth, he had to be flying."

Blanton Collier saw that immediately.

Not long after drafting Warfield, the Browns held an informal workout for him at Lakewood High in suburban Cleveland.

Imagine an NFL team today taking its top draft pick to a high school field, to decide if he were a receiver or a defensive back.

"It was a one-day minicamp," Warfield said. "I had a physical in the morning. Then they did some classroom work just so I'd have a few patterns to run. They gave me a Browns T-shirt, a pair of shorts, and we went out on the field at Lakewood High. They had a guy guarding me named Billy Truax, who was our second-round pick and a defensive end at LSU. They were making him into a linebacker. No way could he guard me.

"I remember making one good catch, and hearing Dub Jones say, 'Forget about being a defensive back.' That made me feel really good."

Jones was the Browns' offensive coordinator, and a star receiver with the Browns from 1948 to 1955. He and Collier stood next to each other, watching Warfield. According to Blanton Collier's daughter, Kay Collier Slone, the two coaches were smiling and winking at each other. They immediately knew that Warfield was special, that he was about to change their offense.

The Browns then hired former receiver Ray Renfro to work with Warfield during training camp.

"Ray had just retired," Warfield said. "He was a great receiver, and he was unequivocally the best teacher I could have ever had. I had the speed and quickness, but I had no idea what it took to be a receiver. Ray Renfro built the fundamental base for me that I used all thirteen years in pro football. By the end of training camp, I know that Blanton and some of the other coaches couldn't figure out why I was doing certain things to get open. They were veteran moves, Ray Renfro's moves."

The two men would head out to the field by themselves. They'd first walk through a pattern, then trot through it. Then run three-quarters speed. Finally, the fourth time, they ran the pattern. Renfro had special drills designed to create fakes and sharp movements to confuse a defensive back and give Warfield just a bit of an opening.

One of Renfro's drills was to count to yourself 1-2-3, while taking three steps in one direction, then 1-2-3 and three steps in another direction. You could still walk to the same place, but you changed directions ever so slightly.

"I did that walking down the street, through hotel lobbies, you name it," Warfield said.

It was a way of coordinating your feet and your mind.

"In my first exhibition game, the first pass I caught went for a touchdown," Warfield recalled. "It was a post pattern."

When the rookie came off the field, he couldn't wait to see Renfro.

"I thought Ray would embrace me," he said. "Instead, he said, 'What are you going to do the next time?'

"I asked, 'The next time?'

"He said, 'The next time. You just ran a post pattern. You think that will work again? Do you have a variation you can use on it?'

"I said, 'I didn't think of that.'

"He said, 'Always think of the next time. You can make your next pattern look exactly like that post pattern, but then cut at the last moment in the opposite direction to the flag. Think about it.'

"People talk about me having a great rookie year. Well, it never would have happened if the Browns hadn't hired Ray Renfro to work with me in training camp."

Or as Chuck Heaton wrote in the *Plain Dealer* on July 16, 1964: "Pay dirt was really struck, however, if we can believe what we are seeing at this camp for rookie receivers and passers. Paul Warfield very well may be the finest football prospect to hit training camp since Jim Brown crashed the scene in 1957. . . . He has the muscular legs of a sprinter and a compact, solid body that should be able to take the knocks of pro football. . . . He runs a 9.6 in the 100 yard dash, but he is more than a track man turned football player. . . . It is a pleasure to watch No. 42 work his way down field."

Dick Schafrath said it best: "Paul was so fluid, he was like an antelope."

Even before his first regular season game, Warfield received this praise from Blanton Collier: "Paul has the potential to be the best receiver I've ever seen in the NFL. If he doesn't develop, it will be a terrible waste of talent."

Collier didn't have to worry, because Warfield left nothing to chance.

The night before a game, Warfield sat in bed and visualized the patterns he'd run the next day. He saw Frank Ryan's passes. He saw the man guarding him. He saw the moves he'd make to free himself, and he saw himself catching those passes from Ryan.

He walked through the hotel lobby thinking, "One-two-three," and doing the slight changes of direction that Ray Renfro taught him. In his hotel room he often paced smaller versions of his pass patterns.

"On game day, I'd go out on the field early, before anyone else was there," Warfield said. "I'd walk through my patterns and moves. I needed to do this to beat the complicated coverages that I'd be facing. I also wanted to feel the turf under my feet. Was it hard? Slippery?"

Now you know why Warfield immediately fit in with the group that was the 1964 Browns. He was a rookie, but his approach was as if he had played for ten years under Mr. Visualization himself, Blanton Collier. He wanted to understand the game. He enjoyed bringing those cold Xs and Os on the blackboard to life.

"I didn't feel under any pressure in 1964," Warfield said. "Not being on the same team with Gary Collins and Jim Brown. Collins already was a star receiver. Jim Brown was Jim Brown. Frank Ryan was established as the quarterback. I just had to fit in."

What Warfield did was lead the team with 52 catches, averaging nearly 18 yards every time he touched the ball. It was the most catches by a Browns receiver since 1952.

"Paul gave us a dimension we didn't have before," Ryan recalled. "He was so fast, and great at getting open. Gary Collins was equal to Paul as a receiver, but if Gary was open, he needed to be *way* open to score. He had good speed, but not blinding speed like Paul. Paul was a guy who could catch a pass and go 80 yards for a touchdown. Now we had receivers on both sides of the line who were tremendous threats, and we had Jim Brown in the backfield. It just opened up the field for us."

By the 1964 title game, Warfield was such a threat that he drew double coverage from the Colts—while Gary Collins was guarded one-on-one, which helped Collins to have such a huge day.

Warfield was a star with the Browns until 1970, when he was traded to Miami for the draft rights to Mike Phipps. It remains one of the worst trades in Browns history.

"I know the Browns didn't want to trade me," Warfield said. "But they felt they had to get a young quarterback because of Bill Nelsen's knees. When the Browns called Miami about trading for the pick, the Dolphins asked who the Browns' untouchable players were. The Brown said Leroy Kelly and myself. They asked for me, and eventually the Browns gave in. The Dolphins knew the Browns were in love with Mike Phipps, and they said they'd draft Phipps and then demand even more than me in a trade later, so the Browns gave me."

Warfield was stunned by the deal.

"When you came to the Browns, there was such an overpowering tradition," he said. "You knew how to behave, and you knew that the team was going to be good every year. I was so proud to wear those colors. Growing up, the Browns were my team. I remember going to Cleveland Stadium for the first time when I was in elementary school. It was so overwhelming, so big, that I never figured I'd be special enough to play there. So when I did get that chance, you can be sure that the last thing I ever wanted to do was be traded."

Especially not to Miami. Not in 1970.

"In 1969, *Sports Illustrated* did an article saying the Dolphins were the worst team in pro football," he said. "And I was just traded to them. I was upset, but I was a good employee."

Just as his father worked whatever shift was needed at the steel mill, Warfield did as he was told in football.

"I didn't think I deserved to be traded, but I had signed a contract and the Browns had the right to do it," he said. "I wasn't a trouble-maker. I had no choice to go, so I went."

And to his utter astonishment, Warfield played in three Super Bowls with Miami, winning two.

"Things worked out great, but Cleveland and the Browns were always my home team," he said.

Warfield is now in the pro football Hall of Fame. For a time, he worked in Cleveland television, and later in the Browns' player person-nel department. He is the kind of dedicated, intelligent man who has been sought for several business ventures. He now owns his own sports marketing company that sells NFL-licensed caps and shirts, mostly in Florida.

"What I remember most about playing for the Browns was the player introductions," Warfield said. "You'd run down that dark tunnel and see the light at the end of it. As we came out and up the dugout steps, those 80,000 fans would roar. I mean, roar. They shook that old stadium. I feel very lucky to have heard those kind of cheers. Few people do."

DICK SCHAFRATH

State Senator Dick Schafrath will tell you that he spends far too much time in a suit and tie. In fact, if you drop in at his office in the Ohio State Capitol after 5 p.m., Schafrath will excuse himself and change into a work shirt and jeans.

"This is how I'm most comfortable," he said. "It's how I grew up."

The man who was a thirteen-year player with the Browns and a six-time Pro Bowl selection never saw a professional football game when he was a kid on a farm in rural Wooster, Ohio, in the 1940s and 1950s.

"We didn't have a TV," he said. "Heck, I never even took a shower until I was in the ninth grade and made the high school football team. All we had was a bathtub at home. The whole family took a bath on the same night, one at a time. I always went last. You weren't allowed to change the water. By the time I got to the tub, it was pretty dirty. I used to take a bath, then to really wash off, I'd head out to the horse and cow trough and jump in. That water was cleaner, even if it was freezing."

Schafrath told this story in his impressive office in the Ohio Capitol, the one with his name in gold letters on the door. He has been a Republican Ohio state senator from District 19. He came to Columbus for the first time in 1985 after winning a close election. Since then, he has been reelected twice with nearly 65 percent of the vote.

When he isn't in politics, he's in the water. He owns a canoe livery in Loudonville, Ohio, which is near Mohican State Park in central Ohio.

"I look around me, and I'm amazed by all this," he said, meaning his office, the Ohio Capitol, and his life today.

Schafrath talked about the 200-acre farm, about growing corn and wheat, and about milking cows.

"We had a phone, but it was one of those party lines that went to ten houses," he said. "You could never have a phone conversation without the entire area knowing about it. We had only three lightbulbs in the entire house. That was a way to keep the light bill low. There were eleven of us kids. The boys slept three to a bed."

Schafrath's father was suspicious of post–World War II America. He refused to own a tractor, plowing his fields with horses and mules.

"When we tilled something small like the vegetable garden, he put the harness on me, and my brothers or sisters would stand on the plow," Schafrath said. "My dad would make the farm chores into a game. When it came to pitching manure, it was, Who could spread manure the fastest? Who could mow hay the fastest? Or shock wheat the fastest? If a guy came down with a tractor, Dad would challenge him to the same work using his horses."

But his father had no use for sports. None whatsoever. Thought it was a waste of time. Couldn't understand why Schafrath was playing sport after sport, and he seldom watched his son play. Watching sports was even a bigger waste of time than playing, even though his son was a three-sport star at Wooster High.

"We weren't Amish, but we were almost like the Amish," Schafrath said. "I had to walk home from school five miles every night after basketball or whatever sport had practice. Then I was up at five the next morning to milk the cows. Occasionally, my father would give me a quarter and I'd be allowed to ride my bike five miles to town. I never even had a date in high school. All I had was my bike, and I always had to be home by ten o'clock. What girl was going to think that would be a great night out?"

How good a high school athlete was Schafrath?

"All the major schools were recruiting me," he said. "Blanton Collier was coaching at Kentucky, and I remember him coming to the farm to meet my parents. But the guy who really made an impression was Woody Hayes. He came on a Sunday, and went to church with our family. Then he and my mother planned a cookout at the farm. There he was with an apron on, flipping burgers. After lunch, Woody and my father headed out to the barn, and they talked for a long time out there with the cows and pigs. Woody hardly spoke to me, he just talked to my parents. When he left, he kissed my mom goodbye.

"A little while later, I told my mother, 'I wasn't real impressed with Coach Hayes and Ohio State. He hardly said a word to me.'

"My mother said, 'Son, you are going to Ohio State.'

"That was it, I went to Ohio State."

Schafrath's mother wanted her son to attend college. She knew there was more to life than the farm and the rolling countryside of central Ohio.

"When I left for Ohio State, my father was convinced it was a break with the family, that I'd never come back to the farm," he said. "Dad had an eighth-grade education. He knew the farming business well. He was groomed so that everything was work, no play."

And he couldn't understand why Ohio State was willing to give his son a free education to play football . . . or why his son would want to move all the way to Columbus and throw away four years on a football field, four years that could have been spent on the farm.

Schafrath insisted he was "eleventh string" as a freshman at Ohio State. He was lonely and lost in Columbus and he wanted to quit the team, but his mother wouldn't allow it. So he intentionally failed two courses, believing that would get him kicked out of school. At this point, he was worried that his father was right—he never should have left the farm. "Right before I thought I was going home for the summer," Schafrath recalled, "Woody told me, 'You are going to summer school to make up those courses.' I said I was going home.

"Woody said, 'You're staying.'

"Then he convinced my mother and father to come to Columbus, and they told me that I had to stay in summer school. Woody was like that. He knew how to get you to do things. One of the courses Woody put me into that summer was something like a Theory of Football course. It was taught by one of the assistant coaches. It was only supposed to be three days a week, but I went five days and they taught me how to become an offensive lineman. I spent ninety minutes every day, blocking. Then I'd play handball about every day, against Woody and his assistants. We didn't lift weights back then, it was all exercises—chin-ups, push-ups, stuff like that."

By his sophomore year, Schafrath was starting, playing on both the offensive and defensive lines.

"I never had a regular position," he said. "Woody used me at every spot on both lines. He once apologized to me, saying, 'You'd be an All-American if I played you at only one position.' But I didn't care. I was so happy just to play. Besides, I never thought about pro football. I knew I didn't have great speed. And I couldn't put on weight. I weighed around 220, but I'd lose twenty pounds during most games—then spend the rest of the week eating trying to put that weight back on."

When the NFL held its 1959 draft, Schafrath paid no attention. He went to Florida with three friends for a vacation. One night, he called home and his mother said, "You've been taken by the Browns."

Schafrath didn't understand.

"The Browns drafted you," she said. "In the second round."

Schafrath was stunned. The Browns had never spoken to him. No NFL team did. But Paul Brown liked having Ohio State players on his team. There was no need for him to talk to Schafrath—he had been watching the kid's career for years.

"I used to think I was a good baseball player, a catcher," Schafrath said. "When I got out of college, I was going to try pro baseball. I wanted to play baseball in college, but Woody Hayes wouldn't let me. If I didn't make it in baseball, then I was going to join the military. All I knew was that I was going to get the heck off that farm."

And Schafrath did, thanks to the Browns.

He spent thirteen years as an offensive tackle with the Browns. You'd never know it by looking at him: He's 6´1˝ and about 210 pounds.

"I played at 250," he said.

How? There is no way. Not on his thin build.

"You have to understand," he said. "If I wanted to play for the Browns, I had to weigh close to 250."

And no one ever wanted to wear the orange and brown more than Schafrath.

Jim Brown tells the story about Schafrath as a rookie, how he weighed only 222 when the Browns drafted him out of Ohio State in 1959. Paul Brown wanted Schafrath on the offensive line, and he wanted Schafrath to weigh 250.

"One day, I looked at Schaf and he was stuffing little weights in his pockets right before he stepped on the scales for the weigh-in," Brown said.

Unfortunately for Schafrath, Paul Brown thought, "This kid can't weigh 250."

So Paul Brown told Schafrath, "Take off your pants."

The pants dropped to the floor with a thud. The scale read: 225. Schafrath promised to eat like a grizzly bear fattening up for the winter.

"Browns players remember Dick having four huge steaks in one sitting," said Kevin Byrne, the Browns' former public relations director. "During training camp, he'd eat sandwich after sandwich at lunch, then stuff himself with bananas. The guys said it hurt just to watch him eat that much."

After his rookie season, Schafrath had a construction job. He told the guys about needing to weigh 250 by training camp.

"They made me an iron jockstrap that weighed about twenty-five pounds," he said. "On the first day, Paul Brown was there and I got on the scale. I weighed 250. Paul made me weigh myself again. Still 250. Then he began to feel around my shirt, then my pants. He found the world's heaviest jock. Paul said, 'Okay, now you need to go out and really put on some weight.' I started lifting weights like crazy, but that wasn't enough."

Schafrath played in an era when athletes weren't supposed to drink water during games. It was thought to cause stomach cramps.

"After most games, I was completely dehydrated and they didn't know how to handle it," he said. "I'd have cramps from head to toe.

Sometimes, they had to take me to the hospital and feed me intravenously. You'll never believe this, but within four hours after a game, I'd drink a case of beer and then a case of pop, trying to put back on the weight I'd lost."

There was more.

"White Castle hamburgers," he said. "There were eight to a box of those little hamburgers. I'd order six boxes and eat forty-eight of them in a sitting."

And even more.

"I drank a lot of beer, I mean beer by the case," he said. "I never drank in high school, but back then people thought beer was a form of food and a great way to put on weight."

Schafrath would have 40-to-50-pound weight swings within a few weeks, but the weight he added was the worst kind.

"Now, I think of what I did to my body and it scares the hell out of me," he said. "But I was so desperate to stay on the team. My first season was 1959, and they had no real position for me. I played offensive end, offensive guard, and defensive end. I had no idea where I fit in."

Before the 1960 season, Lou Groza had to finally give up his job as the starting left offensive tackle. Injuries had reduced him to a full-time kicker. Paul Brown decided Schafrath would replace Groza.

"By then, I got my weight up to 265," he said. "I had to beat out five guys to win the position. Lou Groza was a huge help to me. He could still play football, but his back was bothering him so much that the poor guy couldn't even get down into a three-point stance."

And Schafrath became a great tackle for the Browns.

"When things got tough, Jimmy Brown would ask me, 'Are you ready to be a horse?'" said Schafrath. "I'd tell him that I was ready. I loved Jimmy when he asked me that. I loved the contact. When I played in high school, we had leather helmets and no face masks. My friends tell me that's where I lost my brains. I loved left tackle because it was the toughest position on the offensive line. Because the quarterback is usually right-handed, the man rushing from his left comes from the blind side. For that reason, the left tackle has to hold his block or the quarterback will get killed. The night before games, Jimmy Brown, John Wooten, and myself would get together in a room and we'd go over the plays, figuring which ones would be our 'Attitude Plays,' the plays we really believed would work. Then we'd tell Blanton Collier and

Frank Ryan which running plays would be the most effective against the team we faced that week. Frank Ryan was really responsive. In a key part of the game, he'd ask Jimmy Brown or myself what plays we wanted to try."

The Browns' right tackle was Monte Clark, and he knew exactly what Schafrath was talking about when he said he was the last line of protection for the quarterback.

"Blanton Collier called him 'The Bulldog,'" Clark recalled. "That's because he'd grab on to you and never let go. When he blocked, it was like a bulldog getting his teeth into you."

Schafrath spent thirteen years with the Browns. When he retired in 1971, he had been to the Pro Bowl six different times. He also had put his body through an incredible ordeal.

"Dick played hurt a lot," recalled Tom Melody. "After one game, I had to help him get his shirt on. He couldn't even lift his arm. He told me that when he went home at night, he was too sore to sleep in bed. He just sort of napped in a chair."

Schafrath talks about three broken noses.

He talks about suffering a concussion, thinking he was driving to Hiram, and ending up in Chicago. He believes he had at least six concussions from football.

He talks about tearing a tendon in his right elbow, having it become infected and contracting a form of blood poisoning—yet never missing a game.

And when he stopped playing, he missed the action.

"So I started doing these things," he said.

Like what?

"Like canoeing Lake Erie from one side to another at the widest part of the lake," he said. "No one had ever tried it before. It took me four tries, but the fourth time, I did it. I canoed seventy-eight miles in seventeen and a half hours, nonstop. This was after I had recovered from intestinal cancer. My roommate in the hospital and I used to talk about doing it together. He died from cancer, and I did it for his memory. His name was Sam King."

What else?

"[In 1971] I ran from Cleveland to Wooster," he said. "It was sixty-six miles. I did it in eleven and a half hours, and when I was done, my legs were so cramped up they had to take me to the hospital."

Anything else?

"I used to wrestle Victor the Bear," he said. "Victor was a famous wrestling bear. I used to be able to leg-drop him and get him down, but Victor was too big and round to pin. They wrapped his claws and put a muzzle on his face, but if you hit Victor in the face, he'd get mad and knock you over with one paw. And poor Victor, he had the worst breath you've ever smelled. I mean, horrible! And he was eleven feet when he stood up and weighed 850 pounds, so I really tried to be very nice to Victor when we wrestled."

Remember, this is State Senator Dick Schafrath talking.

"I miss sports and competition," he said. "It's nice to win an election, but in a sport like football, everything can change in a matter of minutes. Every week, you either win or lose a game, and then you come back and play another game. You feel like you're always going forward. But in politics, well, I've worked on some bills for eleven years and still haven't been able to get them passed. You have to lobby. You have to figure out who is telling the truth, who can be trusted. They can take your bill, change it and load it with amendments. It's the opposite of sports, where things are clean. I was elected a state senator, and I'd never been in politics before. So I'm not like a lot of people here, and I've had to learn a lot." He's also paid the price for football.

"It's hard to know if all the gaining and losing weight had anything to do with it, but my heart is in bad shape," he said. "It's fibrillated. Half of it is diseased. I had cancer of the small intestine in 1988, but it was isolated and they removed it. Now I'm fighting prostate cancer. I figure I'll beat that, too."

Doctors tell Schafrath to slow down, to take it easy. He tells them that he'd like to ride a horse from Cincinnati to Cleveland to raise money for charity.

"I loved the physical play on the line, and now I love doing physical things like working on my canoes, lifting and dragging them around," he said. "In a way, I'm a lot like my father. I grew up working hard and I'll probably keep working hard until I drop. I don't know any other way to live."

ERNIE GREEN

Players always preach unselfishness. They talk about putting the team first, about taking true satisfaction from winning. On and on you hear it in professional sports, players telling you that the team matters most.

Fans want to believe them. Fans want players to care about the team as much as they do. They don't want to hear about their contract problems, their disputes with the coach, or how they aren't getting enough commercials.

They want players to think and act like Ernie Green.

"But it wasn't easy being Ernie Green," said Paul Warfield. "He could run the football. He could catch the football. He had the total offensive game. But with the Browns, he had to put all that and his ego aside. He was there to block for Jim Brown."

For a moment, imagine being Ernie Green.

Imagine being in the same backfield as Jim Brown. Imagine knowing that you could gain 1,000 yards in the NFL, if only they'd give you the ball. Imagine knowing that you'd never get the ball—not with Jim Brown there. Not when you and everyone else knew that Jim Brown was the greatest running back who ever lived.

"When I joined the Browns, it was very clear to me that our offense was built around Jim, and that was not about to change," Green said.

Ernie Green didn't debate the point. Green had eyes and a brain. He saw and understood what the Browns had in Jim Brown. But imagine being told that the only way you'll survive in the NFL—or at least with the Cleveland Browns—was learning how to block.

You think about when you played at Louisville, and many considered you the best running back in the history of that school. Your greatest gifts are your speed, your agility, and your intelligence. You not only had to run the ball, you had to know where to run it, how to follow the blockers, when to hit the hole.

But they are asking you to block. Block for Jim Brown. Block for Frank Ryan. Block until you drop.

Furthermore, you know that Jim Brown didn't always appreciate the sacrifices you made. Brown often complimented his offensive linemen, especially guards Gene Hickerson and John Wooten and tackle Dick Schafrath. But he said little about you, something you never quite understood and something Brown never explained.

"Most of us understood what Ernie meant to the team," Paul Warfield said. "He was like most linemen who go unrecognized, unless you happen to be a pulling guard and your picture is there with Jim Brown when Jim ran those sweeps. But Ernie Green spent most of his career in the trenches, where it was dirty, nasty, and tough. On most other teams, he'd have been a featured back. But we had Jim Brown."

If you were Ernie Green, you have spent your life hearing about Jim Brown. Even when someone paid you a compliment, it usually was for your blocking for Brown. Or if you broke free for a long run, it was invariably suggested that you had a huge hole because the defense was keying on Jim Brown. You knew, deep in your heart, that you would never catch a break—at least not as long as you played in the same backfield with Jim Brown.

"That's why we never joked with Ernie about that situation," Warfield said. "I'm sure he wasn't completely happy with it. In his private moments, he had to ask, 'Why is God treating me this way? Why did I end up on the same team as Jim Brown?' But he never said a word. Not one word. He adapted to the situation. He handled it with grace."

Sometimes, Ernie Green had to take a deep breath. Sometimes, he had to say a silent prayer and pretend he didn't hear or see certain things. He had to tell himself not to take slights (real or imagined) personally.

"Ernie was a complete football player," said Jim Ninowski. "But he always caught the brunt of everything. I mean, those defensive ends would go blasting in there—guys outweighing Ernie by fifty pounds— and he'd block them. Blanton Collier loved Ernie because he was so fundamentally sound, and he'd keep Ernie after practice to work with and demonstrate techniques for other players. He worked for the longest time, blocking Bill Glass and the other defensive ends after practice. Blanton did that to teach the defensive ends how to get around that kind of blocker. But in the process, they were beating the hell out of poor Ernie. Let's face it, there had to be times when Ernie knew he was getting crapped on, but he hung in there. I have as much respect for Ernie Green as anyone on that team."

That's why it would have been nice if Jim Brown had said a little more about Ernie Green back in the 1960s. But you can look back through thousands of old newspaper stories quoting Brown on everything from running the ball to race relations, and barely find a word about Green. It may not have been personal. Odds are that Brown simply believed that it really didn't matter who played next to him; he was Jim Brown, he was the offense, beginning and end of story.

But when Ernie Green thought about it thirty years later, he said, "There was no relationship between Jim Brown and me. We were standoffish. Jim is different, always has been, and deserves the right to be different. But Jim Brown was not interested in my opinions, or having someone who was an independent thinker or someone working beside him who didn't idolize him. So we played together in the back-field, then we went our separate ways."

So if you were Ernie Green, that was how it was between you and Jim Brown. It didn't take long for you to figure out that he was Jim Brown, and you were not. And if you were a running back with the Browns and your name wasn't Jim Brown, you'd better be able to block.

"There were times when you could have put a number 60 on my back and put anyone back there to do the blocking," Ernie Green said.

But Green knows better. And if you loved the Browns in the 1960s, you do, too.

As Paul Warfield said, "Ernie Green was very special."

Or as Tom Melody said, "When I covered the Browns, it seemed that I never saw Jim Brown smile—and I seldom saw Ernie Green when he wasn't smiling. Talk about a good man."

Ernie Green grew up in a world that was separate and unequal.

The place was Columbus, Georgia, and the time was the 1940s and 1950s. Green remembers "whites only" restaurants, bathrooms, and drinking fountains. He remembers being relegated to the back of the bus, and told to swim in the town's dirty lakes and streams.

In some ways, this would help him with the Browns. He grew up where life wasn't fair, where you weren't given full credit or allowed to be everything you could.

"I look back now and see that we almost lost an entire region and a group of tremendously bright people because of segregation," Green said. "A lot of the kids I grew up with became lawyers, doctors, and

fighter pilots. One kid went to the University of Maine and became
a major general in the army. But too many kids looked at the world
and just became so disheartened. If you stayed in the deep South, your
opportunities were so limited that it could sap the will right out of you."
Ernie Green was never that way. Ernie Green's parents wouldn't
allow it.

"Recently, I was reading Hillary Clinton's *It Takes a Village*," Green
said. "I thought, that was my neighborhood. We were poor, very poor.
My father drove a truck that delivered feed and supplies to the farms
in the area. I was one of seven kids, and my mother watched us. But
so did every woman in the neighborhood. If you messed up, one of
those ladies was going to rip your butt—and when you got home, your
mother was going to do the same thing. Not every kid was a great kid,
but we just didn't have the problems they do now. We didn't have the
drugs and the violence. I felt protected in that neighborhood."

Green said his mother had faith in the Lord and a passionate belief
that segregation would not prevent her children from succeeding.
Ernie listened. Ernie believed. Ernie Green was the president of his
senior class at Spencer High. He was in the National Honor Society.
He was a great athlete, a good person. And when his father died during
Ernie's senior year, he died proud of his son.

Every major college in the South should have been after Ernie Green.
But this was 1957, this was the South, and Ernie Green was black.

"If I wanted to stay in Georgia, the only schools I could have attended
were the black schools—Clark College, Morehouse, Morris Brown—
those schools," he said. "Most people assumed I was going to Tuskegee
Institute or Florida A&M. But Louisville had recruited a black running
back out of Birmingham named Andy Walker, and he played well for
them. He was about to graduate, and the Louisville coach called Walker's high school coach. That man mentioned my name."

Louisville sent Green a Greyhound bus ticket. Twelve hours it took to
cover those two-lane, blacktop roads through tobacco and cotton fields,
past the Mail Pouch barns, Confederate flags, and the roadside pecan
stands. When Green arrived at the bus station in Louisville, no one
from the college was there to meet him. Remember that he had seldom
ventured away from Columbus, which is on the Georgia-Alabama line.
He was alone and scared. But he also had the presence of mind to look
up the name of Louisville coach Frank Camp in the phone book—yes,

his number was listed. Green called the coach, who sent one of his assistants to pick up the new running back at the bus station.

"They had no film of me and had never scouted me," Green said. "They wanted to try me out. They had a back named Lenny Lyles, who was one of the fastest men in the world in the 200 [meters] at that time. Lyles was drafted by the Baltimore Colts that year. They had me run against Lenny. I beat him out of the blocks, but he caught me down the stretch. I ran some drills for them, caught some passes. It wasn't much."

Then they told Green, "We'll give you a scholarship, room, board, books, and $15 a month laundry money."

"It was the best deal I had," he said. "My mother didn't want me to leave home, but she knew that I had to leave. She knew that Louisville was integrated, that there were more opportunities there. She pushed me to take it."

He did, and he graduated with honors in business.

Oh, he also was a low-round draft pick by the Green Bay Packers.

Most people don't know that Vince Lombardi worshiped Paul Brown. It was Brown who helped Lombardi become the head coach in Green Bay by recommending him to the Packers' owners. Brown often sent players to Lombardi, players who couldn't help Cleveland, but players Brown believed were NFL caliber.

Two of those players were Henry Jordan and Willie Davis, who became All-Pros with the Packers. That was enough for some to suggest that maybe Paul Brown was a little too generous with his young friend Lombardi.

Anyway, Lombardi picked Ernie Green in 1962, and Green found himself in the same backfield with Jim Taylor, Paul Hornung, Elijah Pitts, and Tom Moore. The Packers' No. 1 draft choice in 1962 was Earl Gros, yet another running back, so there was no room for Green.

One day, Lombardi called his mentor, Paul Brown: "Paul, we have a rookie here named Ernie Green from Louisville. He is not going to make my team, but he's good enough to play in the league. Are you interested?"

Brown knew that Lombardi was serious, and Lombardi wanted to return the favor for Davis and Jordan. Until that call, Brown had never given Green a thought. But he looked at his backfield. In 1961, Bobby Mitchell had paired with Jim Brown. But Paul Brown traded Mitchell to Washington for the rights to Ernie Davis, only Davis was already in the early stages of leukemia. Paul Brown was desperate for a running back, so he took Green and agreed to give the Packers a seventh-round draft choice.

"When I came to Cleveland, I was awed by Paul Brown," Green said. "As a kid, I had watched his teams play on TV. He was always in control, and a very sharp dresser with that hat. Before the deal, Vince Lombardi told me how much he respected Paul Brown. Then he said, 'If you demonstrate to Paul Brown that you can play, you'll never have any problems with him.' Paul Brown was a taskmaster. He was demanding. And I never had any problems with him."

In 1962, Green alternated with Charlie Scales as the other back with Jim Brown. When Blanton Collier took over, Green was entrenched as the starter.

"Ernie had a tremendous career with us," recalled Bernie Parrish. "But I remember that there were some guys on the team who thought we should have gotten a big white fullback, a Jim Taylor type, to block for Jim Brown instead of Ernie. I used to argue with those guys, telling them that Ernie was a terrific back, and a helluva blocker, too. The poor guy never got his due."

———

In 1964, guess who led the Browns in touchdowns?

Ernie Green.

And guess who was fifteenth in the NFL in rushing, despite having fewer carries than any of the players ahead of him?

Ernie Green.

Guess who had no idea of those facts?

It's still Ernie Green.

"I knew I averaged over five yards per carry for my career, and that was very good," he said. "But the rest . . ."

After the 1965 season, Jim Brown retired. Green was twenty-eight years old. He was as ready as he'd ever be to become the Browns' featured back.

"Only we had a young man named Leroy Kelly coming along," Green said.

Ah, yes, Leroy Kelly.

Drafted by the Browns in 1964, Kelly was a return man in his first two seasons. But Jim Brown saw that Kelly was something special. So did the coaches. And, yes, so did Ernie Green.

"The difference was that Leroy was a good blocker and he was willing to block," Green said.

If there was a weakness to Jim Brown's game, it was his blocking. He seldom did it. He was carrying the ball more than anyone in the NFL, and taking an enormous physical pounding, so he was not about to block for Ernie Green or anyone else on those few plays when he could rest.

"Even though Leroy was our primary runner, I felt more a part of the offense after Jim left," Green said. "Leroy was my roommate. We were very close, and he's a hard worker. Leroy is just a good man."

And what meant the most to Green was that Leroy Kelly respected him.

"Ernie taught me so much," Kelly said. "He carried himself so well. He was distinguished. He read a lot of books. He spoke with proper English and had excellent diction. He dressed very well and was a nice man. One year, we both went to the Pro Bowl, and I loved that because it meant so much to Ernie."

That was the 1967 Pro Bowl, the first season after Jim Brown retired. Kelly led the NFL with 1,141 yards rushing, but Green gained 750 yards and averaged 5.2 per carry. He also was second on the team with 45 receptions.

In 1967, Kelly gained 1,205 yards to again lead the NFL in rushing. Green ran for 710 yards, and led the team with 39 receptions. In those two seasons, he demonstrated that he was indeed an all-purpose back.

But typical of Ernie Green's luck, he suffered a major knee injury in 1968, and then retired a year later.

"I hurt it in the first exhibition game of 1968," Green said. "I detached a ligament and didn't even know it. I missed half of that season, then limped through the second half while trying to play."

In the meantime, Green had been preparing himself for the day when he could no longer play. While with the Browns, he was a probation officer in the off-season. Then he worked as a provost at Case Western Reserve University in Cleveland, and was thinking about starting his own business.

During the Jimmy Carter administration, Green formed a business where he served as a coal broker, a middleman between utility companies and coal mines. When the gas crunch ended in the early 1980s, the market for coal shrunk. Then he formed EGI—Ernie Green Industries. Green now runs a multimillion-dollar company that makes things such as wheel covers and center caps for the auto industry. He also owns a company in Kentucky that makes parts used in engine mounts and transmission mounts. Green's headquarters is in Dayton. Of all the 1964 Browns who have been so successful in business, his company is the largest and most ambitious.

"Believe me, this is a full-time job," he said. "I can't play golf every day. I work a lot of hours. When I meet people now, some of them remember me from the Browns—but most of them know me from our companies, from EGI. And that's okay, because I'm very proud of what I've done after football."

GENE HICKERSON

If you want to talk to Gene Hickerson, you'd better be ready to get up early.

"I'm a working man," he tells you. "I'm at the office at seven."

He means that he'll see you at 7 a.m.—sharp.

So you arrive at a company called Anchor Tool & Die on Cleveland's West Side. Hickerson is a massive man. You have no doubt that he was once an offensive lineman. He wears an open-collared work shirt and very sensible pants. Nothing flashy about Hickerson or his office.

You sit down and you ask him about playing for the Browns. He starts to tell you about growing up in Memphis. You mention Paul Brown, he talks about playing college ball at Mississippi.

Suddenly, you realize that you don't interview Hickerson, you listen to him tell stories. He has a wonderful drawl and a regal way with words, turning his bleak office on a gray Cleveland December day into a front porch at the Hickerson homestead in Memphis. All that's missing is the front porch swing and a weeping willow tree.

"The most important man I've ever met in my life is Robert Rier," he said.

Who?

"I dated his wife's sister," continued Hickerson. "I thought he was a bookie."

A bookie?

"By the time he was twenty-eight years old, he had a big home, a big car, a speedboat, his own air-o-plane, and a cabin on a lake," Hickerson said. "All of that by the time he was twenty-eight, like I said. That was something for me to think about, especially since Robert Rier worked no more than four days a week."

You want to ask a question, but you now know better.

"I don't worship money," Hickerson said. "I just like having it. And I looked at Mr. Rier and I said, 'I want to make a lot of money, not for money's sake, but for security.' And there he was, right in White Haven—the part of Memphis where I grew up."

And what gold mine did Robert Rier discover?

"He was a manufacturer's representative," Hickerson said, as if he were whispering the secret to the universe. "He had five clients, and he represented five companies. He put them together. He handled paper mills, air conditioning companies, and some heavy industry. Yes, I learned something from Robert Rier."

Then Hickerson walked over to his file cabinet and brought out a set of blueprints.

"My house," he said. "About 8,000 square feet."

Looks like a great place, based upon the blueprint. Then you remember that Hickerson isn't married. He has a son, but the son is grown. He is living in that mansion—alone.

"His home is mammoth," said Dick Schafrath. "You could have three or four families living in there. The chairs and couches are built for giants. I'd sit there and my legs didn't touch the floor."

Then you remember something that Kevin Byrne told you. Byrne is the former Browns public relations director, and he's related to Hickerson by marriage.

"Gene has a huge plot of land out in Avon Lake [a Cleveland suburb] where he built that house," Byrne said. "His concept was that he was going to have five homes around that house, and he was going to pick the people to live in his compound. His son married my sister, and he wants them to live there. He wants [former Browns tackle] Doug Dieken to live there. So far, no one has moved in, but Gene keeps telling them that 'the opportunity is there.' Gene is a good man."

And a very wealthy man, thanks to the lessons he learned from Robert Rier.

"Gene started working for General Motors, then became a manufacturer's representative," Byrne said. "He gets orders from GM for small steel companies in the Cleveland area. He got so much business for Anchor Tool & Die, they gave him an office. He started that business when he was a player for the Browns, and built it up."

———————————

You try to ask Hickerson about his business, and he tells you about his father.

"My daddy was in the lumber business," he said. "He could read all those numbers and add all those lines—twenty sets of numbers and two lines, and he'd add them all up at once. When he was in his eighties, he walked to a shopping center every day. He'd buy some candy and then stop at the elementary school during recess. He'd pass out that candy. All the teachers and students knew my daddy's name."

You came to visit Hickerson to talk about the 1964 Browns team and about his career. Jim Brown told you that Hickerson was the best lineman ever to block for him, and that it's absolutely criminal that Hickerson isn't in the Hall of Fame.

Hickerson played for sixteen seasons. He was All-Pro seven times. He should be in the Hall of Fame. Mention that to him, and he shrugs. He doesn't say a word, just shrugs.

Then he said, "I was a fullback in high school, a 226-pound fullback and a damn good one."

That was in the early 1950s. Being a 226-pound high school fullback forty-some years ago would be like playing that position at 275 today.

"I was recruited by Ole Miss," he said. "You know what they did? They knew that fullbacks were the strongest and fastest people on the high school football team, so they went out and brought in thirty high school fullbacks, and I was one of them."

Thirty fullbacks?

"That was back before the NCAA had any kind of scholarship limits," he said. "Besides, they kept twenty of us, then ran the rest off. They took all of us fullbacks, looked us over, made us sweat and then switched us to different positions. They started me with the fullbacks, but I got tired of running all of those sprints in that sweltering August Mississippi heat. So I asked to change positions.

"They said, 'How about slot end?'

"I said, 'I want a position where I don't have to run as much.'

"They said, 'What do you have in mind?'

"I said, 'Make me an offensive guard or a defensive end. Let me play somewhere that I don't have to run in all this Lord-awful heat.'

"That is how I became a guard."

Later, Hickerson said that his freshman class "had about 100 recruits." He said, "about half of them went home in the first two weeks, left right in the dead of night. You didn't see them, you just heard them dragging their luggage down the stairs [of the dorms]. They made us practice two and a half hours, twice a day in the 90-degree heat and wouldn't give us a drop of water. It's amazing they didn't just kill us. Only reason I stayed was that the food was pretty good."

Hickerson tells you about coaches named "Bruiser" and "Buster." It seems that everyone back at Ole Miss had a nickname. He tells you that the coaches made the players go to class, "or if you skipped a couple, they sent you home." Hickerson tells you a lot about his time at Ole Miss, how he loved his coaches and teammates. But he doesn't talk about himself as a player. He says, "You know, I saved up $5,000 during my senior year alone?"

Say what?

"I had a lot of things going, business things," he said. "I bought a new car for $3,200, an Oldsmobile 98. That was a lot of money back then."

In college?

"My first two years, I worked at the Firestone Appliance Center. But there were things I wanted that I couldn't afford, like that automobile. So in my last years of college, I was a bar salesman. I got up at 4:45 a.m., every morning. I also owned half an interest in a bar."

This was before the NCAA had rules against athletes working?

Hickerson laughed at the mention of the NCAA.

"There was this lawyer who liked to buy tickets from me, football tickets," Hickerson said. "Every game, I'd sell him four tickets—that was four tickets for $100. These tickets cost me $25, so that was a good deal."

No kidding.

"I never met the man, face-to-face, either," Hickerson said.

Then he paused.

"I wasn't thinking about pro football back then," he said. "It wasn't a big deal, not like today. But I was aware of the Browns. Probably because they were so good in the 1950s, and they were on TV most Sundays back in Memphis. Every Sunday on CBS, I'd watch old Paul Brown coach those boys of his."

By his sophomore season, Hickerson was 6´3˝ and 240 pounds. He was a guard who ran like a fullback. He impressed Paul Brown in the 1956 Cotton Bowl. He was big enough to block like a guard, but so fast, so athletic.

But you don't hear this from Hickerson. It comes from other people.

"But I will tell you about how I came to be with the Cleveland Browns," he said. "Bruiser Kinard was our offensive line coach at Ole Miss, and he was friends with Paul Brown in the old days of the All-American Conference. We were on the team bus, on one of those old two-lane blacktop roads out of Oxford, Mississippi, heading up to Memphis for a game. Bruiser Kinard came to the back of the bus, dropped down into the seat next to me and said, 'Paul Brown told me that he's going to draft you.' I looked at him kind of funny. I was only a junior. As I said, the NFL wasn't something we talked about, not like these college kids today. Then Bruiser, he got up and left before I was able to say a word.

"And sure enough, the Browns drafted me in my junior year."

That was a typical Paul Brown move. He'd check with friends about players, decide whom he liked, and then acquire their rights early. He selected Hickerson in the seventh round of the 1957 draft. If he had waited another year, Hickerson would have been a first-rounder. In his senior season, he was named the best offensive lineman in the Southeastern Conference.

"But Paul Brown didn't know that the Canadian League wanted me, too," Hickerson said. "Mr. P. F. Walker was coaching the Montreal team. I remember him telling me, 'Montreal is Sin City, you'll love that.' He offered me a three-year, no-cut contract worth a total of $50,000. That was much more than the NFL."

But Hickerson could not picture himself in the snows of Montreal, Sin City or not. Cleveland was as far north as he wanted to go, and he wanted to go there because of seeing Paul Brown on CBS, and how his family and friends in Memphis would be able to watch him play on TV.

"Paul Brown's first offer was one year at $7,000," Hickerson said. "I made Paul send [General Manager] Dick Gallagher down to Memphis three times before I signed. I got a $1,000 bonus out of them, plus a first-year salary of $10,000. Paul Brown thought $1,000 was a million dollars. Shoot, he only gave Jim Brown a $1,500 signing bonus, and he was the first-round pick the year Paul Brown drafted me. And poor Jim Shofner, he got no bonus at all."

———————

You ask Hickerson about his career with the Browns, and he tells you about being one of Paul Brown's messenger guards, alternating with Chuck Noll.

"One time, Paul gave me a play and I started to run onto the field," he said. "We were playing the Pittsburgh Steelers. I got out a few steps, then Paul yelled and changed the play. I couldn't hear him, but I knew that time was running out, so I better get out there. By the time I got to the huddle, I couldn't remember the first play, and I didn't hear the second one. So I told Milt Plum to give the ball to Jim Brown. That had to be one of the plays, and Mr. Jim Brown carried that ball right in for a touchdown."

What he liked about pro football was the free time, time to go out and make money.

"We played on Sunday afternoons, which meant we had Sunday nights off after home games," he said. "Paul Brown gave us Monday and Tuesday off."

That was when Hickerson set out to become Robert Rier.

"I'd bring clients to our practices on Saturday afternoon at the Stadium, then we'd go to lunch somewhere downtown after the workout," he said. "Then I'd leave them tickets for Sunday. They started telling their friends about it, and soon I had more clients than I could handle."

Hickerson also was up at 5 a.m. on Monday and Tuesday, using those free days "to do some serious business. A lot of those small shops would open by six in the a.m."

Wasn't that tiring?

"I didn't used to eat lunch when we practiced," he said. "I'd crawl into the equipment room and take myself a nap. One day, I woke up and someone had stuffed my mouth with mud."

Hickerson lived at the old Commodore Hotel. A *Cleveland Press* story mentioned that Hickerson's suite was "a stone's throw from Severance Hall, home of the Cleveland Orchestra."

Hickerson has a different memory.

"I had gotten married and unmarried already," he said. "I vowed never to get married again. In that hotel lived about twenty strippers. They got back about two or three in the morning with the food and the spirits they brought home. Those ladies took very good care of me. I'd go visit them at places they worked, which were very nice clubs."

Hickerson paused for a moment.

"We had a lot of opportunities back then," he said. "We'd go into a city for a game, and we'd have a date on Saturday afternoon. Then we'd have a team meeting on Saturday night, and then I liked to have a couple of huge cheeseburgers and watch TV before I went to bed."

For most of the 1960s, Hickerson was the Browns' second most notable bachelor.

"The other was Mr. Art Modell," he said. "You can say that Art and I spent a lot of time in certain places. He and I are in the Theatrical Grill Hall of Fame."

But later, you find out that Hickerson did attend Cleveland Orchestra concerts. He loves theater, especially grand musicals. He used to know several members of the Cleveland Orchestra back in the 1970s.

He is a man full of surprises.

You ask Hickerson why he played so long—sixteen years, until the age of thirty-seven.

"It was good for my other business," he said.

Hickerson was serious about that.

"Gene didn't cash his checks from the Browns for the last five or six years," said Dick Schafrath. "It was like he wanted to prove a point to Modell. He acted as if he didn't need Modell's money now."

But there must have been more to it than that, more than money and business, you tell Hickerson. It must have been fun.

"Fun?" he asked. "The happiest day of the week was Sunday night when the games were over. You have to understand, I have always been a working man."

Then he paused.

"You know that we trained at Hiram College," he said. "They had us in these little rooms in the girls' dorm. You had to go down the hallway to the bathroom, and when you got there, the plumbing was all wrong. They had no air conditioning or TV in those rooms, and in August in Hiram, Ohio, it can be pretty hot and boring. I roomed with Dick Schafrath. We never had a cross word between us, even though he snored too much."

You want to interrupt, to try and get Hickerson back to the point—but you decide he'll take you where he wants, and when he wants to get there.

"Like I said, it was hot at Hiram," he said. "You could buy an air conditioner for $150 to put into the window. So Schafrath and I put in $75 each. And we put in for one of those little black and white TVs, so we could watch it in our room. Our room was cool. We had a TV. We also had about four guys sleeping in there. They brought their matresses from down the hall and put them on the floor. You had to walk over people to go down the hall to the bathroom. You'd think that the other guys would see the light, that they'd buy their own air conditioner and TV, put it in the trunks of their cars, and bring 'em to training camp—but they never did. You tell me if that was fun."

Yes, it does sound fun.

And here is a Hickerson story from Hiram. It comes from a woman named Brenda Wiseman, who worked in the training camp cafeteria. She told Steve King of the *Medina Gazette:* "Gene was a quiet guy with a shy smile. He was more comfortable with one person than a lot of people. He also had a playful side, and we'd get into food fights with radishes . . . but what I remember most was from 1966. I woke up one morning to discover that my dog of thirteen years had died. I was devastated. I got to work, then went out to the back porch and started crying. Here comes Gene, that giant man, not only asking me what was wrong, but then not laughing at me when I told him. He told me how it was okay to be upset and cry, even though other people might figure, 'It was just a dog.' He was one of my all-time favorites to deal with because he was always a gentleman."

And he was a guard for the ages.

"He was an unparalleled pass blocker," said Monte Clark. "His man would never get to the quarterback. He'd make the rest of us look bad. And he was one of the greatest downfield blockers I've ever seen. When he went out on a sweep, his man went down and stayed on the ground.

By the end of his career, he was 265 pounds and he could still run like a high school fullback."

You tell this to Hickerson, and he says, "Mr. Monte Clark was very kind to say that."

Leroy Kelly joined Jim Brown in endorsing Hickerson for the Hall of Fame. That makes Hickerson smile.

"Leroy and I could move just as the snap count was called, that was our secret," he said. "Other lineman worried about getting head-slapped. I never did. Before he [the defensive lineman] could slap me, I'd move and I'd put my head gear right into his chest—send 'em a message. On the line, I'd rather have quickness and speed than brute strength. Some of these linemen today, they are so big, they can't even walk. Their fat hangs over their belts."

Hickerson finally retired in 1973, at the age of thirty-seven; he was the oldest offensive lineman in the league.

"For my last three years, I was going to retire," he said. "I told Art Modell to draft someone at my spot, but he never did. I mean, in my last two seasons, I played every single down on offense. I was ready to go when the time came."

He wanted to say more, but stopped. Hickerson is a huge, sensitive man. He is a Southern gentleman. He acts as if he never left Mississippi and Memphis, yet he has lived in Cleveland since 1960.

"For my last game, they introduced me all by myself," he said. "I ran out on the field and suddenly I felt so stupid. What was I supposed to do, just stand out there and wave? I was glad when I finally could get back to the bench and sit down, although the fans were very gracious and I'll always remember their cheers."

Hickerson tells you that football has "worked out pretty well."

He smiles. He knows it was more than that.

"I started working in the eighth grade," he said. "My job was to push a wheelbarrow full of bricks to a stairway, then carry those bricks up four flights of stairs. As I was doing that, I kept telling myself that there has to be a better way to make a living than this. You understand what I'm saying? That is what my life has been about."

JIM NINOWSKI

If you remember Jim Ninowski at all, it's probably for the wrong reason.

"He threw the ball so hard," recalled Kevin Byrne. "I can still see him firing these bullet screen passes that bounced off Jim Brown's shoulder pads."

Comments like that make Ninowski wince—and he should.

When the 1964 Browns talk about Ninowski, they tell you that he is a great guy. They tell he was a good quarterback, good enough to start for most teams.

Ninowski had one of the best jobs in Cleveland. He was the backup quarterback, which made him the choice of at least half the Browns fans. And if Frank Ryan was having a rough afternoon, Ninowski was the most popular guy in town, despite never taking a snap most Sundays.

Now he is nearly forgotten, an answer to a trivia question: Who was the other quarterback in 1964 besides Frank Ryan?

It's a tough one, because Ninowski threw only nine passes in 1964.

Today, most of the former Browns tell you that "Nino" has made big bucks in business, and that he may be the richest of all of them—which says a lot, because this is a very successful group. His former teammates respect Ninowski because he was a poor kid from Detroit, the son of a man who worked at Ford Motor Company for thirty-nine years. He was a backup quarterback in the NFL. Nothing was handed to him.

As Ninowski said, "My family is Russian-Ukrainian. We had a three-bedroom house. One bedroom for my parents. One bedroom for my two sisters. One bedroom for the four boys. We had two double beds in that one room, and it was so small that to get into bed you had to climb over the end of one of the beds. There was no room between the beds and the walls. Sometimes, we'd get tired of sleeping packed in that room, and one of us would go sleep on the living room floor."

Ninowski now has plenty of room in his house in suburban Detroit. He owns a manufacturing representative sales company, a company that does quite well. He also owns another company that buys and sells international bank securities.

As one of his former teammates said, "Nino is rolling in dough and I'm happy for him."

And Ninowski is a happy man, but talking about 1964 isn't easy for him.

"But there are some things I want to say," he said. "Things I never said publicly before because I never wanted to rock the boat."

Ninowski recalls Blanton Collier calling him "the best backup quarterback in football."

"I guess that was supposed to make me feel good . . ." Ninowski didn't finish the thought.

That's because when Ninowski thinks about 1964, he believes he could have been Frank Ryan. He has nothing against Ryan; he says, "Frank was a fine quarterback." But he still asks himself, "What if . . ."

Ninowski was talking about the 1962 season. He was the team's starting quarterback for the first seven games.

But before he talks about 1962, he tells you something else.

"I didn't want to play for the Browns," he said.

He meant the second time.

Ninowski was drafted by the Browns in 1958, and spent two years as Milt Plum's backup. Then Paul Brown traded him to Detroit before the 1960 season.

"That was a great break for me," he said. "Detroit was my hometown. Bobby Layne had just retired as the Lions' quarterback, and all they had was Earl Morrall. I played with Earl at Michigan State, and I felt that I had a good chance of winning the job. I started for two years (1960–61), and we finished in second place both times. I loved it there, and felt I had established myself in Detroit."

One day, Ninowski answered the phone and it was Paul Brown.

"Nino, I'm going to be in Detroit, and would you meet me at the airport for lunch?" Brown asked.

Ninowski knew that Paul Brown just didn't call you up and invite you to lunch. He wasn't there to tell stories and hear about your family. Paul Brown never did anything unless it was for the greater benefit of Paul Brown and the Cleveland Browns.

Ninowski asked Brown what was on his mind, but Brown said, "I just have a few things to discuss with you."

Ninowski said, "Paul, I appreciate you trading me to Detroit, so I'll meet you at the airport."

But Ninowski was worried. What would Paul Brown want? Paul Brown wouldn't bring him back to Cleveland, would he? He knew that Milt Plum was the Browns' quarterback—the same Milt Plum who had been there during Nino's first two years with the Browns, the same Milt Plum that Paul Brown believed was better than Ninowski. So why would Paul Brown want him back? But why else would Brown want to have lunch?

Before his lunch with Brown, Ninowski visited with Detroit coach George Wilson. Wilson was in a great mood. He told Ninowski, "We believe we have a good passing attack, so we're looking for a running back to help you." Their whole conversation was based upon the Lions' upcoming 1962 season, and Ninowski being the quarterback.

"As I was about to leave, I asked George point-blank if he was going to trade me," Ninowski said. "George said, 'Trade you, why would we do that?' I told him about the call from Paul Brown, and how Brown wanted to have lunch, and why else would he do that unless there was a trade."

Wilson said he had no idea that Brown called, and that no deal was in the works. Ninowski told Wilson that he was relieved. He said he loved playing for him and the Lions, that he lived only ten minutes from training camp and had developed several business interests in Detroit.

Wilson couldn't keep up the charade any longer. "Nino, we traded you."

Ninowski said his jaw bounced off the floor. Then he stormed out of the office. He was mad about the trade, and even more livid about the deception by Wilson and Brown. Why couldn't these guys treat him like a man? Why not just tell him? By the time he met with Brown, his first words were, "Why the hell did you trade for me?"

Brown said, "Aren't you happy?"

Ninowski screamed, "No, I'm not happy. Why would I be happy? I don't want to go back to Cleveland. I've got family here. I have a business here. I'm the number one quarterback. Now why would you disrupt my family and my whole life to take me back to Cleveland?"

Ninowski realized that he was a political football.

Plum had blasted Brown in the newspapers for the coach's rigid play-calling system. Virtually every quarterback had the freedom to call his own plays except the man playing for Brown. But Brown responded that he was better able to make play-calling decisions because he and his assistants could see more of the game than the quarterback. Furthermore, in the previous two seasons, Plum was the highest rated passer in the NFL—so Brown must have been doing something right. At least that was Brown's point.

Then he ended the debate by shipping Plum to Detroit for Ninowski.

Ninowski was fuming, talking about quitting. "But I was twenty-six years old," he said. "What else was I going to do? They were not about to change the trade. If I wanted to play, I had to play for Cleveland."

Right after the deal, the Cleveland *Plain Dealer* expressed this opinion on the editorial page: "Milt Plum, rated No. 1 among NFL quarterbacks the last two years, has been traded to Detroit, and lamentations fill the city. From now on, Paul Brown will presumably be able to call the signals for every offensive play without running into any player criticism—at least not from any player who wishes to remain with the team . . . If the Browns click this fall, fans will forget their present unhappiness. If they fall apart at the seams, Paul Brown will be reminded of the men he traded away just as the Cleveland Indians frequently hear the exploits of Rocky Colavito and Roger Maris."

More than ever, that pushed Brown into the same foxhole with Ninowski. And it took a few months, but Ninowski decided the Browns were a good team, and he was the starter. It could have been much, much worse.

"When I went to training camp in 1962, I was the only veteran quarterback," Ninowski said. "Paul Brown called me in after a couple of weeks and asked me what I thought of the kids we had in camp."

As he told this story, Ninowski began to laugh.

"I told Paul that none of those kids would make it in the league and that he'd better get a veteran just in case something happened to me," he said. "Paul came to me a week later and said, 'I can get one of these guys—King Hill, Zeke Bratkowski, or Frank Ryan.' We talked about the three guys for a while, and I said, 'If you have the chance, you should get Ryan.' Frank was a backup with the Rams, and a week later, Paul traded for Ryan."

Ninowski laughed again.

"Every time I tell someone this, my wife says, 'You and your big mouth. If only you had kept your mouth shut, they would have had some rookie playing behind you and you'd have been the starting quarterback.' Who knows, maybe she's right."

And instead of talking about Frank Ryan, Browns fans would be telling Ninowski–to–Gary Collins stories—or at least that is how Ninowski sees it.

"We won all of our exhibition games that year," Ninowski said. "We opened the season against New York, and we beat them [17–7], and New York went to the championship game that year. So we were playing well. The next week, we played Washington. And it was the kind of crazy thing that happened to me in my career. In that game, I went to throw a pass and my left foot just got caught funny in the ground. As I let the ball go, I was falling forward, and one of the tackles banged into me, and I fell at an awkward angle."

It was more than awkward, it was a torn ligament in his knee. But Ninowski wouldn't know that until months later.

Ninowski played the next month with the torn ligament in his left knee. He could only move in a straight line, and every time he released the ball, his left leg would come down first and his knee would feel like broken glass.

After their first five games, the Browns were 2-3. Ninowski was not especially worried because his knee was starting to feel better. He also knew that Paul Brown had confidence in him, and that Frank Ryan was there only in case Ninowski was carted away in a UFO.

In their sixth game, the Browns crushed St. Louis, 34–7. Ninowski and the team had one of their best games of the season. He thought the Browns were about to make their move, and he believed he'd be the one to lead them. He was twenty-six years old. The previous two seasons, he had played most of the time in Detroit, and the Lions had finished in second place.

"I was entering what should have been the prime of my career," he said.

———————

Then came the seventh game of the 1962 season, one of the most forgotten yet significant games in the history of the Browns franchise. No one knew it at the time, but it was the game that made Frank Ryan a household name in Cleveland.

"I started that game as usual," Ninowski said. "It was in the first quarter, a third-down situation. I went back to throw, and Big Daddy got me in a bear hug."

Big Daddy was Big Daddy Lipscomb, the Steelers' 6′6″, 288-pound defensive tackle. Big Daddy was a huge man for any era, but at 288 pounds, he was Big Foot. He was a monster in 1962, and those who blocked him insisted Big Daddy was more like 300 pounds. Consider that the Browns had no one weighing more than 255 back in 1962. Ninowski said the hit didn't feel like much; it hurt, but it wasn't as if Big Daddy blindsided him. It was a clean tackle, and not especially vicious.

"The only thing that worried me a little is that all his weight came down on my right shoulder," Ninowski said.

"We had to punt, and as I came off the field, I felt a burning sensation in my right shoulder," he said. "I went up to Doc [team physician Dr. Vic Ippolito] and told him about my shoulder. Doc reached into my shoulder pads, felt something and said, 'Oh, man, you're through.'

"I said, 'What do mean, 'I'm through?'

"He said, 'You just broke your collarbone.'

"I said, 'Oh my God.' I was done for the season."

Frank Ryan suddenly realized that the Almighty had just decided to reach down and tap him on the shoulder. He was the starting quarterback for the rest of the year, period. The Browns had no one else.

Ryan completed 58 percent of his passes, 10 for touchdowns compared to seven interceptions. Ninowski had had seven TD passes, eight interceptions, and completed 50 percent. His record as a starter was 4-3, Ryan's was 3-3-1.

Paul Brown was fired after the 1962 season, replaced by Blanton Collier.

"When Blanton took over the team, his biggest decision was who to start—Ryan or Ninowski," recalled Bob August. "A lot of players told me that the two guys were so close, as close as any two quarterbacks they had seen on one team. Blanton kept saying how it was a tough choice, but he seemed to like Ryan from the start. I remember him telling me that Ninowski had a very creative football mind, but sometimes he had trouble focusing. I don't know if that was why he went with Frank, but he did and he stayed with Frank because the team was winning."

Ninowski insists that he went into the 1963 regular season believing he was the starting quarterback. He and Ryan split the job in the 1963 exhibition season. Ninowski recalled a meeting toward the end of training camp when Collier told the two quarterbacks, "Whoever starts the final exhibition game will open the season."

When that game approached, Collier named Ninowski to start.

"Ryan even shook my hand and congratulated me," Ninowski recalled. "We lost that game, 16–7, to Pittsburgh. I didn't play especially well, but I still thought I was the starter. No one told me otherwise. A few days later, I was having breakfast at a rest stop on the Ohio Turnpike. I picked up a newspaper and the headline read: 'Browns to Start Ryan.' I couldn't figure out what happened. Blanton told me that I would start, but he was quoted saying Frank would start. I have the utmost respect for Blanton. He is the smartest coach I've ever played for. As the years went on, we developed a good relationship. But the way he handled that situation always bothered me. He never told me that Frank would start, or why he decided to go with Frank. I guess I should have asked him, but I didn't."

Ryan doesn't remember the details, he just said that both quarterbacks went into training camp in 1963 competing for the job. He was just happy to be given "an equal" chance to battle Ninowski. And for the first time in his career, Ryan knew he could start and win in the NFL. Despite the team's 3-3-1 record with him starting in 1962, those seven games made him believe in himself. He also sensed that Collier was behind him.

The Browns won their first six games in 1963 with Ryan as the quarterback. Suddenly, this was Ninowski's worst nightmare. He was no longer at home in Detroit. He was in Cleveland, and a backup—right where he'd begun his career in 1958. Furthermore, he believed that he wasn't given a fair chance to win the job, and that the team would be playing just as well if he were starting.

After nine games, the Browns were 7–2, but Ryan was slumping. Collier started Ninowski against St. Louis; he completed 15 of 28 passes, but the Browns lost, 20–14. Collier went back to Ryan the following week—and that was it for Ninowski. At the age of twenty-seven, he was relegated to being a backup quarterback. While he played through 1969, Ninowski never threw more than 100 passes in any season.

"It was frustrating in 1964 to watch the team come together and not be a part of it on the field," he said. "But you are a professional. If Frank had a bad game or two, I couldn't show my frustration. The last thing I wanted to do was divide the team. But I'll be honest, there were games where we weren't moving the ball, and I'd be on the sidelines thinking, 'I know this play will work . . . Hell, I can do that.' But you don't say it. You don't even let on that you are thinking it. Every week, I prepared like I was going to play. I watched film with Frank. I suggested plays in our meetings, and I saw the coaches put some of those plays in the offense, and hell, those plays worked, too. Blanton gave me credit for that, and I appreciated it. My wife once said, 'The more you help Frank and the team, the less chance you have of playing.' But that was my job—to help them."

Then Ninowski paused for a moment.

"As far as I'm concerned, that 1964 team was my team," he said. "I helped develop it. I helped bring in Ryan and I helped with the offense. I never said these things before because I didn't want to jeopardize the team chemistry. All of this may sound self-serving, but it is what I honestly feel."

It also is the truth. There were games early in 1964 when Ryan appeared headed for the bench. Ninowski never lobbied with writers, coaches, or other players to push the man in front of him off the gangplank.

"You know, I'm proud of that," he said. "I know that I played the game the right way—even when I wasn't playing."

BILL GLASS

Picture Billy Graham as a 6′5″, 255-pound defensive end who could run over an offensive tackle and knock a quarterback on his can.

Or as *Cleveland Press* columnist Frank Gibbons once wrote, "Everyone knows he is just as hard as the water from an old ranch well."

That was Bill Glass: Preacher. Pass Rusher. Yet another extraordinary member of the 1964 Browns.

While Glass was attending Baylor University, and later playing for the Detroit Lions and the Browns, he was thinking about life after football. In fact, he was thinking about life after life as he finished up his post-graduate studies at Southwestern Baptist Theological Seminary in Fort Worth, Texas. He also was speaking to local churches and youth groups about his faith in the Lord.

Maybe that doesn't impress you. There seemingly are thousands of stories about athletes who give their time and voices to the Lord. Some are sincere; others are doing it because they believe it enhances their image, or because they're coming out of drug rehabilitation and are grabbing for any lifeline they can find.

But very few are like Glass. As he says, "I have spent so much time in prison, I can rob a bank and I wouldn't have to do any time."

Name a jail, and he has been there.

Name a type of convict, and Bill Glass has met him.

Ask him what criminals have in common, and Glass will tell you, "Just about every one of them hates his father."

Bill Glass is the Billy Graham of this country's prison system. There is little glamour or gold to be found behind bars. It won't get you a TV show. It won't bring in big donations.

For Bill Glass, it simply is the right thing to do—he has been doing it since 1972. Furthermore, Glass was not like St. Paul, who was knocked to the ground by the power of the Lord. He never found himself in a gutter or was fingerprinted and booked at the local police station. He was a middle-class kid, born in Texarkana, Texas, and then grew up in Corpus Christi. His father was in the insurance business. His grandfather was a judge, and an uncle was a district attorney.

Glass grew up with a sense of right and wrong, and never strayed far from the right side of the law.

"Believe me, prison ministry was about the last thing I had in mind," he said. "I saw myself preaching to packed stadiums, citywide to the masses. I did some of that when I was with the Browns. When I was in college, I had a growing feeling that I wanted to be in some Christian service, but not as a pastor. I wasn't attracted to conventional ministry. I wanted to do something different and unique with a broader appeal. Because I was an athlete, it was easier for me to do that, because I could speak to a group and they'd listen for a while, just because I was an athlete. I could use my contacts to bring in other athletes as speakers. When I first started, I was a pretty mediocre speaker, but I'd still get invited to functions because I was an athlete."

Glass played twelve years in the NFL. He tells you that he was never a star, but he was good enough to be a first-round draft choice by the

Detroit Lions in 1957. He appeared in four Pro Bowl games. He was a starter on the Browns' championship team, and their most consistent pass-rusher.

Bill Glass could play more than a little football.

By the late 1960s, he was probably the most famous athlete-preacher. He had enough of a following to do it full-time when he retired after the 1968 season.

Then a man named Gordon Heffern changed Glass's life.

"Gordon was president of Goodyear Bank in Akron," Glass said. "He also was active in trying to rehabilitate prisoners. Back then, people thought that if prisoners had a job when they were released, they'd stay straight. Gordon and the others involved in that program used their connections to find the ex-prisoners jobs when they were paroled. Over a five-year period, they found about 5,000 jobs for prisoners and had virtually no success. Jobs or no jobs, these guys would get into trouble and end up back in prison."

One day, Heffern was telling Glass about this. Glass had tremendous respect for Heffern. He served on the board of Glass's ministry. He was a committed Christian, the real thing.

"Bill, why don't you do one of your citywide ministries in a prison?" he asked.

Glass was not really interested.

"Get a group of athletes like you do now, only take them into the prisons, and do exactly the same thing you do on the outside," Heffern said. "Just do it in a more concentrated way. We have to try something different."

When Glass thought of prison, he thought of criminals. He thought of locking them up and throwing away the key. He thought of steel bars. He thought of cold, concrete floors. He thought of dirt and grime and grunge and guys you'd cross the street just to avoid.

"I had no desire to do prison ministry," Glass recalled. "But Gordon told me, 'If you have any guts, you'll go where it's really tough. If you really believe Christ is the answer and Christianity can change a man's life, then you're a wimp if you don't try it in prison. Even if you don't make a ministry of it, this will be healthy for you.'"

Glass didn't agree. Heffern kept bringing it up. Glass tried to picture himself in jail, preaching to the inmates. He had no idea what he'd say to them. He felt he had nothing in common with common criminals.

"Gordon kept needling me," he said. "Finally, I agreed to try it just to satisfy him."

When Bill Glass finally decided to go to jail, he knew it couldn't be one hour and gone. This was not a place to say a few prayers, shake some hands, sign autographs. He knew little about convicts, except that they said you can never con a con.

His first stop was Marion Prison in central Ohio. The warden was Pete Perini, who had played for the Browns in 1955.

"We're going to bring in as many athletes as I can find," Glass told the warden. "We're going to be in for three days."

"Bill, you just tell me what you want," Perini said.

"We want to be there for three days," he said. "We'll eat meals with the inmates. We want to go into the cells with the inmates. We'll bring in fifty counselors, who are just businessmen and other guys willing to come down here at their own expense and talk to the inmates. The athletes will do some clinics in the yard."

"You don't want to go in the chapel?" asked the warden.

"No, I want to go in the yard," Glass said. "A lot of inmates won't go into the chapel, but they will go into the yard."

Before going into Marion, Glass had talked to some friends who had worked in prisons before. He contacted a few recent parolees. He did his homework, and he convinced a lot of friends, football fans, and businessmen to walk through those gates with him.

They didn't know what they would say to these guys. They had no formal training. They just knew someone had to try and talk to these men, to listen to these men. And maybe if they were lucky or if everything went right, they could pray with these men.

In the prison yard was a baseball field. Glass wanted to hold his meeting there. He had recruited a judo and karate expert. He found a world-class weightlifter. He knew the inmates were bored and cynical, and if he just came out and said, "We're here to talk about the Lord," there would be yawns and guys shuffling back to their cells.

"So we put together a little show first," he said. "We didn't know how many inmates would come watch, but they all did. They liked our entertainment. Then I talked about my faith for a while, and said we had fifty counselors there to continue the conversations with anyone who was interested. The response was tremendous. These guys were used to a Christian group going into the chapel and maybe staying for no more than an hour—and not many inmates go to chapel."

Glass and his men were there for three days, sunup to sundown. They only left the prison at night. The warden was thrilled and invited Glass to return anytime. He told other wardens about the program.

Did every prisoner swear off his evil ways and find the Lord?

Obviously not.

Did the presence of Glass and his volunteers cool things down for that weekend, and seem to have a calming effect for the next few weeks?

You bet.

That was Pete Perini's message when he talked to other wardens.

"My phone started ringing," Glass said. "It was wardens from California, Florida—all over the country. But I still wasn't sure I wanted to do it again. I did it once. I proved I could do it, but I doubted my call for prison ministry. What convinced me to continue was the fifty volunteers, they kept calling me asking when I planned to do another prison ministry. They insisted we keep it going."

Glass wrestled with it. He came from a great family. He looked into the eyes of those men and realized their lives were so different than his.

But the more prisoners he met, the more Glass realized these men had no one talking to them. No one was listening. And when they were paroled, they were no more ready to cope with society than they were when they first walked through the prison gates.

"I found myself called to this ministry partly because no one else was doing it and partly because what they were doing in prisons wasn't working," he said. "Most of these men were going to eventually be let out. Someone had to try something to change their attitudes."

Over 1,000 prisons later, Bill Glass still goes to jail about 250 times each year.

"For a long time, I wondered what to tell these men," he said. "But patterns emerged. I'd say 90 to 95 percent of them have a father problem. Either bad fathers or no fathers. They may have had a sorry mother, but they'll make an excuse for her. But nearly all of them just hate their fathers. There is something that makes a man mean when he doesn't have a good father. A person with a father who doesn't give him approval either becomes a criminal or an overachiever. He either goes to jail, or he spends his whole life working like crazy to gain his father's approval. I've seen it over and over."

Glass delivers a powerful sermon called "The Blessing," the essence being that fathers need to bless their children, and too many don't. Either the father isn't around, or he is emotionally distant.

Or he says, "I love you, but . . ."

"Every coach I had was like that," he said. "They hold out their love and approval. They say they like you, but you can do this or that a little better. For a coach, that works. For a father, that stinks."

Glass's message is that fathers should hug and bless their children. Yes, they should teach them. But they also should tell their children that they are loved, period. No strings attached. It's a message he stresses with inmates. Bless your children. Tell them you love them.

"I was on death row in Mississippi, the same prison that was in John Grisham's *The Chamber*," Glass said. "I talked to forty-four inmates on death row. I went to all forty-four cells and asked them how they got along with their fathers. Every single one hated his father. Not one of those guys got along with their dads."

So Glass tells the inmates, "Do you want to keep your children out of prison? Well, bless them. Hold them. Tell them you love them. It is never too late to do that. You can be seventy years old, and you still seek the approval of your father."

Glass tells you how 90 percent of all prisoners are released within three years. Within three months, half of them are back in prison.

"You have to change their hearts," he said. "That's the only chance."

Glass mentions a study conducted by the Billy Graham Center at Wheaton College that showed, "When inmates receive Christ into their lives, the recidivism drops from 75 percent to 32 percent. If the inmate is discipled in prison and mentored after his release from prison, recidivism drops to 10 percent."

Are these figures accurate?

That is impossible to prove. But common sense tells you changing a prisoner's heart and attitude is the only way he'll ever change his life— and if he doesn't change his life, he's going right back to jail.

Glass is armed with statistics. It costs $75,000 to build one jail cell . . . $23,500 a year to house a prisoner . . . lifetime incarceration is about $500,000 . . . building jails and the criminal justice system is the biggest growth industry in the country.

"It's incredibly expensive and it's just not working," he said. "That is why we are welcome in so many prisons. We are up to 13,000 volunteers. We have follow-up programs. We'll go into 250 prisons a year. I know we are getting somewhere with these guys. In all my years going into prison, I've never felt in danger. We've never had one incident with myself or any of our counselors and volunteers. Word gets around. They know we are sincere, so even the guys who don't buy our message still appreciate the fact that we come to see them."

Glass's primary ministry consists of only five full-time people. But there are thousands and thousands of volunteers giving days of their time. They are what make Glass's ministry so effective and unique.

"We are a shoestring operation," he said. "I don't make a lot of money. I never made more than $35,000 in pro football. The best investment I made was after we won the 1964 championship and I took the money and put it down on a 1,172 acre ranch near Hamilton, Texas, which is about two and a half hours from Dallas. I got it real cheap, and sold it several years later. It was the only thing I ever did where I made really good money. I took some of the money from the sale of the ranch and bought thirty acres outside Dallas, which is where I live now. Among the guys on that 1964 team, I probably have been one of the lesser financial successes. But I never really tried to make a lot of money."

Instead, he has helped change lives.

BERNIE PARRISH

The name makes Art Modell's lips curl. He doesn't talk about Bernie Parrish, he almost spits.

"The only negative influence on the '64 team, the only one," Modell said.

That's a harsh thing to say about a guy who helped deliver Modell the only championship of his long career.

And yes, Bernie Parrish had a lot to do with the Browns beating the Baltimore Colts in 1964—maybe not as much as he claims, because he'll tell you that he masterminded that stunning shutout. But this much is certain: Bernie Parrish was more than a shrewd defensive back, he was nearly a player-coach and had input in forming the defensive game plan that so surprised Johnny Unitas and the Colts.

So Modell is out of line when he says, "What I most remember about Parrish that season is him being on the phone in the dressing room, talking to his broker about buying and selling copper futures."

Given the fact that Parrish was a stockbroker during his days with the Browns, he may have indeed been talking investments in the dressing room. But those who know Parrish say that he was obsessed with football, and that he certainly knows more football than his old boss, Mr. Modell.

Now you know why Parrish says, "Owners are petulant, egocentric asses who add nothing to the game. What do they do? What does Art Modell or any of those guys do to win a game? A good GM is worth a helluva lot more than an owner."

That's the nicest thing Parrish has to say about Modell.

Maybe that was why when the 1964 Browns held their thirtieth reunion, the only prominent player missing was Bernie Parrish. He also wasn't there for the twenty-year reunion, or any of the other times this great team gathered to let the beer and memories flow. None of his former teammates had his phone number or had talked with him for years. Some heard he was living in Illinois, others said he was in St. Louis or California. His former roommate, Galen Fiss, did receive a call from Parrish early in 1994. ("First time I'd heard from Bernie in twenty-some years," Fiss said. "He said he was coming to the thirtieth reunion, but he didn't show. He said he was living in Orlando, but I didn't get his address or phone number.")

Orlando is where you can find Parrish, living in an exclusive suburb about a mile from the mansion where Shaquille O'Neal once lived. He's married, with two children under the age of eight. He said he was semi-retired and had done well in the construction business. From the looks of his huge new home and swimming pool, you know that Parrish must have had a hot hand with those old copper futures and his other business endeavors.

But now Bernie Parrish wants more. Now, he wants to reconnect with his old team. He'd like to take one more step back to 1964.

"But to some people, I'll always be a pariah," Parrish said. "Part of it is because of the book. I know some of the people who might like seeing me again—well, they think twice because of my reputation and the things I wrote about the NFL."

Ah, yes, the book.

The title was *They Call It a Game,* and Parrish wrote it back in 1971. No co-author or ghost writer, the man did it himself. There has never been a book quite like it—at least not one written by a former player. The premise is on the first page: "I believe in the American system; but I am also a revolutionary. . . . This book is intended to drive Pete Rozelle, Art Modell, Carroll Rosenbloom, Tex Schramm, Clint Murchison, Lou Spadia and the other so-called sportsman-owners out of professional football. They are my enemies and they know it."

Parrish writes about the impact of gambling on the NFL, and how many of the owners (including Modell) associated with gamblers and other crime figures. He believes that games have been manipulated to comply with the point spreads. He believes football has been and will always be fraught with deceit.

In other words, he thinks too much of it is fixed, and some of the owners are behind it—if nothing else, by their unwillingness to confront these problems. He tells you that he corresponds with people on the Internet such as former FBI agents, and he's planning a revised version of his book, one even more powerful and controversial than his first effort. As you listen to Parrish, you don't doubt his intentions. He has always been a man who needs a mission.

But he doesn't look like the guy who was at the top of the NFL's Most Hated list. He is bearing down on sixty years old, standing maybe 5´10˝ with a prominent, soft belly and half-moon reading glasses perched at the end of his nose. You'd guess for a week before saying that this man was once an All-Pro cornerback. You'd never believe that he was the kind of high-caliber athlete who also played pro baseball.

With his easy smile and soothing, Central Florida drawl, you immediately like him. You are not shocked by some of his outrageous and provocative charges, because they are delivered with an ironic, soft, understanding voice, then a sad shake of the head.

This is the man who took on the NFL, who was the Curt Flood of football?

"That's me," he said.

First, you must understand that Bernie Parrish was at the center of the Browns' defense, a tough, terrier-like cornerback. At the University of Florida, he started as both an offensive and defensive back in football and was an All-American selection. But he was even better in baseball as a centerfielder and third baseman—good enough to sign with the Cincinnati Reds for a $63,000 bonus back in 1958.

That was before baseball had an amateur draft, and it was back when $63,000 was like a $1 million bonus today. You know that Parrish had to have scouts drooling, because it was Cincinnati Reds general manager Gabe Paul who agreed to the bonus. Paul later ran the Cleveland Indians. Gabe Paul didn't like to spend money for stars such as Rocky Colavito, much less on kids coming out of college.

But Parrish was that special, that kind of prospect.

"I played for the Reds in the summer of 1959 for the Albuquerque farm team, but I found that I missed football," he said.

In the meantime, Paul Brown made one of those personnel moves that built the Browns into a powerhouse in the 1950s. Even though Parrish quit school before his senior year to play pro baseball, Brown drafted him in the ninth round. Most teams considered it a wasted pick. Why would Parrish walk away from $63,000 and baseball to sign with the Browns?

But Brown had done his homework. He heard that Parrish loved football, that his combative personality was ill-suited for baseball. So Brown sat back and waited.

One day, this letter arrived at his office in Tower B of the old Cleveland Stadium:

"Dear Coach Brown,

"Being drafted by the Browns was the greatest honor I ever received in football. I don't know you, but you have the best record against the best competition in the world, and that's all I need to know. I want to play for the Browns. I had a 5.5 yards-per-carry average rushing and led Florida in total offense and scoring. I placekicked 14 of 16 [extra points] and averaged 47.3 yards per punt. I like running with the ball, but I think my best position may be defensive back. I am only telling you these things about myself because there is no other way to let you know. Baseball has been a disappointment to me, and I'd like to give pro football a try."

Paul Brown read that, smiled, and told Parrish, "Come on down."

He arranged for Parrish to be flown to Cleveland, where he was picked up by Browns general manager Dick Gallagher, who drove Parrish straight to the Stadium. The Browns were facing the New York

Giants in a few hours. Paul Brown only spoke for a few minutes with Parrish, then arranged for Bernie to watch the game from the sidelines. Brown knew that the Cleveland–New York rivalry was bitter and bone-crunching, exactly the kind of blood-stirring affair that would romance Parrish.

Parrish didn't know the players, but he found himself wanting to be out there, wanting to play for Paul Brown and wanting to help the Browns mop up the field with the Giants. By the second half, he was ready to leave baseball. He received virtually no bonus from the Browns, yet he signed—and then he returned nearly all of his $63,000 to Gabe Paul and the Cincinnati Reds.

"It was the right thing to do," Parrish said. "I didn't earn it."

That tells you something about Bernie Parrish, too.

Want to know the kind of player Bernie Parrish was for the Browns?

On the first day of training camp, Paul Brown designated Parrish as the team's starting left cornerback. That was in 1959, and Parrish remained at that spot until he left the team in 1966.

Paul Brown prized intelligence and courage, and Parrish had both.

"It takes quite a boy to come in and start here," Brown said during Parrish's rookie year. "He is smart, and you start with that in the defensive backfield. He is a real student of the game, and carries out everything he is taught. Opposing players certainly don't do much with him."

To make room for Parrish, Brown moved veteran Warren Lahr from left corner to safety. Brown so liked Parrish's hands that he designated Bernie as the holder for Lou Groza's kicks—but Parrish had to give up that job when he broke his left middle finger during training camp.

It also should be mentioned that Parrish played with that broken finger, and refused to wear a cast. He didn't want to impair his ability to break up passes or catch a football. After the finger healed, his left knuckle was twice its normal size. But he never complained, and never missed a practice, much less a game.

Paul Brown liked that.

"I gave up only one touchdown as a rookie, then two the next year," Parrish said.

Paul Brown liked that, too.

Parrish then convinced Paul Brown to grant a tryout to his former Florida roommate, a guy by the name of Don Fleming.

Fleming was from Shadyside, Ohio, which is near the West Virginia border. He played offensive end at Florida, and was also Parrish's teammate in baseball. Fleming was drafted by the NFL's old Chicago Cardinals, but that didn't work out. When safety Warren Lahr retired, Parrish said that Fleming would be ideal for the Browns, that he'd make a great safety.

Paul Brown so respected Parrish that he made a minor deal to acquire Fleming's rights from the Cardinals. Fleming reported to the Browns and immediately took over as the starting left safety, next to Parrish. Fleming started for the Browns for three years, then was killed in June of 1963. Remember, these were the days of low salaries and little security, the days when players had real off-season jobs to help pay the bills. Fleming was a foreman for a construction company in Orlando. His men were having trouble with a pipe-laying job. Fleming tried to lend a hand, and accidentally bumped against a high-tension wire. He was electrocuted by 12,000 volts.

Fleming was only twenty-five years old.

Talking about the tragedy thirty-three years later, Parrish had a lump in his throat. He fought back tears.

"We were like brothers," he said. "I still miss him."

After Fleming's death, Parrish roomed with Galen Fiss. A veteran linebacker, Fiss was the Browns' defensive captain and the man who called the signals and determined what formations the defense would use on each play. Fiss is as sturdy and straight as his native state of Kansas, a man respected by nearly everyone on the team. But before the 1964 season, Blanton Collier turned the signal-calling job over to Parrish—although Fiss remained the team captain and was still a strong and steady force in the dressing room.

Under most circumstances, Collier's decision to switch from Fiss to Parrish as his defensive strategist would have caused a split between the two men. No way could they remain roommates. But not with Fiss and Parrish. Fiss may not have agreed with the decision, but he trusted Parrish's football mind—and Collier's judgment.

"Bernie was a cerebral player," Fiss recalled. "You have to give him a lot of credit for getting our defense to watch more films. He was the kind of guy who took films home at night, which wasn't done that often back then. He'd watch them over and over. He'd track his receiver's tendencies. Before every game, he'd tell us that a certain receiver would go to the sidelines X times, he'd go deep Y times, and he'd to the post Z times. It reached the point where he forced most of us to watch more film to keep up with him."

Paul Wiggin is a member of the NFL establishment, a fine defensive end with the Browns who has been both a coach and front office executive. When it comes to the politics of the sport, no two men could be further apart than Wiggin and Parrish. But when it comes to football, Wiggin is a Parrish fan.

"By 1964, Bernie was like a player-coach," Wiggin said. "You see players taking films home now? Bernie was the first to do that. He put pressure on us to be students of the game. [Parrish was infamous for breaking up card games in the dressing room and telling players, "How come you're not watching film? Watch this with me."] Blanton gave Bernie quite a bit of authority with the defense. Not only did Bernie have a lot of influence on our defense in 1964, but I think Bernie left his mark on the NFL in terms of how players should prepare themselves."

The Browns didn't have a good defense in 1964, and the weakest spot probably was the secondary. Parrish was the only player of any star caliber, and by this point, injuries and age had robbed him of some speed. He survived more with his wits, grit, and pure stubbornness. Two other starters—Larry Benz and Walter Beach—were ignored by other teams and signed by the Browns as free agents. Ross Fichtner took over for Fleming, and he was a converted quarterback and the last player to make the Browns team in 1960. Things were so desperate that during the 1962 season Paul Brown and Blanton Collier told reporters that they were considering trying halfback Ernie Green in the secondary, because he was a good athlete. It never happened, but the fact that it was even discussed shows how worried the Browns were about their secondary.

It was Parrish who held these guys together. Even his critics admit that.

If you listen to Parrish, he single-handedly shut down the Colts in the 1964 title game.

"People don't want to admit it, but I spent most of 1964 keeping some of the coach's bad ideas away from the other players," he said. "I called the defensive signals. I learned that sometimes the best thing to do was just ignore the bench and call my own game. We on the field knew a helluva lot more about what was going on than the coaches." Which brings us to the 1964 championship game.

"Howard Brinker was our defensive coordinator," Parrish said. "He was a good man, but he worked under Paul Brown. And Paul, he would just abuse Howard. I mean, Paul could barely draw up a 4-3 defense. Paul's specialty was offense, but he'd get all over Howard, and do it in front of the players. Things like that made you not like Paul Brown, and they made you feel sorry for Howard."

But it didn't necessarily make all the players respect Brinker, according to Parrish.

"Howard could be timid," Parrish said. "He didn't like to take chances. He would panic in some situations, and then he'd look to the veteran players to bail him out."

Blanton Collier had to know this, and that probably is why he treated Parrish as a player-coach. He knew that Parrish was aggressive and creative. When Collier was an assistant under Brown in 1962, he lived near Parrish in the Cleveland suburb of Aurora. They often rode together to and from practices, and they constantly talked the game. If anyone understood Parrish's football mind, it was Collier.

With the championship game approaching, Parrish studied even more film than normal. The more he saw, the more he was convinced the Browns would win. He told reporters, coaches, and his teammates just that—and several newspaper stories appeared with Parrish predicting an upset and insisting the Browns' defense (which allowed more yards than any other defense in 1964) was underrated and overlooked.

From the films, Parrish noticed that Colts cornerback Lenny Lyles played right on top of the man he was covering—sort of an early version of the bump-and-run. That was rare in 1964, as most defensive backs gave receivers plenty of room, allowing short-yardage passes in order to protect against the bomb for a touchdown.

"I asked myself why Lyles played that way," Parrish said. "He'd bump his man, try to knock him out of his pattern. I figured that Lenny played that way against Raymond Berry in practice, and it probably was effective—which is why Lyles had become a good player with the Colts after having bounced around with a couple of other teams before."

Walter Beach would cover Berry, and Parrish decided that he'd tell Beach to play right in the face of the Colts' star receiver.

"Howard Brinker was telling Beach to do just the opposite," Parrish said. "He was scared of Berry. The more film I watched, the more I noticed that the few times Unitas struggled was when his receivers were played tight right from the line of scrimmage. Unitas was a great timing passer. He wasn't used to his receivers being bumped off their patterns. But I knew better than to talk about this during the week. Howard Brinker would never go for it."

On the morning of the game, Parrish said he went to Walter Beach, Ross Fichtner, and Larry Benz. He said everyone was going to play bump-and-run.

"Hell, back then you were allowed to bump a receiver out of bounds," he said. "And we did that to Berry, Jimmy Orr, and all those guys."

In the first and third quarters, Unitas also was throwing into a 20 mile-per-hour wind, which aggravated him. Furthermore, the Browns' defensive line led by Jim Kanicki harrassed Unitas all afternoon.

"I like Bernie Parrish, I really do," said Kanicki recently. "But I thought our defensive line had a lot to do with what happened in that game. The Colts liked to run their patterns deeper than most teams, which means Unitas needed a little extra time. We didn't give it to him. Bernie called our defensive signals, but Bernie also was probably the biggest self-promoter I've ever met. He played well that day, but we all did."

Fichtner said that during the regular season, the secondary received a bad rap. "You need a good rush up front to help you," he said. "If you don't get it, the quarterback has all day to pick you apart. I thought the secondary played great in the championship game, but so did our line. They kept the heat on Unitas. As for Bernie, I don't remember him telling us to do anything special that day. We got the game plan in the regular way."

It is fascinating that over thirty years later, these guys still debate Parrish's role.

"Bernie takes credit for changing the defense in the championship game, and I think he's probably overplaying that," said defensive end Bill Glass. "He always liked to insert himself into the coaching situation. Blanton would call him a coach, and Bernie took it seriously."

Glass then told this story:

"Once, Blanton said, 'Bernie, it sounds to me that you'd like to be the defensive coordinator.'

"Bernie said, 'No, you're wrong.'

"Blanton said, 'Why am I wrong?'

"Bernie said, 'I want your job.'

"He actually said that to Blanton's face," Glass said. "Blanton kind of chuckled, and that made Bernie madder because he hated it when people didn't take him seriously."

Parrish was in the middle of the Paul Brown firing, which he still calls "the revolution." Players say that in his early years as owner, Modell often consulted with Parrish, "and Bernie had Art's ear."

So Parrish did like to be in the middle—in the middle of players and coaches, players and management, players and players. He is one of those guys who believe they have most of the answers—and if you give him a little time, he'll come up with all the important questions, too. But someone had the answers for stopping the Colts.

This team that led the NFL in scoring and averaged 31 points per game could not even come close to the end zone against the Browns.

Walter Beach held Hall of Famer Raymond Berry to three catches for 38 yards. Parrish smothered All-Star Jimmy Orr, who caught only two passes for 31 yards. The Browns line of Jim Kanicki, Dick Modzelewski, Bill Glass, and Paul Wiggin forced Unitas to run the ball six times. He threw for only 95 yards.

"Our linebackers were great, too," said Wiggin. "People remember the big hit that Galen Fiss put on Lenny Moore in the first quarter, but I remember watching the film and realizing that Galen played nearly a perfect game that day. But to me, the guy who had as much influence on that day as anyone on the defense was Bernie Parrish. I remember walking down the tunnel at halftime when it was a scoreless tie. I told Bernie, 'This is amazing. We've got a zero up there. We've done pretty good so far.' Bernie told me, 'Don't talk about so far—we've got another half to play and we're going to win this thing.' He believed it. He had an unshakable faith and that rubbed off on us. I'm not pushing Bernie Parrish because he was a great player—he wasn't. But he had an impact on us."

Thirty years later, those are the words that Parrish longs to hear.

He'll sit at his dinner table with salt and pepper shakers, knives and forks, and he'll turn them into the Colts offense and Browns defense. He'll tell you that he called a great game, but wonders what Unitas and the Colts were thinking.

Parrish said, "Unitas was shocked because we blitzed more and played them tighter and more aggressively than we did against any team during the regular season. Yet, you'd think a great quarterback would adjust. Looking at the films, I sometimes got a funny feeling about that game."

Parrish doesn't claim the game was fixed—that would take away from his greatest moment and there is neither proof nor evidence for such a claim—but thirty years later, he still can't fathom why the Colts were so helpless.

He also said, "We felt like we could have played them all day, and they never would have scored."

He also said, "We shocked our own offense. It was like they realized that we weren't going to let them score, and they had better get in the game."

And he said, "To be honest, we got sick of hearing how great our offense was all year. There were times when they left us hanging out there, when they'd go three-plays-and-out, and we'd have to bang our heads out there for a half an hour to stop the other team. I think we wanted to show people—and our own offense—that we were pretty good, too."

Parrish then shows you a story from the December 28, 1964, edition of the *New York World-Telegraph* by Joe King, who stated, "Bernie Parrish, practically unknown safety man of Cleveland, was the brain that thwarted the great quarterback of the Baltimore Colts."

Actually, Parrish was a veteran and well-known cornerback, not a safety. So King had some of the facts wrong, but Parrish still liked the writer's opinion.

Parrish said that 1964 drained him. He said that he appreciated the championship, but something was missing and a lot of things were gnawing away at him.

"By the end of that season, I hated Modell's guts," he said. "I think most of the players did, if they were to be honest about it. The guy was a phony. After you prove you're the best, then what? How long does it take for that feeling to set in after the game? Pretty damn quick, I'll tell you. I spent 90 percent of my time manipulating the coaches and Modell just so we could get on the field and play our game . . . I mean, all the politics just wore me out. It was one big dance between the players, coaches, and the idiot owner."

After the 1964 season, Parrish made headlines when he said that Commissioner Pete Rozelle ought to be fired, and replaced with—of all people—Paul Brown.

This shocked many people who knew Parrish as one of the key Browns who were in favor of Modell firing Paul Brown. But Parrish believed that Rozelle didn't show real leadership in the battle between the owners and the players union about the pension fund before the 1964 championship game. He didn't like Paul Brown personally, but considered Brown to be a man of integrity.

Modell and Rozelle were close friends. Modell lashed out publicly at Parrish, defending Rozelle's record. Then he said that Parrish should take his nose out of commissioner's business and shut up, or he'd be traded. That turned Parrish even more bitter toward Modell and the NFL establishment.

"I said those things mostly to piss off Modell," Parrish said thirty years later. "But I also believed that Paul Brown would have made a better commissioner than Rozelle."

Parrish retired after the 1966 season, and set out to make the NFL's players union a viable force. He saw that football players were almost sheeplike in their willingness to follow the shepherds of the NFL. Part of the reason is that most football players are not told to think for themselves; they are isolated from other members of the team, meeting with players of their own positions and with their special position coaches. Of the major sports, football is the most militaristic and stifles creative thinking.

So Parrish tried to form a huge union of all three sports in the hope that the other union-athletes could carry their football brothers into the twentieth century.

"I talked to Jimmy Hoffa and the Teamsters," Parrish said. "They were interested in representing us if we could bring the sports together. But when we had the meeting of the representatives from all the sports, the football players screwed it up. As some baseball players told me, 'Football players act like owners.' So it didn't happen."

This wounded Parrish deeply. After all, he was a football player. He loved football, even if he hated the owners.

He worked for the Teamsters in St. Louis in the 1970s. He wrote his book, which sold very well. Then he formed his own construction company.

"I remember reading Bernie's book and having no recollection of many of the things he wrote about," said Jim Kanicki. "I kept asking myself why I didn't see these things. Then I realized that Bernie was just an unhappy guy, and I would never see things like he did."

Hal Lebovitz said that Parrish doesn't deserve the attention he has received.

"You can throw everything Bernie Parrish says right into the garbage can," said Lebovitz, Cleveland's most respected sportswriter. "Bernie has no respect for anyone that I know of. He had that telephone installed in his locker so he could trade wheat futures or whatever. Parrish was not a bad player, but he was not a one-man team or a one-man brain."

As time has passed, others view Parrish more kindly.

"I respect Bernie because he was so competitive and he was very thoughtful," Ross Fichtner said. "He was one of those guys who really wanted to coach. But he also was into questioning. He wanted to know why something had to be done that way. I was just the opposite; you tell me what to do, and I do it the best I can. Most football players are like that."

Bill Glass is one of the few Browns who has occasionally spoken to Parrish over the years.

"I've always considered Bernie a friend," said Glass. "But he just likes to irritate and keep things stirred up. He would never let things lie. I didn't think that some of the things he was irritating about were that important. He is a good person, but his nature is to like controversy. He enjoys conflict and being unpredictable. He once told me, 'I make my living being an irritant. It's my job to break up the plans that the offense makes for the game. I have fun messing up their plans.' He had that same attitude toward management, toward almost everybody. But once you understand that about Bernie, it's easier to like him."

Parrish pleads guilty to being the rebel with many causes, but he also insists he is right about men such as Modell.

"Everyone was surprised when he moved the Browns and took a better deal in Baltimore," he said. "Not me. That's vintage Modell."

Parrish now proposes that all NFL teams be publicly owned like the Green Bay Packers.

"Why do we keep building new stadiums for jerks like Modell, and giving them to them, tax free?" he asked. "If we are going to let our tax dollars be used for stadiums, then we should have an ownership in the teams."

Parrish said the answer is to legalize NFL gambling.

"Why make all the people who bet on NFL games into criminals?" he asked. "Do you know that $5 billion is bet on the Super Bowl? Or $50 billion is bet illegally during an NFL season? If $50 billion is bet on this stuff, legalize it. Let the government run it and the money can be used to build new stadiums and help finance teams in the Green Bay model—that would save the taxpayers a lot of money and keep guys like Modell from screwing their fans."

Parrish can talk about these ideas for hours, and some of them have merit. On this subject, he seems to have the interest of the average football fan at heart.

But his heart is still with the 1964 Browns.

"I know that some of the guys considered me to be abrasive," he said. "I didn't continue my friendship with them because I knew they couldn't be friends with me and the NFL and Art Modell all at the same time. It does bother me that only a few players understand what I did for the Browns and what I tried to do for the union. I was going to attend that thirty-year reunion, I really was, but my mother died. I think it is time for me to come back. I think enough time has passed—at least I hope so."

ROSS FICHTNER

Ross Fichtner has a souvenir from his pro football career.

"Epilepsy," he said.

His last seizure was in 1978. He feels fine.

But don't tell Ross Fichtner that a concussion is no big deal. Don't tell him that when a player is hit in the head, it's "just a dinger."

"I was lucky," Fichtner said. "I got out at the right time. I played for nine years. One or two more head injuries—who knows?"

Fichtner's problems began in 1964. The Browns were playing Dallas at home, and he was a safety.

"Frank Clarke was the tight end," Fichtner recalled. "They ran a tight-end reverse, and Clarke was my coverage. They gave the ball to the running back who was headed in one direction, then he handed the ball to Clarke, coming back the other way."

Clarke was running along the sidelines in front of the Dallas bench. "I pushed him out of bounds, but he got my head with the front of his knee," Fichtner recalled. "I went out cold. Jim Houston and some of the other guys who saw it swore it looked as if my head spun around."

"To me, it looked like Ross had broken his neck," Jim Kanicki recalled.

Fichtner was on the ground in front of the Dallas bench.

"I went into convulsions," he said. "I started to swallow my tongue. They stopped that from happening, then rolled me over on my stomach."

Fichtner didn't move. He was facedown, limp, lifeless.

"I thought he was dead," said Jim Houston.

"I was on the field for about a half hour," Fichtner said. "They were afraid to move me. I don't know any of this for myself, because I was out cold. It's what the other guys told me. All this time, the game was stopped. Finally, they carried me into the dressing room, and I woke up about forty-five minutes later."

He was taken to Shaker Medical Center, where he was put in the same room with Browns defensive lineman Bob Gain.

"Bob was in there for a broken leg," Fichtner recalled.

Doctors examined Fichtner, and they were worried. This was no bump on the head, no dinger.

"There was some swelling in my brain," he said. "My left eye had been knocked out of its axis. If I looked at you, my right eye was pointed straight at your face. My left eye looked at your feet. I mean, my left eye would only look straight down."

Fichtner was in the hospital for two weeks. Various serums were pumped through his veins to try and relieve the swelling in his brain.

"The swelling put pressure on my optic nerve," he said. "That was what forced the left eye to look down."

Even after he was released from the hospital, there were problems.

"I was supposed to be fine, but I was seeing double," he said. "I'd look at you, and I'd see two faces, one on top of the other."

Fichtner was out for seven weeks. Every morning, he'd wake up and hope to see the world as he knew it—just one world. But every time he tried to focus on one object, especially something moving, he saw double.

Two faces. Two footballs. Two cars.

He felt pressure to play. He was healthy—no broken bones, no sprains or strains, no blood. He just couldn't see right. In the macho world of football, that isn't the best reason to miss games. Of course, if Fichtner had come back too soon and suffered another concussion, the brain damage could have been fatal. Or the injuries could have been permanent.

He thought about the concussion he'd had in high school. There was another one in college. But his last concussion was five years earlier. Fichtner had endured so much just to make the NFL. He was a promising quarterback at Purdue, but he broke his shoulder during his senior year. He played the final few games, but he could hardly throw. He also played defensive back, and when the 1960 NFL draft came, the Browns selected him in the third round.

He was nearly cut by Paul Brown, playing only three games as a rookie. In 1962, he led the Browns in tackles on the special teams—and he wasn't even supposed to be on the special teams.

"On our kickoff coverage teams, we had a lot of veterans like Galen Fiss," Fichtner said. "He'd go down on the opening kickoff, and then he would look for a younger player to cover the remainder of the kickoffs. He was the starting linebacker, and he wanted to rest. So I'd go in for Galen, or anyone else who'd let me. It was the only way I could get on the field. That was how I ended up with all those tackles, even though I wasn't on the depth chart."

That attitude impressed both Paul Brown and Blanton Collier. It inspired them to give Fichtner a chance to play safety. He became the starter in 1963, and never gave up the job until he was traded to New Orleans before the 1968 season.

———————

Fichtner was a four-year pro when he suffered that concussion in the Dallas game in 1964.

He was pleased and surprised when he returned to action and discovered he had no fear of suffering another concussion. He played in the Browns' last two regular-season games, and in the championship victory over Baltimore.

"The only thing was, the muscles around my left eye were sort of loose," he said. "When I ran, my left eye bounced. That was why I'd see two footballs coming at me. If my right eye focused on the ball first, then I was okay—I knew that was the ball to catch. If not, I just guessed. I told the Browns about my double vision, but I didn't tell them about the eye bouncing."

Fichtner was like virtually every other player in this era. He didn't want his team to know the full extent of his injuries for fear they'd find someone else.

Those who saw Fichtner in the final games of the 1964 season never guessed the serious extent of his injuries. Certainly, there was no reason to imagine this guy had double vision.

"I'm proud to say I played great in the championship game," he said.

Given how the Browns' defense shut down the Colts and how Johnny Unitas couldn't seem to find an open receiver, Fichtner and the entire Browns defensive secondary probably played the game of their lives.

In 1965, Fichtner returned to the Browns, and the double vision was almost gone. It occurred only when running, and not every time or with every step.

"I was feeling very good, and we were playing the L.A. Rams in an exhibition game," he said. "I tackled Les Josephson. I don't even know where I hit him, or how he hit me. I just know that I went down. I was awake, but I couldn't move. It was like feeling you were knocked out, only your eyes stayed open."

Because Fichtner's eyes were open, the Browns dragged him off the field.

"They were trying to save a timeout," he said, matter-of-factly.

Think about that. Here was a guy who'd had a major head injury the year before, and he was down again. This was only an exhibition game, so it didn't even count. And they dragged him off the field, just to save a timeout.

"All teams did it back then," he said. "Later, they put in a rule that the game must be stopped until the player was on his feet or helped off the field. No dragging people, because if they had a back injury or something, it would just make everything worse."

When the team returned to Cleveland from the game in L.A., Fichtner went back into Shaker Medical Center.

"They had just come out with this new machine to do brain scans," he said. "They put me through that, and found I was okay to play. There was no brain damage. But they discovered I had a bad, uneven bite. Basically, my jaw was uneven, so when I'd get hit on the field, even in a place like the shoulder, my jaw would slam shut. Because it was uneven, it would put pressure on the temple, and my brain would just shut down—I'd be out cold."

The medical people designed a special mouth guard.

"That allowed me to play for four more years," he said.

But the Browns were starting to worry about Fichtner and the concussions.

"They traded Mike Lucci because of me," he said. "Mike was a friend, a good guy and a good linebacker. But he was part of a deal that brought Erich Barnes to us from New York, because they wanted Erich to play safety. They said they couldn't count on me anymore."

Thirty years later, Fichtner was bothered about the deal.

"I was able to play safety, so we didn't need Erich," he said. "He was moved to cornerback. But we lost Lucci, who ended up having a great career in Detroit."

While he was with the Browns, Fichtner owned part of a radio station in Ashland, Ohio, and he'd do sports reports. He still is part owner of the station, but lives in Plymouth, Michigan, where he works for the Fellowship of Christian Athletes.

"I remember what the doctors said to me after that brain scan in 1965," he said. "They told me that I was okay now, but down the line— maybe fifteen years—'you may have some problems.' It was not something I dwelled on, but it was in the back of my mind. Fourteen years later, I had a grand seizure. They discovered I had epilepsy. I haven't had another seizure since 1978, but I take Milontin every day and I have a brain scan every few years. But I consider myself lucky. Some of the guys I played with, all the back and knee injuries they have and how they can barely walk today—I got off pretty easy. That's how I look at it."

GALEN FISS

Galen Fiss has a confession to make.

Remember his great play in the 1964 championship game? The play where Fiss roll-blocked Lenny Moore for a loss in the first quarter?

That play is on every Browns retrospective highlight tape. Lenny Moore catches a screen pass, and Fiss cuts the legs out from under the running back, sending him for a five-yard loss back on the Baltimore 30 yard line.

When that play was shown at a banquet for 500 fans during the thirtieth reunion of the Browns' 1964 team, people cheered and whistled. All Fiss could do was blush.

"It really wasn't a great play," he said.

People don't agree. In fact, it is the only defensive play fans still remember from the game.

"I know that," Fiss said. "But I'm telling you, I was scared to death. I mean, my heart was in my throat."

Why?

"I was out of position," he said. "I could see the screen pass coming. They had it set up well, and I was playing too darn deep."

Fiss was the linebacker on the right side. It was his job to sniff out screen passes, and then close quickly on the running back just as he caught the ball.

"I was too deep, and I also knew there was no one behind me," he said. "If Moore got past me, who knows?"

Fiss didn't think. He didn't worry about his heart pounding or his throat feeling like someone had squeezed it. Suddenly, he just felt his legs moving like pistons, pumping up and down. He didn't know the last time he'd moved so fast, he just knew something was carrying him.

"Only way I can explain it is fear," he said. "When you have that kind of fear in you, you can do things."

What Fiss did was run right past a Baltimore blocker and bear down on Moore.

"Lenny was fast and shifty," Fiss said. "I was afraid if I just tried to tackle him normally, he would give me a fake and I'd miss him. I could try to put a shoulder into a guy like that and come up with nothing but air." Fiss's body took over. Before he knew what was happening, he had thrown himself at Moore's kneecaps. He was like a human saw, cutting down a tree.

"It's called a roll-block," he said. "Lenny was still going a little sideways, trying to turn the corner. I got a good angle on him, and I took him down."

Not just.

He flattened Moore. He had the sellout crowd on its feet. He brought out a roar from those people, the kind that shook the Stadium. He had the Colts asking, "What got into the Browns' defense?" He had the Browns saying, "Our defense came to play today."

It was a remarkable play.

"But people don't realize how close that play was to a total failure," he said. "The defensive backs were way behind me. Moore would have had a lot of open field if I didn't get to him. It could have been a big play for them because Lenny was tremendous in the open field. When Lenny went down, I felt relieved more than anything. At least I knew I wasn't going to be the one who gave up the first touchdown."

On that day, none of the Browns did.

"We kept the pressure on Johnny Unitas all afternoon," he said. "Jim Kanicki really played the best game of any of us. Jim Parker was supposed to kill Kanicki, but Kanicki came into his own."

That's typical of Fiss, crediting someone else.

Fiss is from Johnson, Kansas.

"It's the heart of the Dust Bowl," he said. "It's out there in the western corner of Kansas, twenty-seven miles from Oklahoma and thirteen miles from Colorado."

This is John Steinbeck, *Grapes of Wrath* country.

"It's where farms were just blown away," Fiss said. "People saw their whole lives go up in dust."

Fiss was born in 1931. His family was one of the few in the area who didn't pack all they owned on the back of a truck and head out for California. This dry, dusty land was their land, and they planned to stay. They weren't quitters. They believed in themselves, in their ability to get something out of the land.

"We had it better than some farmers," he said. "Our wheat crop had some good years, even during the Depression. We also had a few cattle.

When I was a kid, I spent ten to twelve hours a day on a tractor. My brother, my father, and my grandfather—all of us worked the farm. It was all we knew. I loved it. I couldn't think of a better way to grow up."

In Johnson, Kansas, the sky is the limit and the sky seems to go on forever. The ground isn't just flat, as most people think. There are small, rolling hills. But there are few trees, few buildings, few roads. You look out and you are sure you can see for a hundred miles, but all you see are fence posts and farmland. You see rows of corn. You see dust in the distance being kicked up from a dirt road as a clanky truck makes its way to a distant farmhouse. At one time, this was buffalo country, with long, brown grasses. When farmers decided to let some fields go, just not plant for a few years and let nature take over, the grasses came back. If you have a sense of history, you can look at those fields, that grass, and imagine when there was nothing here but the sky, the chirping birds, and the buffalo.

At night, the sky was huge, black, full of stars. That's because there were so few lights. Virtually no streetlights. No neon signs. And in the 1930s, many farms didn't even have electricity. So when darkness fell, it was a black curtain. When the sun came up, it was as if God smiled on the land. Storms could be fierce. Lightning. Wind. Tornadoes. Barns shuddering in the gusts. Children with wide eyes. Adults with grim faces. In this part of Kansas, you grow up realizing the power of the land and weather. You couldn't make it rain. And when it did pour, and off in the distance you saw funnel clouds, you couldn't stop that, either. You couldn't stop the snow, and the wind that cut through your bones like a hacksaw.

In this barren land of clouds and sky, you learned your limits.

You also learned decency, and looking out for your neighbor. You had to take care of each other, because there were so few of you around.

Today Johnson, Kansas, has a population of 1,244.

"It has changed," said Fiss. "They've got two traffic lights now, one at each end of Main Street."

Galen's people became the First Family of Johnson. They kept their farm, but they also opened a garage and automobile agency in town. Fiss & Sons. Galen's dad ran the repair shop, his uncle sold the cars and trucks. Another uncle also helped out.

"The kids worked on the farm," he said. "Dad thought it was good for us. I just remember planting and plowing . . . plowing and planting. I shoveled grain. I baled hay. Everything was physical, and I ended up the biggest boy in the family. It was like lifting weights while growing up."

Galen was also a star athlete. His father thought sports were healthy for a young man. But the entire Fiss family was surprised when the University of Kansas offered Galen a football scholarship. Boys from Johnson didn't go to college; either they stayed on the farm, or they sort of drifted off and were never heard from again. But Kansas wanted Galen, and his family was thrilled to see their son so honored.

Galen played four different sports in high school. In the 1940s and 1950s, coaches from Kansas simply recruited the best athletes in their state, and decided which sport the kid could play once he showed up in Lawrence. They did the same with Bob Dole, a strapping kid out of Russell. Dole gravitated toward basketball, while Fiss found his calling as a fullback—although he also lettered in baseball and basketball in college.

"I loved where I grew up, but when I went away to college, I decided that I didn't want to work on the farm or live in a real small town," he said. "I wasn't sure what I wanted to do, but there were a lot of things out there. I wanted to see some of it myself."

In the summers, he returned home to Johnson to help out on the farm. He also played baseball for a high-powered amateur team in Garden City, Kansas.

"My dad let me have a car and let me off work on the farm so I could drive to the games," he said. "Garden City was about eighty miles away. I wouldn't get home until two or three in the morning, and I'd get up early to work on the farm. But my father was very supportive. He was a fan and he wanted me to play ball while I could."

But no one—not even Galen—expected sports to become his living. Athletics was just a chance to live a little before earning a degree and going to work.

After he graduated from Kansas, Fiss was offered a contract by the Cleveland Indians. They wanted him as a catcher. He signed, and spent the summer of 1953 in Fargo, North Dakota. One of his teammates was Roger Maris.

"You can say that Roger had a better swing than me," he said.

In 1952, Paul Brown drafted Fiss in the twelfth round. But the

Browns didn't immediately offer a contract, which was why he tried baseball in 1953. Then he had to spend two years in the Air Force.

In the fall of 1956, Galen Fiss showed up at the Browns' training camp. He was twenty-five years old, an Air Force veteran who had risen to the rank of first lieutenant. The Indians wanted him back in the summer of 1956. But, remember, he was twenty-five years old. He was married. He didn't want to play in the low minors for $400 a month.

"When I got out of the service, Paul Brown called and offered me $7,500," Fiss said. "He kept tabs on me. But I had no idea if I could play pro football. I had never even seen a pro game. I hadn't played football for three years. I was kind of scared, because I figured I didn't know anyone—but the money was too good not to try it."

But he did have a friend on the Browns.

"Mike McCormack was there," he said. "We had played together at Kansas."

Fiss would walk away from a practice battered and confused. He wondered if maybe he should just go back to Kansas and start a life at home.

But Mike McCormack would tell him otherwise. Mike McCormack was an established NFL starting tackle, and he told Galen, "You are good enough. You are my friend, and I wouldn't say that unless it was true."

Fiss stuck it out. McCormack taught him the routine. He tutored him about the ways of Paul Brown. The coach moved Fiss to linebacker, where he backed up Chuck Noll in 1956. By 1957, Fiss was starting. Two years later, he and McCormack were team captains.

In 1965, the *Plain Dealer* ran a story that tells you so much about Fiss.

Unbeknownst to Fiss, a Roman Catholic priest named Thomas Cullen called the newspaper with this information:

At Shaker Medical Center was a four-year-old boy identified only as Brian. He was to have surgery the next day and was staying down the hall from Fiss, who was in the hospital with a leg injury.

Fiss was hobbling down the hall on crutches. He heard the boy crying and went into the room.

"What's wrong?" Fiss asked.

The boy was too upset to answer.

"What's your name?" he asked.

"Brian."

"Well, Brian, I bet you miss your mom and dad," he said.

The boy nodded.

"But I bet you are a brave boy, too," he said.

There was another nod, not quite as certain.

"Well, I have a son just about your age," Fiss said. "I miss being with him tonight just like you miss being with your mom and dad."

The boy stared at him, wide-eyed.

"Suppose tonight, I take the place of your dad and you take the place of my son," Fiss said. "Then we can help each other."

"That would be swell," Brian said.

Fiss found a chair in the boy's room. He sat and talked until Brian fell asleep. Then Fiss hobbled back to his room. The boy had no idea who the man was, and Fiss would tell you this was what people in Kansas did every day. They took care of each other.

The story only came out because Father Cullen was making his rounds and discovered the two talking.

––––––––––

To Fiss and most of the 1964 Browns, playing pro football was an honor. They didn't believe anyone owed them a living just because they worked in front of 80,000 people on Sunday afternoon.

"We were making more money than most people," he said. "But it wasn't like today, where a pro athlete makes a hundred times more than the average guy. To us, pro football was just a part of who we were. We knew it would end, and then we'd have to go to work. That's why so many of us had real jobs while we were playing. Mike McCormack had gotten involved in the insurance business in Kansas City, and he told me that I should go into it with him. We formed a partnership. He retired after the 1962 season, but then he went into coaching, and I kept the business. Still have it to this day. My son runs it now."

Fiss retired from football after the 1966 season. He made $25,000 that year, his highest salary with the Browns. He moved full-time to Kansas City. He coached his sons in Little League, and volunteered at the YMCA to work with kids.

"Galen Fiss was a true leader," Jim Kanicki said. "He wasn't one of those rah-rah guys, but he had an honesty about him. He could talk to everybody—the white guys, the black guys, the city guys and the farm guys."

Fiss made the Pro Bowl twice. He was like most of the 1964 Browns, a good player but not great. His real strength was his character.

Or as former Browns public relations director Kevin Byrne said, "You see Galen now, and he's some balding, chunky insurance man from Kansas City. But his teammates talk about him almost reverently. On the 1964 defensive team, you had three players who became head coaches in Monte Clark, Paul Wiggin, and Dick Modzelewski. You had an evangelist in Bill Glass, defensive end. But who was the captain? Galen Fiss."

Fiss said he had a couple of chances to return to football as an assistant at either the college or pro level.

"But I looked at those guys, and most of them had to uproot their families, keep moving from city to city," he said. "That wasn't for me. It wouldn't have been fair to my family. I missed football a lot, but I was lucky because both of my boys played football at the University of Kansas. That was a happy time of my life, going to watch my boys play for my alma mater. Now, I'm just a businessman from Kansas City. I still go to the Kansas games. I'm a big fan of the Jayhawks."

Then Fiss paused.

"I came from the Dust Bowl," he said. "I played eleven years in the NFL. I've had a good business and a great family. I've made tremendous friends. Every once in a while, someone asks me about the Browns. I know I've been lucky."

GARY COLLINS

Of all the key members of the 1964 Browns, the one who has the least to say about that team is Gary Collins.

"He is just very bitter about the Browns situation," said veteran Cleveland broadcaster Casey Coleman. "He's bitter about Art Modell. Things just haven't been easy for him. I know that the Browns had a very hard time convincing Gary to come to Cleveland for the thirtieth reunion of the team back in 1994."

Collins lives in Hershey, Pennsylvania. He was the only player who declined to be interviewed for this book. He now works in insurance and financial planning.

Collins was first contacted right before the 1994 reunion. He had decided to come and sounded excited about seeing his old friends. He seemed happy to be interviewed.

He talked about predicting a Browns victory before the 1964 title game: "We were such a big underdog that no one gave us a chance. I was still very young, only twenty-four. What did I know? I was cocky. I believed we could beat anyone. So I told every reporter I saw that we'd win. Why not? If we lost, no one would remember what I'd said. Besides, I really did believe we'd win."

He talked about the Colts taking the Browns lightly: "I don't know if it's true, but I heard that a few days before the game, the Colts' owner took the team to Las Vegas for a day. At least, that's the story the players told, and it just made us even more determined to beat them. It was like they weren't even taking us seriously."

He talked about Frank Ryan: "He was all business in the huddle. He talked to the guys, but in the end, you knew that he'd make the decision. I respected Frank very much."

He talked about the three TD catches: "The first one was on a broken pattern. My only concern was that Frank's pass might hit the goal post. The second one, I was wide open. The defender slipped. On the third one, I went over a 5′ 11″ guy to catch it. I should have made the catch, because I'm 6′ 4″."

He talked about the 1964 Browns: "It was only years later I realized how good a team we were, and it was years later that I had people telling me how good a player I was."

He talked about Jim Brown: "He led with his determination and silence. He is the greatest athlete who ever played the game and it was an honor for me to be on the same team as him."

———————————

Collins's closest friend on the Browns was Dick Schafrath. "I'm not sure why Gary doesn't want to talk about 1964," he said. "But Gary has always gone his own way."

Other than that chat before the reunion, Collins refused to share any of his memories. He didn't respond to letters. He wouldn't even come to the phone, leaving his wife to say, "Sorry, Gary says he doesn't want to talk to reporters." The one time he answered the phone, he immediately hung up when he heard the subject was the Browns.

"Gary Collins could be a strange cat," recalled veteran Cleveland radio talk show host Pete Franklin. "One day, he was, 'Hey, how are you? Glad to see you.' He acted as if he were your best friend in the world. The next day, he'd just walk right by you without a word. But say this much for Gary, he was one helluva football player."

Longtime Browns equipment manager Morrie Kono once told reporters, "I always thought Gary was mad at me. It was from the way he looked. I couldn't tell if Gary was moody, sulking, or angry. But once I got to know him, what a guy. What a sense of humor."

That is how Schafrath remembers Collins.

"We both lived in Aurora and we rode together every day to practice at League Park," he said. "I had an old VW Bug, and Gary hated riding in it. He'd say, 'Schaf, the truck tires are higher than our car. This thing scares the hell out of me.' As we went to the park, Gary would tell me that we didn't throw the ball enough. I can still hear him say, 'Dammit, Schaf, enough of this running crap.' I'd remind Gary that we did have Jim Brown on our team."

The argument would continue.

"Schaf, I'm open on every play," Collins said. "I mean, I could catch twenty passes a game."

"I know you're open," Schafrath said. "But you're open because we are running the ball, because we have Jim Brown. Don't you get it?"

"But I'm still open," he said.

Schafrath said that Collins had to get in the last word. During games, he'd pester Ryan about calling his number.

"Frank, I'm open," he said. "Just throw it to me. Go ahead, I'll catch it."

"Gary said that on almost every play," Schafrath said. "And Paul Warfield was just the opposite. He never said a word. But in practice, both of those players had the same attitude. I'd watch them catch fifty passes in a row during drills. If they dropped one, then they had to catch ten more to make up for it."

Yet Collins told anyone who'd listen, "I hate practice." In fact, one of his coaches at Maryland [Tom Nugent] wondered if Collins would make it in the NFL because of his attitude about practice. Nugent also called Collins "the greatest athlete I've ever coached."

In a 1964 profile, the *New York Times* wrote that Collins "is known as a friendly neighbor who plays catch with local youngsters and is always ready to put his beefy shoulders against someone's snowbound car."

That is typical Collins: nice to kids, there when you need him.

But also there is the Gary Collins who liked to look cool.

As Milton Gross wrote in the *New York Post*, "Collins does not believe that missing a pass requires a guy to go into a dying swan act on the field and pound his fist in the turf."

"Am I supposed to grimace and groan if I miss one?" Collins asked Gross. "Am I supposed to be a phony and an actor instead of a football player?"

Or as Jim Brown once said, "Gary gives the wrong impression, like he doesn't give a damn. You see some of those speed boys running around the field, and Gary can't compare. But when the game comes, he makes the catches."

The Browns learned to let Collins talk. Let him complain, let him blow off steam, or let him act as if he had little interest in what was going on. They knew he'd do the work, even if he was telling you there was no reason to do it at the same time.

"A lot of people think I'm cocky," Collins once said. "I'm not. The truth is I'm a sensitive, nervous, restless guy. I'm a fitful sleeper. Things bother me. I'm very conscientious deep down."

Collins was born in Williamstown, Pennsylvania, a town of about 2,000 located thirty miles north of Harrisburg. Collins told Cleveland sportswriter Hal Lebovitz that his father worked in the coal mines, leaving at 6 a.m. and working a twelve-hour shift. His grandfather also worked in the mines and lost the vision in one eye from all the dust.

"When I was thirteen, I went down in the mines for the first time," he said. "I saw what it was like and I said, 'Forget this.' I never went down there again."

Collins was an excellent athlete, but his parents refused to sign the permission card for him to play football. His older brother (Dale) had made the high school football team, but it was a tradition for the first-year players to have their entire bodies painted red. Dale Collins became sick from the paint, and his parents didn't want the same thing to happen to Gary. Collins faked his parents' signature on the card so he could play. His hazing was him getting tossed into some pricker bushes and smacked with wet towels. He told Lebovitz those experiences convinced him never to take part in any hazing of rookies when he was with the Browns.

At 6´4˝, Collins was a football and basketball star. He believed sports were his ticket to college, and college would ensure him a living that did not include putting on a helmet and going underground after coal. He even asked to play fullback, hoping to score touchdowns and get his name in the newspapers so college scouts would notice him.

It worked, as eighty different colleges offered him scholarships to play football. The University of Cincinnati and Loyola of Chicago also wanted him to play basketball, and both schools were building strong basketball programs when Collins was a high school senior in 1958. He decided to go to Maryland, and he married his high school sweetheart.

In addition to playing wide receiver, Collins was a punter.

"I was fourteen the first time I punted in a game," Collins told Bill Scholl of the *Cleveland Press*. "I was scared. On the previous series, my older brother had punted and three guys came in and hit him after he got off the punt."

Collins's brother never punted again as Gary took over the job for the high school team.

At Maryland, Collins was a first-team All-American. He set school records for pass receptions and touchdowns, both for a season and a career. He averaged 45 yards per punt and played linebacker on defense.

During his senior year, the Maryland football guide said Collins "has to be considered the most brilliant end ever to play for any Maryland football team. . . . He does everything and does it better than anyone else. He catches the ball sensationally and effortlessly. He blocks brilliantly. He tackles superbly. He punts exceptionally well. . . . He has the finest pair of hands for catching a football ever seen at College Park. He has the finest pair of hands ever seen at any stadium."

For one of the very few times, the hype from a college sports information office turned out to be correct.

The Browns made Collins their No. 1 pick in the 1962 draft. They also acquired top pick Ernie Davis, a running back from Syracuse, in a trade with Washington. The Redskins wanted Bobby Mitchell and Collins in the deal for Davis. Paul Brown refused. They asked again. Brown wouldn't do it. Finally, Brown convinced Washington to take Leroy Jackson, a running back from Western Illinois, rather than Collins.

"Collins is an all-around great athlete, and with his fine speed, he should strengthen our receiving," Paul Brown said after drafting him. "He has great hands and he's aggressive."

Brown also was in the market for a punter, and he believed Collins could fill that role. He loved the idea of two for one, obtaining both a receiver and a punter with one draft pick. That also meant he did not have to save a space on the roster for a punter.

As a rookie, Collins caught only 11 passes. By his second pro season, Collins was the team's starting flanker and set a team record by catching 13 touchdown passes. He also averaged 41 yards per punt.

"After he drafted me, Paul Brown said, 'I understand you have an attitude with you,'" Collins recalled. It was all Brown said, and Collins got the message. If he planned to play for Paul Brown, he had better keep his mouth shut—which he did.

―――――――――――――

Collins played with the Browns from 1962–1971.

He was a textbook receiver, as his eyes would follow the ball right into his hands. That sounds elementary, but many receivers take their eyes off the ball just as they are making the catch. They either look at the field to see where they can run, or they search for the defensive back who wants to knock their head off.

"Gary was so tough and determined," Frank Ryan said. "He'd hang in there and fight the defensive back for the ball."

Quarterbacks love that because it prevents interceptions. If Collins couldn't make the catch, he was going to do everything within his power to make sure that no one else caught the pass, either.

"Part of Gary's success was he thought he was the best receiver who ever played," said Bernie Parrish. And that confidence carried over to his teammates, especially the quarterback. That was why Ryan went to Collins so often in clutch situations. One of every five catches by Collins went for a touchdown.

Despite his stellar college career, there were doubts about Collins when he came to the Browns. Too slow. He needed too long to get open.

"Gary's first step wasn't quick," Paul Warfield said. "But once he got going, he surprised you. He was as strong as any receiver I've seen, and no one had better hands than Gary Collins."

Collins also punted in his first six years with the Browns.

"It wasn't easy," he said. "We'd have a third-down-and-14 situation, and I'd go out for a long pass. It would be incomplete, and I'd have to come back to the huddle and punt. By the fourth quarter of most games, my legs were starting to tighten up."

Bob August once wrote in the *Cleveland Press*, "Collins is a powerful man known to offer transportation over the goal line to several tacklers, but after he punts, he becomes surprisingly fragile. If an opponent even brushes him, Collins is inclined to crumble dramatically [hoping to get a roughing-the-kicker call], his pain so obvious that it seems advisable to inform his next of kin. Once a penalty has been called, he recuperates amazingly."

Collins's best seasons were from 1963 to 1967. After that, he had a series of injuries, everything from broken ribs to a severely bruised back to jammed fingers to pleurisy.

In Browns history, only Jim Brown (126) and Leroy Kelly (90) had more touchdowns than Collins (70). The 46.7 yards per punt he averaged in 1965 was the best ever by a Cleveland punter in a single season.

Yet he left the Browns at the age of thirty-one, released because injuries had worn down his body.

He didn't play in 1972 or 1973, but returned as a player-coach with the Florida Blazers of the old World Football League. That lasted one season.

For a while, Collins raised Appaloosa horses. He later owned a small farm. He spent a year as an assistant junior college football coach. In 1982–83, he did pregame radio reports for the Browns.

"He didn't seem very happy," Browns public relations director Kevin Byrne recalled.

In a 1981 interview with reporter Phil Porter, Collins said, "I was shocked after I retired. It was the first time I'd waited in a doctor's office in years. . . . It's difficult to live up to expectations and many people treat you differently because you were a pro athlete. . . . I made big money at a young age and it can screw you up. . . . When the special treatment is gone, it is difficult to get used to."

JIM KANICKI

Imagine Grizzly Adams running a small steel company.

That's Jim Kanicki today.

He greets you wearing a work shirt, jeans, steel-toed shoes, and salt-and-pepper beard. He is a huge man, 6´ 5″ and 250 pounds, but he has one of those smiles that make you believe you have a new best friend. Then you shake his hand—and your hand just disappears in his grip. His hand knows the meaning of work; it's a hand that is lined and hard.

Dick Modzelewski talked about that hand, how Kanicki used it to head-slap offensive lineman.

"He'd ring your bell," Modzelewski said. "He had huge arms and enormous hands. Jesus, Mary, and Joseph! Jim Kanicki was a big man. A nice man, but he could knock you into next week with those paws of his."

That was when Kanicki was a defensive tackle for the Browns, playing next to Modzelewski in 1964 to form the heart of the line. Today, it's hard to imagine this nice man ever hitting anyone.

Since 1985, he has owned the Arthur Louis Steel Company in Ashtabula, a town in eastern Ohio on the shore of Lake Erie. His company has two buildings and forty employees.

"My father loves this," Kanicki said, meaning the steel business. "He always wanted me to own a good company, a company where he'd like to work. He keeps telling me that I should hire him, but he's eighty-five years old. He still likes to walk around our buildings, then go out and check on some of the jobs we've done. He says this is the kind of job he wished he'd had—where he'd be the boss and the owner."

Kanicki's father worked for fifty years at a foundry in Saginaw, Michigan.

"The man had an eighth-grade education," Kanicki said. "He was a millwright. I love my father, but he was in charge of the family, and all twelve of us knew it."

Twelve children?

"I was the fifth child," he said. "There were ten boys. All of us felt the same way. When we got in trouble at school, we'd tell the teachers, 'Do whatever you want to me, just don't tell my dad.'"

Kanicki laughed about his father, who emigrated from Poland. "Imagine working at the same company and pretty much in the same job for fifty years," Kanicki said, shaking his head.

Then Kanicki talked about his mother, who grew up on a farm—and how even though his dad worked in a foundry, they lived on a farm. "It was outside Bay City, Michigan," he said. "We had a hundred acres, and planted things like corn and potatoes. The great thing was that it was a real farming area. All the neighbors helped each other with the harvest. With ten Kanicki boys, we always had a few strong bodies available to work on someone else's farm."

Kanicki learned how to drive a tractor not long after he started to walk. He was raised with his hands in the dirt—planting, picking, watering, and checking the crops. The brothers played games behind the barn. "For twenty-two consecutive years, there was always at least one Kanicki boy playing football at Bay City Central High," he said.

Kanicki talked about the farmhouse, the one with three bedrooms. How could you put a family with twelve kids in three bedrooms?

"My parents had one room," he said. "The two girls had another room."

That left one bedroom for ten boys?

"Five bunk beds, but the oldest boy got to sleep on the porch," he said. "That was special, because it was like having your own room."

Kanicki smiled and shook his head.

"Get this," he said. "We had only two bathrooms."

Just two?

"One of them was outside," he said.

Come on.

"I kid you not," he said. "Two bathrooms. One inside, one outside. In the mornings before school, the time limit for everyone was five minutes. Those were great times."

With that wonderful smile coming through that gray beard, you know Kanicki means it.

While all the Kanicki brothers played football, none of them played as well as Jim. He was big and quick, 6′4″ and 225 pounds as a senior in high school. Most major colleges offered him a scholarship, but he wanted to stay close to home and attended Michigan State.

Some of the freshmen complained about the small rooms and the bathrooms down the hall. Kanicki missed the open spaces of the farm, but he thought his room was great. The fact that you could walk down the hall and get into the bathroom anytime you wanted . . . that you could stay in the shower until the hot water ran out . . . that you could eat as much as you wanted in the cafeteria—well, there was a lot to like about college life.

And football?

"I liked to play," he said. "But I never thought of it as a career. I was at Michigan State to get a degree."

In his three years under coach Duffy Daugherty, he played a grand total of 190 minutes.

"I held a lot of tackling dummies," he said. "I was only sixteen when I graduated from high school. Duffy Daugherty liked me as a player, but he kept saying he didn't know where to play me. He wanted me to attend one of those military prep schools for a year, and then go to college. But I wasn't interested in that. If I was going to go to college, I wanted to go to college."

Freshmen were not eligible to play varsity sports in the 1960s. As a sophomore, Kanicki was slotted as a center. He also discovered center was the deepest spot on the team, as the Spartans already had two All-American caliber players there—Dave Manders and Dave Behrman, both of whom later played pro football.

"There were some weeks when I didn't even make the traveling squad," he said. "That was when the Big Ten demanded that its players go both ways, offense and defense. I was lucky to play ten minutes a game, and that was only if someone got hurt. The frustrating thing was they wouldn't let me play on the scout teams because I messed up their preparation for the games. There was no one who could block me."

Kanicki wanted more playing time, but he never considered transferring or complaining to the coach. "If it hadn't been for football, I never would have gone to college," he said. "I was grateful for that and just wanted to get my degree."

Even though Kanicki played little, pro scouts knew of him. They attended the practices of most Big Ten teams. They knew the coaches and they all immediately were intrigued by Kanicki because he was so big.

After his senior year, several pro scouts asked that Kanicki be invited to play in the North-South college all-star game. In that game, Kanicki played and played a lot. He was a defensive tackle and recovered two fumbles. The North team said it didn't have a kicker, so Kanicki volunteered.

He booted an extra point and a 40-yard field goal.

"I used to kick in high school," he said. "But we had a good kicker at Michigan State, and they didn't need me."

Kanicki also played in the Senior Bowl, and once again he had scouts wondering why this guy spent three years on the Michigan State bench. Here was a huge defensive tackle who was such a gifted athlete that he also could kick? He seemed like a nice enough kid, but maybe something was wrong with him, something we don't know. Besides, it's pretty hard to stand up and say your first-round pick is a guy who was a third-string center at Michigan State, even if you planned to play him on defense.

But this was the kind of player Paul Brown loved, a true sleeper. By the end of his senior year, Kanicki was 6′ 4″, 270 pounds, and he had yet to turn twenty-one. Sure, some of that weight was baby fat, but he was still a kid. When it came time to pick in the second round, Paul Brown never hesitated—he took James Henry Kanicki.

The Buffalo Bills of the rival American Football League also drafted Kanicki in the second round.

"Buffalo got to me first," he recalled. "They offered me $20,000. That sounded like a million bucks to me. I signed."

But Kanicki still wasn't twenty-one, so the contract wasn't legal.

"They invalidated the contract," he said. "So I signed with the Browns for $14,500."

But that contract wasn't valid, either. So now Kanicki could pick again, Buffalo or Cleveland.

"Buffalo had Dave Behrman on their roster," he said. "I didn't want to play behind him again like I did at Michigan State. So I signed with Cleveland."

This time, his father co-signed.

"Not long after I signed, Paul Brown was fired," Kanicki said. "I was worried about where I stood, but Blanton Collier called me. He said they would have drafted me in the first round, but they needed a receiver so they took Tom Hutchinson. Blanton told me, 'I've followed you all the way back to high school when I was coaching at Kentucky and we were thinking of recruiting you.' The fact that Blanton knew me was reassuring."

The Browns saw Kanicki as a defensive tackle. He was supposed to play behind veteran Bob Gain and learn the pro game slowly. But Gain had several injuries in 1963.

"I played more as a rookie with the Browns than I did in all three years of college combined," he said. "By then, I weighed 282 pounds. I could bench-press 500 pounds. I just went out there and tried to beat the hell out of people."

Kanicki was a strong, raw rookie who had little idea of the technique or footwork needed to be an effective lineman. But he was a smart and willing student, and Collier loved to teach. No detail was too small, no concept too obscure. After the 1963 season, Collier traded for Dick Modzelewski so the veteran lineman could continue Kanicki's education.

Kanicki's first four years with the Browns were a dream. He was healthy. He was playing for a team that was beloved by the town. He played in two title games, winning once. Football was fun.

In 1967, Kanicki found the NFL to be a cruel place, where some men whom he trusted had hearts of stone.

"I hurt my ankle early in the year," he said. "I could hardly walk on it, but I took a shot and played every single week. I couldn't practice. I was limping around, but I took a shot and went out there every Sunday and played."

At the end of the season, the Browns wanted to cut his pay.

"They said I had a bad year," he said. "No kidding. But I played hurt. That was something I learned. They tell you to do the best you can, to play through the injuries. You do it, and they tell you that you're not playing as well as you once did."

In 1968, the ankle had healed, but Kanicki dislocated his left shoulder.

"I could barely lift my arm over my head," he said. "But I kept playing." More shots. More pain. More frustration.

In 1969, it was a slight tear of the Achilles tendon.

"They told me that I pulled a calf muscle," he said. "It didn't feel like a pulled muscle to me, but I kept playing. I took cortisone, novocaine, all kinds of painkillers. They never said it, but you knew the deal was: No play, no pay. The team expected you to play. Your teammates expected you to play. So I played."

But Kanicki wasn't the same player.

After the 1969 season, the Browns traded him to New York in a multiplayer deal bringing receiver Homer Jones to Cleveland.

"Art Modell was ready to trade Paul Warfield for the rights to Mike Phipps," Kanicki recalled. "Then he wanted Jones to replace Warfield, so I had to go. At least that was how Art explained it to me. Being traded to New York was the low point of my career. I loved Cleveland and I loved the Browns. I never wanted to play anywhere else. I was a farm kid from Michigan. I didn't want to live in New York."

The Giants discovered that Kanicki's "pulled calf muscle" was really a torn Achilles. It was surgically repaired.

Kanicki played two years with the Giants, another year in the World Football League, and then retired at the age of thirty-two.

———————

Like so many of the 1964 Browns, Kanicki never counted on football to take care of him for the rest of his life.

"I sold insurance," he said. "I was a manufacturer's representative for an industrial tool company. For a few years, I owned an appliance store. All of this was while I was still playing."

Kanicki's top football salary was $43,000. He was never an All-Pro player, but always a starter.

In 1964, he was earning $15,000 when the Browns won the title.

"I took the $8,000 from our share of the championship game and I put it down on 150 acres of land outside of Ashtabula," he said. "The total price was $20,000. We still live on that property today. I left eighty acres of it as woods. We had a river running through it, and all kinds of wildlife. For a while, we had horses and about fifty head of cattle. The kids belonged to the 4-H club. It was a great place for them to grow up."

Kanicki never moved from that farm, even after he was traded.

When his career was over, he returned to Ashtabula. He went to work for the steel company there and learned the business. Then he bought it.

"I still love the Browns," he said. "I had tickets right up to the time they moved. That tore my heart out. They were my team. This will always be home for me. When they moved to Baltimore, it felt like I was traded all over again. It just was something I never thought would happen."

LEROY KELLY

"Jim Brown saved my career," he says.

You wait for Leroy Kelly to explain. You figure that perhaps Kelly means Brown's decision to retire after the 1965 season.

"That's not it," he said. "You needed to see me in 1964."

Kelly meant that he was a scared kid out of Morgan State, an eighth-round draft choice. He'd never seen an NFL game in his life.

"I didn't even know that I was picked by the Browns until the day after the draft," he said. "A friend of mine came up to me after class and told me the Browns had taken me.

"I told him, 'Man, don't play with me.'

"The guy said, 'Look, it's right here in the newspaper.'

"I took the paper from him and there was my name. I was so relieved, because I wanted to play pro football, but I had no idea if I'd get the chance. The old American Football League held their draft a few weeks before, and they passed me up. I was sure they'd pick me, so I had no idea what to think about the NFL."

Kelly was worried that he was hidden playing at Morgan State, a small school near Baltimore. In 1964, most NFL teams had only one or two full-time scouts. They primarily relied on the word of friends and coaches. Morgan State was hardly the mainstream of college football. It was a black school, and virtually all of the NFL coaches and assistants were white. Besides a high-profile program such as Grambling, it was rare that a black school was even scouted. But thanks to Paul Brown, the Browns had more contacts and heard more whispers about college players than any other team. In fact, one of the people who mentioned Kelly to the Browns was Indians pitcher Jim "Mudcat" Grant, who was a football fan and had once seen Kelly play.

The Browns had Kelly's name. By the eighth round, all the players they really wanted were long gone, so they took Kelly simply because he was one of the few familiar names still available.

"I didn't even know what position the Browns wanted me to play," Kelly said. "I was both a running back and a defensive back in college. I also was a pretty good punter. When I reported to minicamp in the summer, I heard they were looking for defensive backs, so I thought they'd use me there."

Blanton Collier thought otherwise.

He saw Kelly's speed and agility. He saw that Kelly had excellent hands when catching kickoffs and punts. Jim Brown had told Art Modell that he planned to play only two or three more years. Eventually, the Browns would need another running back. Being from a small school, Kelly was raw. But he also was an athlete.

"When you come back to veterans camp, you'll stay at running back," Collier told Kelly. "Now go home and see if you can put on another ten pounds."

Kelly had only 180 pounds on his 6-foot frame.

Then came Hiram. There was Jim Brown. To Kelly, Jim Brown was a god. He was 6´2˝, 230 pounds of muscle. He had a forty-seven-inch chest and a thirty-two-inch waist. He was faster than a locomotive. He leaped over tacklers. He also seemed quiet, but very wise.

"Superman," thought Kelly.

"If all running backs are like him, then I'm not gonna last very long in this league," thought Kelly.

Four days into camp, Kelly thought his career was over.

"Leroy came at me, full speed," said Jim Kanicki. "It was a dive play up the middle and Leroy was trying to block me."

Kelly still weighed no more than 180. Kanicki was a 270-pound defensive tackle.

"He was some little rookie running back trying to block me," Kanicki said. "So I crunched him. His body and legs just got twisted."

Kelly tried to get up and grabbed his left hamstring. It felt as if the back of his left thigh was on fire.

"I was so scared," he said. "I had never had an injury like that. It was just a pull, but I could hardly run. I kept trying to play on it. Rookies had to keep practicing. I roomed with another rookie, and after a couple of days, they cut him. I was afraid they'd do the same to me."

Jim Brown had been watching Kelly. He saw the hamstring injury. He saw Kelly limping through drills and he saw the fear in the rookie's eyes.

One day after practice, Brown approached Blanton Collier.

"Why don't you give Kelly a few days off to heal that hamstring?" Brown told the coach. "Maybe we should rest him until after our West Coast trip."

Collier agreed with his star runner. He also was impressed by the fact Brown thought Kelly was worthy of special treatment.

"Jim was very astute," Kelly said. "He was always evaluating the young players, trying to decide if they would help the team. When I did come back and play, I had a terrible last exhibition game. I fumbled two kickoff returns. Now I was convinced I was going to be cut. I hadn't played much because of my injuries, and in the last game I was awful. After the second fumble, Jim came over to me on the sidelines and told me to hold my head up. He said I had good hands, and not to worry about it."

Kelly went into the final days of training camp wondering if he'd make the team. The Browns had five running backs—Ernie Green, Charlie Scales, Kenny Webb, Jim Brown, and Kelly. Green, Brown, and Scales were assured roster spots. Collier planned to keep only one more running back, and Webb had been a backup in the league for six years.

"I thought I was the odd man out," Kelly said. "But on the last day of training camp, Kenny Webb still had not signed his contract. It was lunchtime and we were having sandwiches outside. The next thing I knew, I saw Kenny Webb carrying his equipment out of the dressing room. 'See you guys later,' he told us. Turned out Art Modell wouldn't give him the money he wanted, so he left the team."

And Kelly stayed.

Kelly probably would have made the team anyway, although on the taxi squad, where he'd practice but not dress for games.

"Jim Brown had a lot of influence with Blanton and the coaches," Kanicki recalled. "And we knew that Jim liked Leroy very much, so I don't think he was ever in danger of being cut. Leroy was supposed to be Jim's backup, which was a thankless job because Jim never came out of the game."

"It wasn't long into Leroy's rookie year that I remember Jim telling me that one day, Leroy would take his place," recalled John Wooten. "I know he was worried about Leroy being from a small school, and then getting caught up in the nightlife. Jim would tell me, 'We've got to make sure this kid doesn't get into any trouble. We don't want the wrong people getting ahold of him.' Leroy didn't know it, but even in 1964 Jim was grooming him to take his place."

Kelly recalled another time Jim Brown intervened. During a practice, he received a cut over his eye.

"The trainer stitched me up, and I thought I was done for the day with practice," Kelly said.

"What are you going to do?" asked Brown. "Let that cut and a couple of stitches keep you out of practice?"

"He didn't tell me to get back on the field," Kelly said. "But I got the message."

Kelly's first contract with the Browns was for $12,000, and that included a $7,000 bonus for signing.

"Seemed like I was rich," he said. "I used some of that bonus money to buy a 1964 Malibu convertible. It cost me $3,600. I tried to save the rest of it. I moved in with two other players, Sidney Williams and Walter Roberts. We rented the top floor of a house from a lady. Her husband had just died, and she was taking in boarders. We thought it was great because the rent was cheap and each of us got our own room."

In fact, Kelly didn't move into his own apartment until his third year in the NFL, when he also took over for the retired Jim Brown in the backfield. It was only then that he began to feel secure.

Kelly grew up in Philadelphia. His father, Orvin, worked at a quarry where he ran a machine that poured lime into bags.

"I had three brothers and three sisters, and he made sure all of us worked," Kelly said. "When I was in grade school, I had a wagon. On Friday nights and all day Saturday, I delivered groceries. People would call in an order to the store, and the clerk would pack the bags and I'd take them to the house in my wagon."

When Kelly was in high school, he was a busboy at a local cafeteria.

"I was good at it," he said. "I started making 75 cents an hour, and I remember getting a raise to $1.20. Then my father got me a job at the quarry. I loaded fifty-pound bags of lime into trucks. I did that every summer while I was going to college."

That was why Kelly took nothing for granted with the Browns. It was why he was willing to play behind Jim Brown, and why he performed with such single-mindedness on special teams, where he was one of the Browns' best at running downfield and making tackles on the kickoff squad. To him, just being in the NFL, having a car and a room of his own was more than he had dared dream.

Then the 1966 training camp opened, and Jim Brown was in England making a movie.

"From England, I wrote Blanton a letter," Brown said. "I explained that I was retiring, but that he'd be set at running back. I told him to keep Ernie Green blocking, and that he had a runner who was going to be unbelievable. In that letter, I told Blanton to give the ball to Leroy Kelly."

Collier did just that.

He called Kelly into his office. He explained that Jim Brown was retiring, but the team had no intention of bringing in another runner. Collier told Kelly he'd replace Jim Brown. In his soft, soothing voice, Collier explained that the great offensive line was still in place. He said Ernie Green was there to teach him and to block for him. He assured Kelly the team had "every confidence in the world in you."

Kelly walked out of that meeting thrilled, excited, and scared. But Kelly never doubted he'd be a success, at least not after the way Collier explained the situation.

"I was a natural halfback," Kelly said. "Jim had played fullback. Blanton moved Ernie Green from halfback to fullback, and then let me play halfback. That was another thing that really helped, Ernie switching positions like he did."

Kelly rushed for 1,141 yards and scored 15 touchdowns in 1966, his first year as a starter. He was named to the Pro Bowl and went on to make the Hall of Fame.

While he relishes his ten years with the Browns, he doesn't like to hear the name of Art Modell.

"I thought we had a good relationship," Kelly said. "In my last few years with the Browns, I had a personal service contract whereby I was supposed to work for the team after my career was over. In my final season [1973], I was making $90,000, but it was clear they were breaking in Greg Pruitt at halfback. I wanted to play another year or two as his backup, but Art wouldn't go along with it. He didn't want to pay that kind of money. So he put me on waivers, and I never did get a chance to work for the team."

Kelly retired in 1974. Along with his brother Pat (a major league outfielder for fifteen years) and his nephew, Kelly owned and operated three Burger King franchises in Philadelphia for fourteen years. They sold the franchises in 1993, and now Kelly goes to some card shows and has an interest in a mortgage security company.

"Art came to my Hall of Fame induction and things between us have softened a little over the years," Kelly said. "Then he moved the team to Baltimore, so I feel the less said about Art Modell, the better."

FRANK RYAN

The quarterback had a Ph.D. in math, and that was why most sports-writers had no idea how to cope with Dr. Frank Ryan.

"I came quickly not to like the media's interpretation of my interest in math," Ryan said. "It was pretty demeaning of what I was trying to do. I don't think that I ever acted like the 'flaky egghead' they called me. It shows you how deficient the sports world was that they had to seize on those sorts of hooks to get a story out. It was pretty pathetic journalism."

What Ryan did was perhaps unique in the annals of sports history. In December of 1964, he quarterbacked the Browns to the NFL title. Five months later, he received his Ph.D. in mathematics from Rice University.

Sportswriters were stunned to learn he was studying for his doctorate while playing in the NFL. Ryan graduated from Rice in 1958, where he majored in physics, but his professors believed that he had better aptitude in math, so he pursued that in graduate school.

Maybe that is why some sportswriters insisted he was a "nuclear mathematician." Others called him "an autotomic mathematician."

They had no clue. They couldn't see that Ryan was like most of his Browns teammates in this era—he knew the world didn't begin and end with football. He knew that in a few years he'd have to go out and get a real job, because football wasn't going to pay the bills forever.

Sportswriters could understand Galen Fiss, Lou Groza, and Jim Houston selling insurance. That's because most sportswriters figured if they ever were canned by their papers, they could sell insurance, or become a stockbroker like Bernie Parrish, or a manufacturer's representative like Gene Hickerson.

Jim Brown wanting to be an actor? Why not? Big money there. Who doesn't want to be in the movies?

But how could Frank Ryan be passionate about math? Not 2+2=4 kind of math, but a course where you spend a full year on a problem—a problem you may never solve?

Sportswriters thought that was "kooky" and called him such.

"Now, you see players packaging themselves into marketable personalities, such as Deion Sanders," Ryan said. "These players create their own image and play up to it. But when I played, there was no reason to package yourself because there was no consumption of the package."

Ryan and the rest of his peers were not about to sign contracts with Nike or Pepsi worth millions of dollars. They couldn't sell out to advertisers, because no one was buying.

"But sportswriters did try to package me in a way that was an easy story for them," he said. "I suppose they did it because, frankly, writing about sports is pretty boring. But I disapproved of how they packaged me."

They wrote that Ryan had a "genius IQ of 160."

Ryan never knew his IQ and never bothered to find out. He did believe he was not even close to a genius, at least not compared to the people he studied with and under at Rice. These folks had published major books and papers before they were thirty. In the classroom, they sometimes made him feel very average, and he believed that only perspiration rather than raw intelligence would save him.

"If I have one gift, it is my ability to concentrate," he often said.

Ryan's wife, Joan, said most people couldn't comprehend what it took for her husband to earn his doctorate. He began his graduate work in 1958, and didn't finish until 1965. He did it by staying up late, often until one in the morning, to study math during the football season. He did it by cramming extra coursework into the off-season. He did it with "an incredible stamina for studying," according to Joan Ryan. "A lot of times we told people we couldn't go out or go to dinner because Frank had to study."

Ryan said he could "turn on a switch" and tune out everything else but math. He wanted to be Dr. Frank Ryan eventually, teaching math at the college level—and he was willing to put in the time and work to make it happen.

"There seems to be an impression that Ryan was handed his doctorate on a platter," Dr. A. J. Lohwater of Rice told the *Saturday Evening Post* in 1965. "Nothing could be less correct. The man worked hard for his degree. He worked for seven postgraduate years under Dr. G. R.

MacLane, one of the best geometric-function theorists and a man of uncompromising standards. Frank wrote an excellent paper as well."

Ah, yes, the paper. Sportswriters loved the paper.

His thesis was called: "Characterization of the Set of Asymptotic Values of a Function Holomorphic in the Unit Disc."

That appeared in countless stories about Ryan.

Many also quoted the thesis, which began: "As is well known, a Blaschke product f(z) in (z–x 1) has radical limits f(e) of modulus one almost everywhere on (z=1). The object of the present paper is to give a partial answer to the question: how many times does f(z) assume a given radical limit."

Many sportswriters approached the subject as the *San Francisco Examiner*'s Prescott Sullivan did in an August 25, 1963, article: "As it happens, we worked on much the same problem with the same results that Ryan reaches in the brilliant conclusion to his thesis. That is to say, a Blaschke product is a useful thing to have around the house, but can be harmful when taken in quantity and should be kept away from children."

Or took the route Jack Gallagher did in the *Houston Post:* "The Cleveland Browns quarterback is a bit of a kook."

Those comments had to depress Ryan. He knew that sportswriters were just trying to be funny, but math was serious business to him. It was his business, his future. While he was still playing for the Browns, he taught a course in "Applied Complex Analysis" at Rice, and was said to be an effective teacher and communicator.

Yet he could never get across this message about what math meant to him, not even to the Browns' front office. In the media guide, the Browns wrote he had a "near genius IQ." Ryan read that and reached for the aspirin. They wrote he played chess by mail, sometimes having ten games at once going with people around the country. When Roger Kahn wanted to interview Ryan for the *Saturday Evening Post*, Browns general manager Harold Sauerbrei told him, "I'm sure Frank will talk to you, but that doesn't mean you'll know what he's talking about."

That's a cruel insult. It means that Ryan—the Browns' quarterback—was too smart or too much of an egghead to communicate with the average guy, and that wasn't fair or true.

"Right after the Browns traded for Frank Ryan, Mike McCormack and I ran into him at a rest stop on the Ohio Turnpike," recalled Galen

Fiss. "We had a Coke, then went back to our respective cars. The first thing McCormack said was, 'Well, I didn't think Frank Ryan was so damn smart, did you?'"

Fiss insisted that McCormack was serious.

"Most people never understood that what I did in math and at the university had nothing to do with what I did on the field," Ryan said. "Math and football take different points of view and attitudes in order to accomplish things. Mathematics was not just a satisfying pursuit for me. It was building a potential professional career."

No one could blame Ryan for that. He attended Paschal High in Fort Worth, Texas, and he once said, "I was the fifth best of the six quarterbacks in our conference." Coaches named Jim Shofner as that conference's best quarterback; Shofner later became a defensive back and a teammate of Ryan's with the Browns.

Ryan had impressive size for a high school quarterback in 1954 at 6′ 3″ and 175 pounds. Legend had it that he threw the ball 73 yards to prove a point to a professor, who claimed the laws of gravity and such meant that no football could be thrown more than 50 yards. While he wasn't an accurate passer, Ryan was tall and had a strong arm. Rice was one of the few major colleges interested in him; the Owls had an extra scholarship and an excellent academic reputation, so they recruited this true student-athlete. His grandfather, Dr. Frank Beall, was a noted surgeon. Ryan was the first member in three generations of his family not to attend Yale.

But the Rice quarterback everyone knew was King Hill.

"That year, Rice recruited Frank Ryan, myself, and another quarterback, who was supposed to be the starter because he was all-state," Hill once said. "But they made that kid into a halfback, so it was Frank and I. We always thought that there wasn't any difference in ability between us, but Frank got his knee banged up in his sophomore season and he couldn't play defense. [Coach] Jess Neely always was an ardent believer in playing both ways, so he used me and spotted Frank on offense."

About all that Ryan recalls about his senior year was that he "played little." Hill was an All-American, a first-round pick by the old Chicago Cardinals. Ryan applied to graduate schools and was accepted at places such as UCLA and UC Berkeley. He was stunned when the L.A. Rams picked him in the fourth round of the 1958 draft. He thought his football days were over. Pete Rozelle was the Rams' general manager, and he liked Ryan's size and arm strength. He viewed Ryan as a project, a guy who might develop into a decent backup. Ryan wasn't even sure if he should bother with the NFL, given his lack of success at Rice and his desire to become a mathematician. But Rozelle said, "Frank, give it a shot. You've already been accepted at UCLA, so you can go to grad school there and play for us at the same time."

Sit for the Rams was more like it; Ryan played a grand total of 19 minutes as a rookie. In the next three seasons, he sat behind Billy Wade and Zeke Bratkowski. There were a few games where he did start, only to be yanked for throwing an interception. With the Rams, Ryan was known for his ability to scramble, which will come as a shock to those who only remember Ryan in his stiff, banged-up final years with the Browns.

He was traded to the Browns in 1962, another great deal by Paul Brown. Of course, Brown was primarily looking for a quarterback to play behind Jim Ninowski. When he showed up with the Browns, Dallas sportswriter Blackie Sherrod wrote that Ryan was "lanky, shambling, a mat of limp, graying black hair. Looks more like Jimmy Stewart playing the role of a struggling lawyer than a professional quarterback. . . . Mostly, the pro people looked at him and shoved him into the file marked: Average. Sorta kookie guy who understands about Xs and Ys and pi and cosines and all such animals. Plays chess by mail with other kookie guys."

As for Ryan trying to be a quarterback, Los Angeles sportswriter Mel Durslag wrote, "That is tantamount roughly to Albert Schweitzer working in a drug store."

That implied being a quarterback was beneath Ryan. He quickly rejects that, and tells you that establishing himself as a starter was the hardest thing he ever did in his life.

He wasn't a star high school quarterback. He was a backup in college. He was drafted by one of the worst teams in the NFL, didn't receive a dime as a signing bonus, sweated out the final cut just to make the Rams—and then hardly played over the next four years.

He then asked to be traded, but not to Cleveland.

"When Frank heard of the trade, he slumped down in the nearest chair," Joan Ryan wrote in her *Plain Dealer* column. "His reaction was, 'That's the last place I want to go.'"

Joan Ryan told her husband how the Browns were a fine team with great players such as Jimmy Brown and a great coach in Paul Brown. But Ryan looked at it from a different angle. He was twenty-six when the Browns acquired him in July of 1962. Ninowski had just been obtained by Paul Brown, and Brown had named Ninowski the starter. Like Ryan, Ninowski was twenty-six. Only Ninowski had broken into the NFL with the Browns and under Paul Brown. He had been the starter for the previous two years in Detroit.

Where did Ryan fit in?

Ninowski started the first seven games of the 1962 season. Then he broke his collarbone and was out for the season.

"At that point, the Browns had to play me because they had no one else," Ryan said. "It was the first time in my career where I knew I could play through my mistakes."

He played relatively well. Not great, but he showed enough to inspire Paul Brown to actually gush. A man who handed out compliments as if they were $1,000 bills, Brown said late in the 1962 season: "If Ryan continues to improve, the deal with Los Angeles could dwarf all the others. I don't want to build this out of proportion, but the more I see of him, the more I like. He doesn't lack for courage. He's no schoolboy."

No, he was more than that. Frank Ryan was the last quarterback to lead the Browns to a title, even though Paul Brown was not around to see it.

Blanton Collier took over for Paul Brown in 1963, and that coaching change made Ryan's career.

Ryan had nothing against Paul. He said he wasn't in Cleveland long enough to get to know Brown, and he now appreciates the faith Brown showed by trading for him. But Brown wasn't a coach who did a lot of hands-on instruction, getting into the heads of his players. He left that to assistants such as Collier, only now Collier would also make all the final decisions about the offense.

"Blanton had a lot of theories about every position, and they usually were pretty simple," Ryan said. "What he did for me was to break throwing the football down into small parts and technique. It gave me some rationale to base my performance upon."

Collier cut down the Browns' passing playbook, and then told Ryan, here are the primary receivers on each play, and here is the man to look to next, and so on.

"Blanton figured it out for Frank," Art Modell recalled. "If there was a blitz, he'd tell Frank, 'Just throw the ball to the tight end, or throw it to Ernie Green.' I remember standing next to Blanton when Frank was throwing the ball on the sidelines; he'd quietly tell Frank, 'Pick out a target. It's like shooting a rifle, just zero in on the chest.' Over and over, he told Ryan that: 'Zero in on the chest, hit the man between the numbers.' He had tremendous faith in Frank."

Collier told Ryan not to watch the ball in the air after he threw it. In the past, Ryan fretted when his passes weren't perfect spirals; Collier believed that Ryan was so anxious about seeing his passes in the air, he was taking his eye off the receiver too soon just so he could watch the ball.

That's also why Collier often stood near Ryan as the quarterback warmed up for a game, to remind him to watch the target, throw to the target.

Collier believed that just because Ryan was becoming a doctor of math, it didn't mean he was a genius on the football field. Collier was a former high school algebra teacher, and knew there was little connection between football and math. In math, you're presented with a problem and you have plenty of quiet time to find an answer. You can take one road, erase it, then try another. You think things through.

Not in football. Not with a 250-pound lineman bearing down on you, and with variables changing every second as assignments were carried out or missed, or your receiver fell down, or your foot stuck in the mud, or a running back forgot the play.

With the Rams, Ryan became so obsessed with all these details and potential problems that he nearly paralyzed himself.

Hal Lebovitz probably understood Ryan as well as any sportswriter, as is evident in a column he wrote in the *Plain Dealer* early in the 1965 season when Ryan was struggling: "Remember that Frank Ryan was second string. This led to a certain insecurity on the football field. Even now, the fear of a secondary role haunts him. . . . He doesn't want to lose his job. He tries to ignore injuries for this season. He's afraid that once he's benched, he'll never make it back to No. 1."

Collier agreed, and that's why he stuck with Ryan after bad games, when fans were demanding that Jim Ninowski be given a chance.

Collier publicly said that he didn't believe in juggling quarterbacks; privately, he knew that a benching of Ryan could destroy all the confidence he'd gained in Cleveland.

Lebovitz saw Ryan's insecurities in the quarterback's concern about the press: "Frank Ryan is a shy, sensitive guy," Lebovitz wrote. "What is written has been known to disturb him immeasurably. Sometimes rightfully, sometimes almost childishly, not at all in keeping with his fine, mature analytical mind."

But Ryan had one of the key ingredients of an athlete: courage.

"Frank came to the Browns with this reputation as a brilliant guy, the math genius, and all of that," recalled Bernie Parrish. "He was not brilliant in terms of his play-calling. But Frank Ryan was the guttiest quarterback that I've ever seen. He'd stand in that pocket and damn near let those linemen kill him before he threw the ball—he held on to the ball until the last possible second waiting for Gary Collins to finish his post pattern."

"Frank wasn't a great football mind," said Bill Glass, who was Ryan's roommate. "But Frank didn't have to be brilliant on the football field. Blanton Collier was brilliant. Frank was an intelligent guy off the field who was gutsy and a gambler on the field."

"Frank was the best I've ever seen at scoring from inside the 20-yard line," added Parrish. "That's the measure of a quarterback."

"Frank had tremendous confidence that he could put points on the board," recalled tackle Dick Schafrath. "He communicated well in the huddle. There was always a little bit of having to pull Frank back, because he loved to throw the ball. Jimmy [Brown] would occasionally tap Frank on the shoulder, just to let Frank know that he was there and it was time to run the ball. But I can understand why he wanted to throw; in Gary Collins and Paul Warfield, Frank had two great receivers and they made it a lot of fun."

"Frank was a very tough guy," said guard John Wooten. "He'd stand in that pocket and take a hit, then throw the ball. We [linemen] really admired that."

"Frank is the quarterback who makes our team move," Jim Brown once said. "Frankly, I don't know why. He's not a natural. He just has the ability to move our team in the clutch."

Or as Leroy Kelly said, "The Doc was cool."

As time went on, Ryan began to talk about football in very unmathematical terms.

He once said that a football game "is like a painting must be to an artist. Other people can observe the painting, but nobody else can feel what the artist felt when he made it."

And he once said, "There are times when it seems as though I can think the ball right to the target. It seems so easy to pass. Other times, it's like I'm throwing a shotput."

And he also said, "The ideal quarterback must have serendipity. Why does he make the consistent good play? By training? By accident? By coincidence? Or some sixth sense? The times when I felt the best on the football field—the championship game for instance—my mind was following no logical conscious thinking pattern. There was no effort to analyze, to evaluate, to review, to study the patterns and tendencies of the defense. Something just came to me like a flash and it worked—not just once or twice, but almost every time."

Gary Collins gave this example: "In a game against New York, Frank went down on his hands and knees and drew up a play in the dirt for me to catch a pass. It was the kind of thing you do when you're kids. I thought it was funny, drawing in the dirt and him being a doctor and all. But I ran the pattern he drew, and we scored."

Collier would hear these things and smile. The coach was an advocate of *Psycho-Cybernetics* by Maxwell Maltz. The theory is that everything can be broken down into small parts. You practice each part, then you put it together into the whole. You also visualize how you'll perform each component.

"I wasn't part of the cult that went with that," Ryan recalled. "I think we all employ some technique that is really rehearsing mentally for a positive performance. You imagine doing things the right way."

While Frank Ryan—in the words of veteran Akron sportswriter Tom Melody—had "a chip on his shoulder about sportswriters," he also found himself married to one.

During the 1964 season, *Plain Dealer* sports editor Hal Lebovitz hired Joan Ryan to write columns for his paper, the idea being that Joan could add some special insights on the team and her husband. She also handled the language well.

Ryan would say that Joan was "one sportswriter you could trust." He once was surprised when Joan was at a banquet and asked to name her favorite player. She replied, "Bernie Parrish."

Ryan looked up, a bit startled.

Then Joan explained that there was a story in that week's newspaper headlined: "Parrish Interception Keeps Ryan from Bench." (Ryan had not seen the story because Joan had been hiding the sports pages that week.)

"Her writing was never a problem for me," Ryan recently said. "After we left Cleveland, she wrote for the *Washington Star.* Then the *Washington Post* raided the *Star* and hired her. She kept writing until we moved to New Haven [when Ryan was named athletic director at Yale]."

"I used to tell Frank that I was the only ballplayer willing to go out with him at night," Gene Hickerson said. "And I told him it was because of his wife—she was nice."

Ryan did try to be one of the boys with the Browns. He once called Galen Fiss, but identified himself as a sportswriter; for a few moments, he had the Browns' defensive captain convinced he had been traded. For the 1963 team publicity photos, he posed throwing the ball left-handed; it was only after the pictures were developed that the Browns noticed Ryan had the ball in the wrong hand. Another time, he stuck a dead seagull in Lou Groza's kicking shoe, which was stuffed in the bottom of a duffel bag and flown with the team to St. Louis for a game. Groza had to disinfect the shoe before he wore it.

"Frank was smart," Hickerson said. "He just tried to act normally around us dummies, but he really didn't know how. I loved to tell him that he was terrible. I'd say, 'If you're really a doctor, then you've got to be the dumbest doctor I know to keep playing football.' Another time, I asked him, 'How good could you really be? I mean, you were a second-string quarterback at Rice!' We'd argue back and forth, and he loved it."

Hickerson said Ryan drove "this Javelin, drove it 150 miles an hour. I told everyone never to get into a car with him. He could outrun the police."

But Ryan also is the guy who heard that the members of the Independence High academic challenge team were feeling blue after their appearance on the old Cleveland television show *It's Academic,* so on

October 27, 1965, Ryan wrote a letter to the students and the moderator, stating, "I can appreciate how you must feel, for several weeks ago the St. Louis Cardinals defeated the Browns, 49–13. I played one of the worst games of my career, and no one can convince me that I didn't let my teammates down with my atrocious performance. Our defeats, yours and mine, are hard, cold facts of life, and we should anticipate that these are not the only defeats we'll encounter. What's important is our developing the ability to rise above our setbacks and fix our teeth firmly into the next task at hand."

A copy of this letter was found at the bottom of the old Frank Ryan file as the Cleveland Browns were packing up and moving to Baltimore.

At the end of the 1964 championship game, Frank Ryan proved that a smart guy could do a very dumb thing. The Browns were leading the Colts, 27–0. As the final seconds ticked down, the officials seemed content to let the clock run out.

But Ryan said, "Give me one more play, I want another TD."

This surprised the officials. It also enraged Baltimore defensive lineman Gino Marchetti, and after the game Marchetti vowed to "get Ryan" in the Pro Bowl Game a week later.

"We were feeling our oats," Ryan recalled. "We were about on their 15-yard line. The fans had started piling onto the field. There were about 20 seconds left, and the officials asked me if I wanted to end the game. I said I wanted one more play, and I threw a pass into the end zone to our tight end, John Brewer, who hadn't caught any passes. I thought throwing him a pass would make him feel more a part of the team. The pass was incomplete. Gino Marchetti had overheard me talking to the officials, and he had a very justified reason to be angry with me."

Which Marchetti was.

Even Frank's favorite sportswriter, Joan, wrote, "In defense of Frank, let me say that his motives were noble, though misdirected. . . . Frank admits that his remarks were ill-advised."

Joan Ryan wrote that on January 13, 1965. By then, her husband had a separated right shoulder, courtesy of Mr. Marchetti. In the Pro Bowl game—Marchetti's final game before retirement—Marchetti was the first to grab Ryan as he tried to pass. He had Ryan around the neck.

Then Roger Brown hit Ryan in the back, and Willie Davis joined in the tackle. Ryan went down under about 750 pounds of defensive linemen. Afterward, Marchetti insisted he had no intention of injuring Ryan. The Browns and Ryan also believe it was "one of those things, good, hard football."

But Ryan's shoulder was a mess. While he led the Browns back to the 1965 championship game, and then into the 1967 playoffs, Ryan was never quite the same after that play.

"After that play [in the Pro Bowl game], they took me into the dressing room as the game was still going on," Ryan recalled. "The doctor taped my shoulder so that it went back into place—he could clearly see that it was separated. He then sent me to the hospital. When they went to X-ray my arm, they lacerated the skin because they couldn't get the tape off without tearing my skin off. Then they couldn't operate, because [the skin injuries] created a danger of infection. I was so mad and frightened at the same time, because my professional livelihood was my right shoulder. They ended up putting me in an upper body cast and sending me back to Cleveland."

At this point, Ryan was twenty-eight years old. He was becoming a celebrity, on the cover of national magazines. (Still, he stumped the panel on *I've Got a Secret;* Ryan was presented as a math professor who had another career, and they couldn't guess that he also was a pro quarterback.)

He had thrown for 50 touchdowns in 1963 and 1964. He had 25 in each season, tying a Browns team record set by Otto Graham. Despite never being known as a runner, in 1964 he averaged nearly six yards per carry—only Fran Tarkenton gained more yards than Ryan among quarterbacks.

Now they wanted to keep his arm in a brace. Surgery was debated, but the Browns and their physicians advised against it.

"I wore that thing for two months," Ryan said. "I couldn't even take a bath during the two months. What a lamentable state of athletic medicine."

Once out of the brace, the Browns put Ryan on a weight program. His elbow began to hurt. The Browns said, no big deal, it's just a "tennis elbow."

"I went two years before it was discovered that I'd torn a muscle in my right forearm," Ryan said. "They said I had a tennis elbow, and the intense pain would go away by itself. They started giving me injections of painkillers and cortisone. That was supposed to take care of the pain, but, of course, there is a great deal of difference between a tennis elbow, which is an inflammation, and a muscle tear."

Ryan kept playing with this injury through 1965 and 1966. Collier noticed that Ryan's passes just didn't have the same zip, and that his arm motion was different. He was throwing more sidearm, which was a way of taking some of the strain off his aching arm. The fans became very harsh with Ryan, calling him "gimpy-armed" and demanding that Ninowski play. But Collier stuck with Ryan, and Ryan somehow kept playing—and winning. It was the same dogged determination with which he earned his doctorate. Ryan willed himself to deal with the pain, and he was scared to rest because, as Lebovitz pointed out, he feared he'd lose his job, since he knew he had major arm problems.

The remarkable thing is that in 1966, he was ranked as the third-best passer in the NFL and set a team record with 29 TD passes.

"That year, it was a situation where I took a shot every Wednesday so I could practice, then another shot on game day to play," Ryan said. "By the end of the 1966 season, it was apparent that there was something terribly wrong and the shots weren't helping. I convinced Modell to let me see some specialists. I went to the 1966 Pro Bowl, but I literally could not throw. The doctors couldn't find anything wrong. Finally, I had exploratory surgery done in Oklahoma City, and it was discovered that the biggest muscle in my right forearm was hanging from my elbow by a thread. They did reconstructive surgery, which allowed me to play for a few more years."

For those final three years, Ryan was a backup, ending his twelve-year career with the Washington Redskins in 1970.

"The injury didn't come from another player, but from my weight program [after the separated shoulder], and then every time I threw I simply exacerbated it even more," he said. "I ended up with this blue blotch on my inside right elbow that was constantly hemorrhaging from the injections I received. Once, they were probing around to give me an injection in my arm, and they imbedded the needle in my bone. It stuck there, and the doctor kept trying to push the plunger on the syringe—and the damn syringe exploded. He then pulled it out, and then went back in [with another syringe] to give me a shot so I could play."

Ryan told this story calmly, as he if were talking about someone else. "When I came back from that operation, everything was corrected and the pain was gone," he said. "But the whole use of the arm was different. I had changed my delivery. . . . Those things happen. It's too bad that I had to go through all that, because I think it really curtailed my career. But sometimes, I think I should have stopped a lot sooner, anyway. By the end, I was pretty beaten up."

But Frank Ryan couldn't stop, not until he knew it was over. You see, Dr. Frank Ryan, Ph.D. in math from Rice, loved football. He loved being in the huddle and hearing Jim Brown tell him, "I'm ready," or Gary Collins saying, "I can beat my man," or the expectant looks from his teammates as they waited for him to pick a play. He was willing to stand in the pocket, to be bludgeoned by linemen, just to give his receivers one more step to get open—and then put the ball in their hands.

As Ryan said, "If you started flinching, you weren't going to get the ball to them."

You must say this for Dr. Frank Ryan, who now teaches math at Rice University: He never flinched.

AFTERWORD

A few days after the Browns crushed the Colts in the championship game, the *Plain Dealer* ran a story under this headline: "A New Browns Dynasty?"

"The shutout at the Stadium very well could mean the start of an Eastern Conference domination similar to the one enjoyed in the 1950s until Otto Graham's retirement," wrote Chuck Heaton.

Heaton's point was that players such as Paul Warfield, Frank Ryan, Leroy Kelly, Ernie Green, and Jim Brown were all under thirty. Collier was a great coach. Why not more titles?

But 1964 would be it.

In 1965, the Browns were even a better regular season team with an 11-3 record. They faced Green Bay in the championship game, a game that still haunts many of the players today,

"It was really snowing," Frank Ryan recalled. "Lambeau Field was a frozen tundra. They'd installed a bunch of heat coils under the grass hoping to melt it. It snowed heavily the night before the game, and all the following morning. The snow was just abating when we got to the field. There was a helicopter blowing snow off the seats. On the field, which had not been covered, there were jeeps with brooms on the front, pushing the snow off to the side. When they got the snow off, the field looked nice and green."

Then Ryan stepped on the field.

"It was like mush," he said. "Those heating coils had turned the turf to a quagmire. This was going to be the Slop Bowl. When you see films of the game, everyone is coated in mud. As the game went on, it just got worse and worse."

Many of those in the game believe Collier made a mistake, but it had nothing to do with his game plan.

"Blanton wanted to stay away from the city of Green Bay so we wouldn't be around all the activity surrounding the game," recalled center John Morrow. "We stayed in a crummy Holiday Inn near Appleton, about forty minutes from Green Bay. We worked out on the field on Saturday, and the turf was frozen and fast. We thought we'd be able to run the ball and play on a quick surface when we went to bed Saturday night. When we woke up, it had snowed like crazy. No one had bothered to get a weather report, because then we could have left earlier for the game. All of sudden, we were backed up in traffic, bumper-to-bumper."

Veteran sportswriter Hal Lebovitz takes it a step further.

"The Browns lost the game on the bus to the field," he said. "The traffic was awful. It was a little road and people were driving slow because of the snow. The bus would stop, creep a little, stop again, creep some more. A lot of players like to get to the game early; they have special rituals, things they do before the game. By the time the bus finally got there, most of the guys were basket cases because they were out of their routines. Jim Brown was the only one who was stoic. There were other reasons the Browns lost that day, but I'm convinced the bus ride played a big part."

The field was indeed muck.

"No championship of any sort should be decided under the conditions that prevailed," Arthur Daley wrote in the *New York Times*. "Inclement weather has interrupted the World Series for as long as a week. Golf championships are postponed when the course becomes unplayable. . . . Only in professional football must the show go on—come rain, snow, hail or Presidential assassination."

The Browns were left asking themselves, What if they had stayed in Green Bay instead of near Appleton and there had been no long bus ride? What if the game had been played on a dry field? What if they simply had had an earlier wakeup call and had missed the traffic?

None of those questions will ever be answered.

The bottom line is the Packers beat the Browns, 23–12, and that did signal the start of a dynasty—one for Vince Lombardi in Green Bay.

Then Art Modell blew it with Jim Brown.

After the 1965 season, Jim Brown went off to make movies. He said 1965 might be his final year, but he also hinted about coming back in 1966.

He was in England, filming *The Dirty Dozen*, and Art Modell was furious that Brown was putting his movie career ahead of training camp. In truth, you could even say that Brown considered making movies more important than the team in 1966.

But he still was willing to play in the regular season.

If you were Art Modell, what would you do?

How about bringing the team together and asking them what they thought about Jim Brown missing training camp? Was it okay with them? Modell could have then left the players by themselves, let them vote or whatever—and then deliver his teammates' decision to Jim Brown.

Instead, Art Modell acted like Paul Brown.

Remember, he had fired Paul Brown because the coach was too rigid, because he had lost touch with the players. Paul Brown's supporters don't want to hear it, but player after player who won that 1964 title will tell you the team never would have done it with Paul Brown. Yes, Paul Brown had assembled most of the talent; there is no denying that twenty-five of the forty-two players who appeared with the team in 1964 were obtained by Paul Brown. Of the regulars, only Paul Warfield, Monte Clark, Dick Modzelewski, Larry Benz, Jim Kanicki, and Walter Beach didn't play under Paul Brown. So Paul Brown trained the players, mentored the coaches, and his system remained in place.

But the divide between Paul Brown and the players was too wide, and it took a fatherly Blanton Collier to bridge the gap.

Art Modell knew that you didn't push Jim Brown against a wall and expect him to back down. So what did Art Modell do? He pulled a Paul Brown. My way or the highway. Jim Brown said, "Fine, I'll go to Hollywood."

The Browns let Jim Brown walk away in 1966, when he was still in his prime at the age of thirty. While Leroy Kelly became a star, he was no Jim Brown. No one would ever be Jim Brown. In 1966, the Browns were 9-5, a good team again. Yes, Frank Ryan was experiencing arm problems. Yes, the defense was aging. Yes, there were other problems on the team. But if Jim Brown had played in 1966, maybe they'd have gone to one more championship game.

We'll never know.

But this much is certain: Art Modell should be faulted more for his handling of Jim Brown's retirement than for the firing of Paul Brown.

———————

The Modell and Paul Brown families never reconciled. Blanton Collier found himself in the middle and never was able to talk at length again with the man who used to be his best friend.

"After Daddy took the head coaching job, he told us, 'You need to understand that an era has ended in our lives. I know Paul and I know he will never forgive me.' And Paul never did," said Kay Collier-Slone.

"I remember when we were playing Cincinnati," Modell said. "Blanton was still coaching, and Paul Brown was coaching the Bengals. Before the game, both coaches were on the field, watching their players warm up. I saw Blanton inching closer to Paul, just trying to get a sign of recognition, a little 'Hello,' or something. He got closer and closer, stealing looks at Paul. But it was fruitless. Paul was not about to acknowledge him."

Paul Brown returned to football with the expansion Bengals in 1967. He was part-owner, general manager, and head coach. "Complete control," was what he called it. At the age of sixty-three, Paul Brown coached the Bengals into the playoffs in only their third year of existence. He quit coaching at the age of sixty-seven; his final season record was 11-3.

"In retrospect, Art Modell might have done Paul a favor because it was like a wake-up call," John Morrow said. "Paul was always a great football man, and the years away from the game allowed him to really study it. Then he came back and did a tremendous job putting together the Bengals."

When the Bengals and Browns played, it was a holy war. When Modell won, he'd hug his players. Paul Brown would seethe. When Paul Brown won, as was more often the case, the old coach was stoic yet satisfied. Modell was devastated.

In 1979, Paul Brown published a book in which he was very critical of Modell.

"I had Paul on my show for a couple of hours when his book came out," said talk show host Pete Franklin. "This was 1979, seventeen years after he was fired by Modell, and he was still so bitter about it. It would never go away. He thought Modell was a piece of garbage, a meddler."

Modell wrote letters to the NFL, complaining that Paul Brown had violated the league's bylaws which stated, "No member . . . shall publicly criticize any member club or its management personnel, employees or coaches." Modell was complaining about Brown's book. In that same letter, Modell's lawyers wrote, "Paul Brown has seen fit not only to criticize Art Modell in his book, he has launched a scurrilous and unfounded attack upon Art Modell's character, integrity and morality. . . . Art Modell has been portrayed as a man ignorant of the profession, who knows no bounds in furthering his own self-interest. A man who cannot be trusted to live up to his contracts and obligations. . . ."

The same charges were levied against Modell in 1995, when he moved the franchise to Baltimore.

The NFL sided with Modell, fining Paul Brown $10,000 for his book. But that actually helped Paul Brown. Modell's protesting and whining about the book became public; so did the fine. All the controversy just spurred book sales. But Modell kept writing letters to NFL commissioner Pete Rozelle about Brown's book, and he still hasn't resolved his feelings about the Hall of Fame coach.

"I helped him get the franchise in Cincinnati," Modell said. "I lobbied for Paul. I was trying to be nice. I had hurt the man. I hurt him terribly and I wanted to try and make it up to him."

Paul Brown's son, Mike, said this was true. Modell didn't stand in the way of expansion to Cincinnati or the Brown family being the owners—and Modell could have used his clout to make it difficult for them to secure a team.

"I would have handled Paul differently now," Modell said. "I bet he would have handled me differently, too. We were at a dinner in the early 1970s. It was in Phoenix. I toasted him and said, 'I deeply, deeply regret what I did in 1962. I'm sorry it didn't work out. You and I would have made a helluva team.' Paul didn't say anything, but I could see he was touched. I also can say if I had to do it over again, I wouldn't fire Paul Brown today."

Yes, Art Modell would.

First of all, if Modell believed that dinner and toast in the early 1970s resolved matters, why did Paul Brown write the book in 1979? Why did Modell protest so loudly and take the criticism to heart?

"Art so wanted to mend fences with Paul Brown and his family," said former Browns coach Sam Rutigliano. "He wanted Paul to like him. But Paul Brown went to his grave, and he never forgave Art Modell. . . . As the Bengals became more successful, I found that if you wanted to survive as coach of the Browns, you had better beat Cincinnati. It meant so much to Art. When Art fired Forrest Gregg as coach, Paul Brown hired Forrest to coach the Bengals, and there was even more sizzle to the rivalry."

In the end, Paul Brown won. His Bengals went to the Super Bowl in 1981 and 1988. Paul Brown was not the coach, but he was the owner and general manager. He picked the players. He picked the coaches. It was his team, a team that went to the Super Bowl two more times than Art Modell ever did.

"I worked for both Art and Paul," said Dick Modzelewski. "I think those two never would have gotten along, so being fired was best for Paul in the long run. It set the stage for him to have his own team in Cincinnati, and he could be happy because he could do things his own way."

And Modell?

Things went pretty well as long as Blanton Collier was coach. But no one lasts forever.

Blanton Collier coached the Browns through the 1970 season. He never had a losing record. He was 7-7 in 1970, his worst season. Those who played for Collier and knew him well insist he was a Hall of Fame caliber coach with the Browns.

He also saved Art Modell's professional butt.

If Collier had been a lousy coach, taking over for Paul Brown, the guns would have been aimed at the owner who fired the legend. Instead, everyone liked Collier. The team won. Everyone likes a winner, so Modell was accepted.

But Collier had his own problems, especially with his hearing. The older he became, the harder it was for him to hear even normal conversations in quiet rooms. At the Stadium in the heat of battle with all the crowd noise, it was nearly impossible. After the 1970 season, Collier went to Modell. This humble, gracious man admitted he no longer could hear well enough to coach.

"Daddy just didn't want to do anything to hurt the team," Kay Collier-Slone said. "Art wanted Daddy to coach one more year, but Daddy just knew . . . he was so afraid of making a mistake that would cost the Browns."

"Art was heartbroken when Blanton came to him," Pete Franklin recalled. "Art knew he would never be as close to another coach as he was to Blanton."

Modell will never forget the day Collier delivered the news.

"I can't even hear my players anymore," he told Modell.

Modell tried to talk him out of it, even though the owner had watched the deterioration of Collier's hearing.

"Finally, I asked Blanton to stay with me as a consultant, assistant coach, anything he wanted," Modell said. "We went to every specialist we could find. No one could help him. In the end, he was lip-reading all the time, and with the face masks the players had on their helmets, he couldn't read their lips. It was so sad."

Blanton Collier's final record with the Browns was 79-38-2, a .675 winning percentage. No Browns coach after him would even approach that mark.

"Daddy would never have spoken a disloyal word about Art," Kay Collier-Slone said. "My father never said a word about it, but it bothered my mother that the Browns never had a day for Daddy. They didn't give him a car or anything special after he retired. He just received his pension. When Daddy retired, he took his projector, his game films, and all the wonderful words the sportswriters wrote about him. The people who knew him just poured their hearts out. We always heard from Art; he'd send us cards, nice notes, and he praised Daddy to the sky. To Daddy, that may have been enough. He never said anything about it. But it did bother my mother and the rest of the family that there wasn't a tribute to Daddy. When she was dying, my mother told me, 'I don't care what he [Modell] does, he didn't recognize your father properly.' Art did send her some long-stemmed roses for her eightieth birthday, but she just thought Art didn't handle Daddy's retirement correctly."

If Modell knew the Collier family felt this way, it would cause him considerable pain. He never meant to hurt the Colliers.

Blanton Collier died of prostate cancer in 1983. He was seventy-six years old.

"He had it for seven years and never told anyone," Kay Collier-Slone said. "Mother knew, but he would not allow her to tell us until October of 1982. He died in March of 1983. He lived on a lake [in Texas] for the last seven years of his life. He enjoyed his retirement, playing golf and visiting with friends and family."

Forman Collier died on January 20, 1996. She was buried next to her husband in his hometown of Paris, Kentucky.

"Before she died, my mother knew of the Browns' move," Kay Collier-Slone said. "That bothered her terribly. After her death, the family went through her things. She had so many Browns items. Here we were, picking through them, knowing Art had moved the team to Baltimore. Every member of the family picked something they wanted. There were hundreds of things.

"But there were two items no one would take. One was an autographed picture of Paul Brown with a very loyal inscription to Daddy. The other is the silver bowl that Art gave Mother when they won the 1964 championship.

"That picture and that bowl are still in the house. They are two heartbreaking pieces, those two things and the move of the Browns. They speak so much about broken loyalties and broken promises."

Despite their contract squabbles and other problems with Modell, most of the 1964 Browns liked the team's owner.

"One time, Monte Clark and Art were about $200 apart on a contract," recalled Jim Kanicki. "Monte was 'holding out,' but still working out with the team in training camp. Art called Monte into his room at Hiram. They talked about the $200, and finally Art said, 'Let's split it—and be sure you don't tell anyone.'

"Monte said, 'Don't worry, Art, I'm just as embarrassed by this as you are.'

"I think Monte was making about $18,000 back then, so $200 was a lot of money."

Kanicki told the story with a smile. He considered Modell a friend.

"I always liked Art, too," said Bill Glass. "Overall, I thought he was fair-minded. He was a more lenient leader than Paul Brown, and that made him relatively popular with the players."

"You had to be in Cleveland in the late 1960s and early 1970s to remember how the Browns owned the town," said Pete Franklin. "Year in, year out. They were competitive. It was like the whole town wore brown and orange, and Modell was the owner. He reveled in it. When Blanton was the coach, I don't think Art was as much a meddler as he later became. He was happy to go to dinner with the coach once a week. But after Blanton left, Art seemed to think he knew a lot more football than he did."

Jim Ninowski offered an interesting insight into Modell.

"Look at the coaches he had after Blanton," he said. "A couple of times, he tried to find his own Paul Brown. Once, he did it by hiring Marty Schottenheimer. Again with Bill Belichick. Two tough, no-nonsense guys. Then he tried to find another Blanton Collier. First it was with Bud Carson. Now, it's with Ted Marchibroda in Baltimore."

Ninowski certainly is right, at least with Marchibroda. As Modell said, "My wife told me that we have another Blanton in Ted. I think she is right."

There is little to gain from rehashing Modell's decision to move the team to Baltimore. Fans blame him and his greed. He blames the politicians for not treating him the same as they did the Indians and Cavaliers. They built new facilities for the baseball and basketball teams, but they stalled on getting a new stadium for Modell—or, at least, that's his version.

Modell had also vowed he'd never move the team. Then, in November of 1995, he proclaimed that promise "null and void." He took a sweetheart deal and packed his bags for Baltimore.

"People say they never thought Art Modell would do that," Jim Brown said. "Well, this man threw Paul Brown out of his office, then he fired Paul. To us, that was like firing God. Then Art cut Bernie Kosar, one of the most popular players in the history of the franchise. When the politicians tried to play hardball with Art, they picked the wrong guy."

Brown was on Modell's staff as a $50,000 a year consultant when the move was announced. He was not surprised to see it happen.

"I would love to embrace the Browns fans and tell them, 'Art is no good,' and all that," Jim Brown said. "But Art's deal with Baltimore and the NFL are what America is all about. It's the free enterprise system. My heart hurts for the fans, but I understand what Art did, too."

Most of Jim Brown's 1964 teammates can't make the same statement.

"I had what turned out to be unfounded respect for Art," said Frank Ryan. "We had our differences when I played for him, but I always wanted to believe Art was a positive force. So I am very disappointed by this."

For Lou Groza, it was worse than that. He cried.

"I felt like I lost a close relative," he said. "It was hard to believe the move would happen because our attendance was so strong. I remember when 40,000 was a good crowd. Now, a bad Browns team would average 70,000. I played twenty-one years for the franchise. I remember when Art bought it for $4 million, and now what is it worth? Maybe $150 million? Or $200 million? Wouldn't you say the Browns fans had something to do with enhancing the value of his franchise? Wouldn't you want to give something back to the community, if you were in that situation?"

"If my father were alive, he'd be grieving about the Browns moving," said Kay Collier-Slone. "He and Lou Groza would sit in the same room and cry those same tears because their concept of loyalty was so huge."

Or as John Morrow said, "Modell doesn't have the right to screw with the team the way he did, whether he owned it or not. Do you own the country? I'm sorry, Art, you made some bad moves. I know the politicians probably didn't come through when maybe they could have, but you don't just take the team away from the fans."

Hal Lebovitz was very close to Modell for thirty-five years. No more.

"He kept the Stadium going when the city didn't have the money to operate it," Lebovitz said. "By taking over the Stadium, he helped keep the Indians in town. He saved the Stouffer Hotel, which is downtown next to Terminal Tower. He did so many wonderful, charitable things. To me, there was nothing in Art Modell's manner or personality to indicate he would move to Baltimore. I knew there was trouble between Art and the city, but Art was the guy who was always blasting Al Davis and those other owners who moved their teams. I had never known Art to lie or be a hypocrite. But with this . . . by moving the team, he killed all the good works he did over all the years in one fell swoop."

From the day the move was announced, Lebovitz promised never to speak to his old friend, and he's stuck to that vow.

No one ever expected Cleveland to be anything other than a Browns Town.

No one imagined the 1964 team would be the last true champions. Certainly, no Browns fans would ever believe the team they so loved would end up in Baltimore, of all places. Thirty-one years after the Browns beat the Colts 27–0 for the NFL championship, the Browns would move to that very city?

There will be a new football team in Cleveland by 1999. It will play in a new stadium. It will be called the Browns and have the same colors. "But I just don't know if it will be the same," said Lou Groza. "All that history . . . it hurts to talk about it."

Only the memories soothe some of the wounds.

"I've traveled all over this country," said John Wooten. "No fans are like Browns fans. None. No one has their passion, their loyalty. Once you play for the Browns, you are always a member of the Browns in their eyes. I loved that old stadium, the colors and the tradition. Nothing can ever take that away from me."

Over and over, you hear words like that from the 1964 Browns and others who played for the team.

They talk about passion and loyalty. They talk about snowy Sunday afternoons. They talk about the roar of the crowd, how it embraced them, carried them.

"Suppose I had a chance to do it over again," Paul Wiggin said. "Suppose I was asked if I wanted to play my eleven years anywhere else but Cleveland. Would I want to play on Vince Lombardi's great teams in Green Bay? Or anywhere else? Suppose I had a choice. Well, it would be no choice. I'd do it all over again, all eleven years with the Cleveland Browns. Not just the team, but the people, the town, those wonderful times in the 1960s. If I could do it over again, that is what I'd do: I'd pick to play one more time for the 1964 Cleveland Browns."

ACKNOWLEDGMENTS

This book is dedicated to Nev Chandler, the veteran Cleveland television and radio personality who died of cancer in 1994. Chandler was the radio voice of the Browns for eleven years. He not only told you what happened in the game and why, but he did it with the enthusiasm of a fan at his first game. He was also a close friend, and a day seldom passes when I don't miss him. The Browns' 1995 media guide was also dedicated to Nev Chandler, as was the team's football season. We all know what happened in 1995: At midseason, the team announced it was moving to Baltimore. Some tribute to Nev Chandler, right? Chandler was a lifelong Clevelander who said it was the 1964 Browns that really made him a football fan. This is a subject Nev loved dearly, so this book is for him.

There are many people who do research for authors, but no author has a better researcher than Wally Mieskoski of Action Media in Cleveland. Wally made this book his own, living with microfilm and other documents from the 1964 Browns. He is accurate, meticulous, and caring. So many of the interesting facts about this 1964 team were dug up by Wally.

As usual, Jeff Neuman was the Jim Brown of editors. This is the ninth book on which we have worked together, and every time I realize how blessed I am to have him as my editor and Simon & Schuster as my publisher. Faith Hamlin was the agent for this book, but calling her an agent is like saying all Frank Ryan happened to be was a quarterback with a Ph.D. in math. She is an extraordinary person and wonderful friend.

OTHER BOOKS OF INTEREST . . .

Things I've Learned from Watching the Browns

Terry Pluto

Veteran sports writer Terry Pluto asks Cleveland Browns fans: Why, after four decades of heartbreak, teasing, and futility, do you still stick with this team? Their stories, coupled with Pluto's own insight and analysis, deliver the answers. Like any intense relationship, it's complicated. But these fans just won't give up.

"For dedicated Browns fans [the book is] like leafing through an old family photo album." – BlogCritics.com

False Start
How the New Browns Were Set Up to Fail

Terry Pluto

A hard look at the unhappy beginnings of the post-1999 Cleveland Browns franchise, this book chronicles the backroom deals, big-money power plays, poor decisions, and plain bad luck that dogged the venerable franchise after Art Modell skipped town in 1995. How long should fans have to wait for a winner? A book the NFL does not want you to read.

"[A book] NFL fans in general and Browns' fans in particular will definitely want to read . . . a fascinating, behind-the-scenes look at how the new Browns were created and what's kept them from making the progress everyone expected." – Houston Chronicle

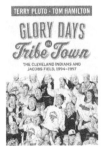

Glory Days in Tribe Town
The Cleveland Indians and Jacobs Field 1994–1997

Terry Pluto, Tom Hamilton

Relive the most thrilling seasons of Indians baseball in recent memory! Cleveland's top sportswriter teams up with the Tribe's veteran radio announcer and fans to share favorite stories from the first years of Jacobs Field, when a star-studded roster (Belle, Thome, Vizquel, Ramirez, Alomar, Nagy) and a sparkling ballpark captivated an entire city.

Read samples at **www.grayco.com**

OTHER BOOKS OF INTEREST . . .

On Being Brown
What it Means to Be a Cleveland Browns Fan

Scott Huler

What makes Browns fans so . . . different? These 33 essays explain: It's about pride. It's about desire, tempered by crushing disappointment. It's about tradition, rivalry, and electrifying victory. It's about longing. It's about heart. Includes interviews with Jim Brown, Lou Groza, Paul Warfield, Ozzie Newsome, and other legends.

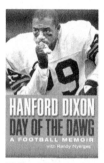

Day of the Dawg
A Football Memoir

Hanford Dixon, Randy Nyerges

The popular and outspoken NFL cornerback offers an inside look at the turbulent, exciting, and frustrating Cleveland Browns seasons of the 1980s. Dixon, a three-time Pro Bowler and co-inventor of the Dawg Pound, recalls both roller-coaster on-field action and a culture of drug use that permeated the NFL and led to the tragic death of a teammate.

"A fun ride down memory lane for any Browns fans over the age of 35. For those under that age it's a reminder (painful perhaps) of what you've been missing while watching the current state of the Browns." – News Herald

Browns Scrapbook
A Fond Look Back at Five Decades of Football, from a Legendary Cleveland Sportswriter

Chuck Heaton

Sportswriter Chuck Heaton looks back at 47 years covering the Cleveland Browns, including Hall of Famers Jim Brown, Leroy Kelly, and Bobby Mitchell; legendary coach Paul Brown; fabled trainer Murray Kono; even notorious Browns rivals. Longtime fans will fondly recall the old days; younger Browns fans will learn why everyone still longs for them.

Read samples at **www.grayco.com**

Made in the USA
Middletown, DE
12 December 2021

55404974R10179